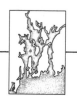

A Cruising Guide to Narragansett Bay

Best wishes
Lynda Childers

A CRUISING GUIDE TO NARRAGANSETT BAY

Lynda Morris Childress
Patrick Childress

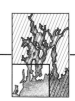

INTERNATIONAL MARINE PUBLISHING COMPANY
Camden, Maine

This book is dedicated
in memory of
JOHN WALSH

☐

Published by International Marine Publishing Company

10 9 8 7 6 5 4 3 2 1

Copyright © 1990 International Marine Publishing Company

Library of Congress Cataloging-in-Publication Data
Childress, Lynda Morris.
    A cruising guide to Narragansett Bay / Lynda Morris Childress.
Patrick Childress.
        p.   cm.
    Includes bibliographical references.
    ISBN 0-87742-989-8
    1. Pilot guides—Rhode Island—Narragansett Bay.   2. Yachts and
yachting—Rhode Island—Narragansett Bay.   3. Narragansett Bay
(R.I.)—Description and travel—Guide-books.   I. Childress,
Patrick.   II. Title.
VK982.N37C45 1989   89-20003
623.89'22346—dc20   CIP

International Marine Publishing Company offers software
for sale. For information and a catalog, please contact TAB
Software Department, Blue Ridge Summit, PA 17294-0850.

Questions regarding the content of
this book should be addressed to:

International Marine Publishing Company
Division of TAB Books, Inc.
P.O. Box 220
Camden, ME 04843

Typeset by Crane Typesetting, West Barnstable, MA
Printed by Fairfield Graphics, Fairfield, PA
Edited by Claire Cramer, T. P. McCarthy
Unless otherwise noted, all maps by Alex Wallach.

DESIGN BY LURELLE CHEVERIE

Contents

Preface

To sail on Narragansett Bay and be unaware of its richly patterned past is like admiring a diamond in the rough. The more you learn about the bay, the more brightly it shines as a cruising ground. Having spent considerable time cruising the bay, we knew a bit about its history. But many an evening, as we swung at anchor in one peaceful cove or another, questions arose: How did this place get its name? Who inhabited that abandoned house, or strolled along that old dirt road? What did it look like here hundreds of years ago?

The bay is full of wonderful relics of times past that prompt such speculation, from a mysterious tower said to have been built by the Vikings to forts, lighthouses, and homes dating back to colonial times. On several islands, buildings that housed troops and supplies as recently as World War II stand silent and empty, inviting exploration and conjecture about their past.

Aboard our sloop, we carried several cruising guides that covered (but did not focus on) Narragansett Bay. All offered nuts-and-bolts advice on how to round the buoys or where to get fuel or ice—information that was only marginally useful to us as locals. Those guides left us wanting to know more about the origins and history of the places we visited by water, as well as the best activities to enjoy while we were there. Over the years, cruising friends came to visit from faraway ports, full of questions about the bay, and as we attempted to find answers to their queries as well as our own, the idea for this book was born.

This guide is a bit different from most conventional cruising guides and we hope it will be useful and enjoyable for local Narragansett Bay boaters as well as visitors. It is a compilation of almost two years of research, both on the water and at libraries, historical societies, museums, and city and town offices around the bay.

Assuming familiarity with use of a nautical chart and tide tables, navigating on the bay is, in general, fairly clear-cut. In addition to basic cruising information and lists of transient dock and mooring space, this book gives readers an equal taste of local history and legend, flora and fauna, food and people. We also share our perspective, based on experience, on the best places to drop the hook and the best things to do ashore once the anchor is securely set.

We have visited at least once every anchorage mentioned, and our opinions are straightforward. If we liked a place, you'll know it, and if we didn't, we'll tell you that, too.

The popular port of Newport lures many sailors to the mouth of the bay. But most fail to realize they can see much more on Narragansett Bay than one resort town. With this in mind, we provide information on the entire bay—from Point Judith to Providence and Sakonnet Point to the Taunton River. The guide focuses on the bay as a destination rather than a brief stop on the way north or south along the New England coast.

It has been our observation that people tend to cruise the bay by area rather than by coastline or island. For this reason, we have divided it into four regions: the Lower Bay, including Block Island, the Middle Bay, the Upper Bay, and the Sakonnet River. Individual ports are listed alphabetically in the Index. We have made every attempt to keep information accurate and up-to-date; however, the pace of change is rapid and some discrepancies may occur. Readers who wish to share their own observations are encouraged to write to us in care of the publisher. We will make every effort to incorporate pertinent material into any future editions of the book.

The quotes that appear throughout the book come from a wonderful book called *Narragansett Bay* by Edgar Mayhew Bacon (New York: G.P. Putnam's Sons, 1904). The book is long out of print, but Bacon shares a perspective on the bay that is both refreshing and timeless, and we felt his lively commentary was worth sharing with readers.

We would sincerely like to thank all the people in shoreside communities baywide—from harbormasters and dockmasters to launch drivers and librarians—who took an interest in the project and generously shared information and local knowledge on a wide range of subjects.

Those of us who cruise under sail or power are drawn to the sport for a reason—the desire to explore new and exciting destinations by water and to learn all we can about each place we visit.

Whether you're a regular cruiser of the bay, or visiting for a few days or an entire season, we hope this guide will teach you something you didn't already know, and in so doing, enhance your exploration and enjoyment of one of the East Coast's greatest cruising grounds.

How

to

Use

This

Book

☐

General Information

The first three chapters of the book contain pertinent information for all bay cruisers, from wind, weather and cruising conditions to bay history and the reasons behind some of the area's difficult Indian names. To fully enjoy your cruise on the bay, we suggest you begin with these before reading about the ports of call.

Regions

The bay may look small on a map, but it has hundreds of anchorages. The easiest approach is to divide it into four regions: the Lower Bay,

Regions of the Bay

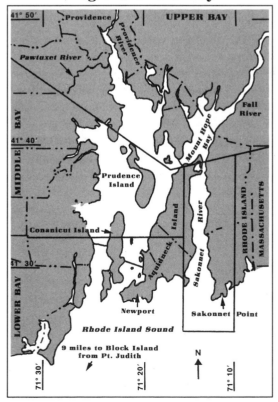

SCALE: 1″=9 MILES

including Block Island, the Middle Bay, the Upper Bay, and the Sakonnet River. Detail maps accompany discussions of each region, which are listed in the Table of Contents.

Charts

We have made every effort to provide information that is accurate and up-to-date, but it is impossible to guarantee complete accuracy. This guide should be used as a supplement to official U.S. charts.

Charts necessary for each area are included under each harbor listing. The best one to use for each harbor is in boldface type. For a cruise of Narragansett Bay, you will need the following National Oceanic and Atmospheric Administration (NOAA) Charts:

13217 Block Island
13219 Point Judith Harbor
13221 Narragansett Bay
13223 Narragansett Bay,
      East and West Passages
13224 Providence River and
      Head of Narragansett Bay
13227 Fall River Harbor and
      Taunton River

The Better Boating Association (BBA) chart kit for Narragansett Bay includes all necessary charts.

Resources

In addition to the appropriate charts, we suggest you carry the following volumes aboard your boat for a cruise of the bay:

Eldridge Tide And Pilot Book (published annually by Robert Eldridge White, 34 Commercial Wharf, Boston, MA 02110; phone 617-742-3045; price $7.50). This is the annual reference guide to tides and currents on the East Coast and is full of useful piloting information.

United States Coast Pilot 2, Atlantic Coast: Cape Cod To Sandy Hook (published annually by the U.S. Department of Commerce, National Oceanic and Atmospheric Administration, National Ocean Service, Rockville, MD 20852; price approximately $16.50; available at chandleries and marine bookstores). This annually updated reference supplements navigational information on government nautical charts.

NYNEX Boaters Directory, Massachusetts/ Rhode Island Edition; (published annually by NYNEX Information Resources Co., 201 Edgewater Drive, Wakefield, MA 01880; phone 800-648-8660; price: $7.95). A boater's telephone directory to all marine services.

Anchorage
Ratings

Within each region, anchorages have been given a rating for Beauty and Interest; Protection; and Facilities.

Beauty/Interest

 Beautiful, interesting, or both. Not to be missed.

 Very attractive or interesting. Worth a stop.

 Attractive or interesting.

 Nothing special.

 Not very attractive.

Protection

5 Best protection available; hurricane hole.

4 Well protected under most conditions; good anchorage.

3 Well protected for prevailing southwest winds.

2 Reasonably protected for prevailing winds; some exposure.

1 Exposed in two or more directions; okay as temporary anchorage.

X No protection.

Facilities

 Slips, moorings, or both

 Fuel (gas, diesel, or both)

 Water

 Repairs

 Groceries within ½ mile

 Laundromat

 Shower

 Restaurant

 Phone

 Ice

 No anchoring

Sketch Maps

Where appropriate, sketch maps are included to help you identify anchorage and mooring areas or locate shoreside services. Under no circumstances should they be used as substitutes for government charts or for navigation.

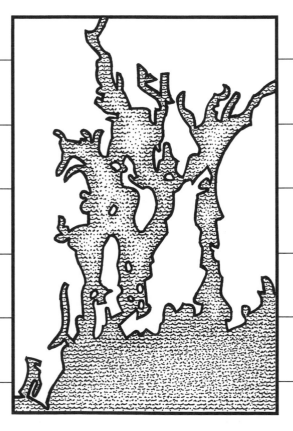

Background
On
The
Bay

Where Is Narragansett Bay?

MASSACHUSETTS

Boston

Cape Cod

RHODE
ISLAND

CONNECTICUT

Providence

Narragansett Bay →

New Bedford

Buzzards
Bay

New
London

Mystic

Vineyard Sound

Rhode Island
Sound

Martha's Vineyard

Nantucket Island

Block Island Sound

Block Island

Long Island
Sound

Montauk

Long Island

Ocean

Atlantic

N

SCALE: 1"=28 MILES

Welcome

to

Narragansett

Bay

"We can crow loud enough," the Rhode Island man says, "even if we do have to go outside the state to flap our wings."

Every resident knows the scenario: Mention to a non-New Englander that you hail from Rhode Island and the response is likely to be, "Rhode Island? Isn't that part of New York?"

For centuries, Little Rhody has fought for recognition. Narragansett Bay has fared better—almost any Northeast boater is familiar with the name. Thanks largely to the bay, which bisects Rhode Island, extending 28 miles inland and up to 12 miles across, the nation's smallest state has a coastline that measures nearly 400 miles.

For boaters, these numbers add up to almost endless opportunities for exploration by water.

Narragansett Bay has lured mariners for centuries. Its early discoverers sailed across the Atlantic from Europe and Iceland and, years later, the state's colonial founders fled from Massachusetts across the rivers and streams of the bay's northern tributaries. While early visitors didn't have the transportion options available today, exploring Rhode Island by water remains one of the best ways to discover its attractions.

Narragansett Bay lies 41°40′ north of the equator and 71°20′ west of Greenwich, England. Its waters run north to south, dividing the mainland of Rhode Island and extending inland half the length of the state. On the west side of the bay, coastal communities nestle against rural Rhode Island and Connecticut; and on the east side, the shore blends without fanfare into Massachusetts. Between the two mainland coasts hunker about 36 large and small islands, the largest of which are linked to the mainland on either side by a network of bridges.

There are various interpretations of the bay's boundaries. Roughly speaking, if you drew a line from Point Judith, on Rhode Island's southwestern shore, to Sakonnet Point, which juts out from its southeastern shore, the waters to the north constitute Narragansett Bay. The terrain is a pleasant and scenic mix of white sand and pebbly beaches, rolling green hillsides, rocky cliffs tumbling to the sea, woodlands, salt marshes, and sheltered rivers and coves.

Like Chesapeake Bay, Narragansett Bay is an estuary, a semi-enclosed body of water fed by freshwater rivers and streams. The Chesapeake, one of the world's largest and renowned estuaries, is four times larger. As estuaries go, Narragansett Bay is small to medium-sized, yet it covers 10 percent of the state's area and bites two-thirds of the way into its borders—the water's just a hop from virtually every Rhode Island community.

If you took a taste of the bay, you would find the water is more brackish than the water outside in Rhode Island Sound. But the water here is saltier than it is in most estuaries, ensuring excellent fishing and swimming. Salinity is about 29 parts per thousand (ppt) in the bay as opposed to 32 ppt in the ocean. It never dips below 20 ppt, interesting when compared with other estuaries such as the mostly freshwater Chesapeake, which has an average salinity of 8 to 12 ppt. On average, the bay can be counted on to

flush itself every 25 days, though times can vary from between 40 days during dry spells to a quick 12 days when rain is plentiful and river runoff is high.

The lower bay is divided by large islands into three main arteries: West Passage, which, as the name implies, forms the westernmost arm; East Passage, which threads through the middle; and the misnamed Sakonnet River, which is not a river at all but a strait or passage, as it was properly called on early maps. The Sakonnet forms the bay's easternmost saltwater channel. In the northern reaches of the bay, a series of lesser bays and rivers run like capillaries all the way to Rhode Island's capital city of Providence and filter east across the border into Massachusetts.

The entrance to the bay has been marked since 1962 by the 87-foot Brenton Tower. Named for the point of land and treacherous reefs that lie just to the east, the tower, which replaced the Brenton Reef Lightship, achieved recognition as a start and finish line for many long distance races and voyages, and has guided many a mariner safely into port on dark and foggy nights. However, it is in a sad state of disrepair, and the Coast Guard is in the process of replacing the tower with a 12-foot-high lighted buoy equipped with an electronic horn and radar beacon. The buoy's flashing strobe will be visible for 8 to 9 miles, and its steady passing light at 6 miles. The signals will operate 24 hours a day. The Coast Guard expects the new buoy to be in operation by the end of 1990, at which time the tower will be dismantled.

Dozens of islands, most of which are accessible by boat, lie within the sheltered waters of the bay. The two largest, Conanicut and Rhode Island, are home to a significant portion of the state's population. The third largest, Prudence Island, is linked to the mainland only by a small ferry. It is sparsely populated by humans but is home to one of New England's densest herds of white-tailed deer.

The name Narragansett is an Indian name meaning "people of the small point." The bay is named for the tribe of Algonquins who roamed the forests long before the area was settled by

A sloop beats up the bay beneath the span of the Newport Bridge, a familiar Narragansett Bay landmark.
STEVEN KROUS PHOTO

Pilgrims. Many places still carry Indian names, particularly the bay islands. Many places also carry colonial names, which can cause endless confusion and pronunciation dilemmas for visitors.

Highest on the list of confusion-causers is the bay's largest island: Rhode Island, locally known as Aquidneck (Ah-KWID-neck). A friend from the U.S. Virgin Islands cruised the bay almost an entire summer before finally wondering aloud who "Aquidneck" was. She thought the man must be quite important to have so many sites on Rhode Island named for him.

Indeed, on nautical charts, Aquidneck *is* called "Rhode Island," which is correct if you adhere to the name given by the colonists. After landing on its northern tip in 1638, they replaced the Indian name with Rhode Island after the Greek isle of Rhodes. However, when the island and the neighboring Providence Plantations united, the region's official name became the cumbersome "State of Rhode Island and Providence Plantations" and remains so to this day. For obvious reasons, the state's name has been shortened in common usage. To avoid confusion between the state and the bay's largest island, Aquidneck is the more popularly used name.

Conanicut (Co-NAN-i-cut) Island is also a common cause of name confusion. Named for the Narragansett chief Conanicus, the island is known locally as Jamestown—the name of the island's sole town.

Because virtually every resident lives near water, Rhode Island is a state that revolves around the ocean. For those who live along its shores, the bay is a primary focus of seasonal activity—up to 30 percent of Rhode Islanders own boats. The state is home to many boatbuilders and yacht designers. Fishing and shellfishing are large and important contributors to the state's economy—large Rhode Island clams called quahogs (KO-hogs), provide a quarter of the nation's shellfish quotient. The Ocean State lists the quahog as its official shell. The state emblem is the anchor. Newport, at the mouth of the bay on the tip of Aquidneck Island, has long been known as the "Yachting Capital of the World."

In other words, Rhode Islanders love the ocean and boats. During a cruise on the bay you will find not only picturesque, sheltered harbors with atmosphere, history, and excellent swimming and shellfishing, but every convenience available to yachtsmen—and a warm welcome to accompany it.

Cruising
Conditions

□

To sail among the islands and explore the arms and tributaries of Narragansett Bay is as fascinating a pastime as an inshore sailor can desire. The long stretches of open water give ample searoom for small boats and the winding channels that must be picked out by chart and buoy, range and beacon, call for the exercise of just those faculties that contribute to the keenest physical enjoyment.

Narragansett Bay is one of the deepest and finest natural harbors in the world. Fair breezes and fair skies prevail in summer and few other sailing grounds offer as wide a variety of interesting places to visit within an easy afternoon's sail. Navigation, except in fog, is not complicated. Most areas are well buoyed, hazards are well marked, and land is never out of sight. Basic piloting skills and a chart are all you need to cruise the bay in good weather. Safe harbors with all the conveniences are as plentiful as secluded coves, making it easy to pick up or drop off crew or spend a day provisioning or doing laundry.

The average depth of the bay is 26 feet, with East and West Passages offering the greatest depths, and Greenwich Bay and the Sakonnet River the shallowest. Holding ground in the bay is almost without exception soft mud or sand, with few rocks or reefs to foul anchors. The Danforth-type anchor, which embeds itself well in the muck, and the plow are the anchors of choice in these waters.

Most of the bay offers delightful and refreshing swimming, with Upper Bay water noticeably warmer than the cooler water near the entrance to Rhode Island Sound. On average, water temperature in summer is 68° to 72° Fahrenheit; in winter, it drops to a frigid 32°F and grudgingly warms during the spring. June is the coldest summer month for swimming, but the water warms up nicely as the summer progresses, making bathing in August and early September a most pleasant pastime.

Generally, the boating season in southern New England begins around Memorial Day and extends into October, though the tenth month can usually be counted on to dish up a mixture of northeasterly gales as well as balmy days with temperatures in the 60s.

Weather

New England weather is notorious for its fickleness. As the saying here goes: "If you don't like

Weather Signs

	Fair Weather	Falling Temp.	Rain/Snow	Weather Deteriorating	Rising Temp.	Fog
Wind shifts to W or NW	•	•				
Decreasing clouds	•					
Barometer steady or rising	•					
Heavy dew or frost at night	•					
Light winds, clear sky	•	•				
Thickening, lowering cirrus clouds				•		
Rapidly moving lower clouds				•		
Chaotically moving clouds				•		
Barometer falling steadily			•	•		
Approaching front			•	•		
Cloud bases increasing	•					
Cold front has passed	•	•				
Darkening western sky			•	•		
Increasing S wind			•	•	•	
Overcast night sky					•	
Wind shifts to S				•	•	
Warm front has passed					•	
In advance of warm front			•	•		•
Southerly flow of warm air over colder water						•

NOTE: Weather signs, while only a rough guide, can have some predictive value.

COURTESY OF THE UNIVERSITY OF RHODE ISLAND SEA GRANT PROGRAM.

the weather, wait a minute." The weather here does change, and any one weather pattern is unlikely to linger for more than a few days, making it likely that your two-week cruise will be predominantly sunny. Other areas of the country, such as the south and west, are not so lucky in this regard.

Southern New England weather is largely influenced by the Gulf Stream just offshore and the Bermuda High, which pushes warm, moist ocean air in from above the waters of the stream. To the west, cool dry air pools over Canada. Contrasts in temperature between the two are accentuated by atmospheric circulation processes, producing fronts that are responsible for much of the weather on the bay.

Cold fronts usually move into the area traveling from west to east. Watch for a fall in the barometer and an increase in south to southwest winds with an accompanying increase in cloud cover from the northwest. When the front passes, winds may die before shifting to the north or northwest and increasing in strength. Clearing usually follows, bringing clear, crisp air, blue skies, and puffy clouds. Winds may remain north or northwest for several hours after the front passes, until the seasonal sea breeze pipes up and the wind switches southwest.

Warm fronts move into the area from the southwest or southeast and are almost always preceded by northeasterly, southeasterly, or easterly winds. If it blows out of the east in these waters, you can bet something is brewing and wind and rain are likely to follow as moist air sweeps in from the Atlantic. You may notice high, filmy clouds that cover the sun like gauze, making it look as if it is shining weakly through ground glass. Again, the barometer will begin to drop. As the front passes over, winds, which can sometimes be quite strong, will continue to blow from a general easterly direction but fluctuate north or south a bit depending on the location of the center of the storm. When the warm front passes, skies will clear, with winds coming from the southwest and a general rise in temperature.

Occasionally, but not often, a stationary front will cause unpleasant weather to linger for a few days, but this is unusual in the summer months.

On average, the summer weather on the bay is quite pleasant, with fair days outnumbering rainy or cloudy ones by a margin of three to one. The cooling sea breeze keeps daytime temperatures in a comfortable range of about 75°, while at night on the water, temperatures dip into the low 60s and sometimes lower. Be sure to pack a wool sweater, long pants, socks, and a wind-breaker along with your shorts and bathing suit. Especially in May and June, the cool water and wind can keep temperatures on the water downright chilly.

Fog. Fog is a probability during any summer cruise on the bay, but mariners will be pleased to hear it averages only two days per month—much less than on Cape Cod or the islands, or farther Down East in coastal Maine. Since colder water brings a higher incidence of fog, the areas near the mouth of the bay are more likely to experience fog than cruising grounds in the Upper Bay. The farther you go up the bay, the less likely is fog, with Providence experiencing very little during the summer. Often we have basked at anchor in a sunny Upper Bay cove and gloated at the fogbank blanketing Newport and Jamestown. Usually, fog burns off by late morning or early afternoon; if 1 P.M. rolls around and you're still socked in, the fog is likely to linger. If your boat is equipped with radar and Loran, try head-

Fog is a probability during any summer cruise on the bay, but it is far less likely here than on Cape Cod and the islands, or farther Down East in Maine. LYNDA CHILDRESS PHOTO.

ing up the bay. You may be surprised at the difference in the weather. On the other hand, if the morning is clear when you awake, but the breeze stays south or switches southeast instead of southwest, it is frequently the harbinger of an onslaught of ocean fog—be prepared.

Thunderstorms. Anyone cruising the bay in spring and summer will encounter an occasional thunderstorm. While thunderstorms should not be taken lightly, they are generally less severe and less frequent on Narragansett Bay than on Long Island Sound or Chesapeake Bay. There is almost always plenty of warning, leaving time to get safely into harbor before the storm hits.

Most summer storms approach from the north or west, moving south-southeast over the bay from the direction of Providence or Fall River, though occasionally one will approach from the southwest. Watch for building cumulonimbus clouds with telltale flat "anvil" tops or cottony, mushrooming cumulus clouds and a sky that develops a blue-black or even pinkish cast.

It's advisable to find the nearest cove and drop the hook or head for home port at the first indication of an approaching storm. Rain accompanying thunderstorms can be heavy, decreasing or eliminating visibility. Winds, which usually come from west or north in a thunderstorm, can be strong and erratic, and sailboats caught out should drop all canvas and proceed under power.

Occasionally, severe thunderstorms may be accompanied by microbursts—severe downdrafts —such as those believed to have sunk the tall ships *Pride of Baltimore* and *Marques*. Although this phenomenon is relatively rare, it is something to be aware of.

Just as infrequent but equally treacherous are waterspouts, which on rare occasions have been sighted spinning their way up the bay. Waterspouts are the by-products of severe thunderstorms, and boaters should take all action to avoid them.

Hurricanes. The hurricane season in the North Atlantic stretches from June to November. Although the official season lasts six months, when

a hurricane heads this way it usually does so in late August or September.

Hurricanes do occasionally strike here, but they are by no means frequent. On average, tropical storms and hurricanes have threatened the state in only one out of every five years. Looking back over the last 350 years, hurricanes have affected Narragansett Bay on the average of only one year in every 15.

Fortunately, in recent years the National Hurricane Center in Miami, Florida, as well as local meteorologists, have provided ample warning of approaching storms, leaving mariners time to haul out their vessels and batten them down or head to a good hurricane hole, lay out plenty of ground tackle and exercise prudent seamanship. The bay has several good hurricane holes. More in-depth information on hurricanes that have hit the region are discussed in the chapter, "Hurricanes and the Bay" on page 148.

Winds. In summer, the prevailing wind here is the "smokey sou'wester" that drew the America's Cup races from Long Island Sound to Rhode Island for 53 years, until America's defeat by Australia in 1983. Unlike many windless summer cruising grounds, the wind on Narragansett Bay is dependable, so much so that locals tell time by it. Almost without exception, calm mornings are followed by catspaws that skitter across the water. By noon or 1 P.M. the trusty sea breeze springs up, taking a while longer to filter up the bay.

Often, we have sat with sails slatting just above Newport Bridge for as long as an hour, watching boats off Newport reaching along at smart angles of heel with sails full and drawing. Sailors will be happy to know it is rare to be becalmed for long on Narragansett Bay. You can see full sails on all parts of the bay by 2 P.M. or 3 P.M. on any summer afternoon. At times the breeze can arrive with startling speed, sending surprised sailboat crews scurrying to the sheets and scrambling up to the windward side.

The southwesterly sea breeze is usually strong at the southern end of the bay. Because it blows so consistently over a distance of considerable

fetch, there is usually a good-sized swell running at the bay mouth. The swell can persist even though the wind direction may intermittently switch, causing confused seas and lumpy conditions. A change of tide can compound this. Within the bay, wind and boat wakes can whip the water into an uncomfortable chop, but unless it's blowing 20 knots or more, waters in the bay remain relatively smooth.

Wind speeds most days range between 10 and 20 knots. The hotter it is, the stronger the sea breeze is likely to be. At times it can pipe up to 25 or 30 knots on sunny summer afternoons. Another rule that is true more often than not is that the earlier it starts to blow, the stronger the breeze will build by late afternoon.

The Narragansett Bay sea breeze pattern repeats itself like clockwork during periods of fair weather, making these waters unrivaled for sailboat racing and cruising. The wind can be expected to die at sunset, peacefully leaving boaters to enjoy sundowners and barbecue dinners in the cool of the cockpit. If the wind does not die at sunset, it usually means something is brewing and you can expect a change in the weather.

In spring and fall, westerly winds prevail, making any route up or down the bay a painless beam reach for sailboats. Especially in September, westerlies are often accompanied by marvelous, clear, sunny weather. With such delightful wind and weather, and the crowds of summer gone, September may well be the month of choice for a cruise on Narragansett Bay.

Although the summer wind direction is consistent, the twists and turns of the landmasses in the bay sometimes make it briefly veer, back, or fluctuate in strength. In Newport, boaters may notice an increase in the wind strength while entering the harbor. It's not your imagination, but a phenomenon known as "harbor breeze," caused by wind funneling or deflecting off narrow harbor entrances. Sailing near the Jamestown shore or under the bay's two largest bridges, the Newport and Mount Hope, you may experience windshifts and williwaws. In the Upper Bay, Mount Hope itself combines with the bridge carrying its name to cause fairly dramatic wind shifts, often

Region Winds and What They Mean

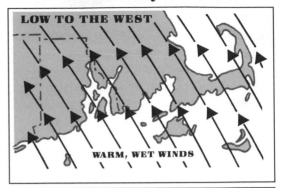

LOW TO THE WEST

WARM, WET WINDS

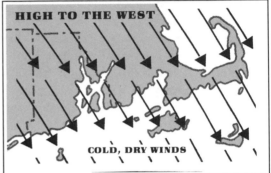

HIGH TO THE WEST

COLD, DRY WINDS

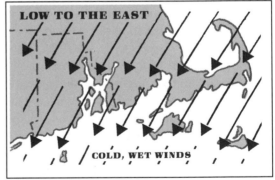

LOW TO THE EAST

COLD, WET WINDS

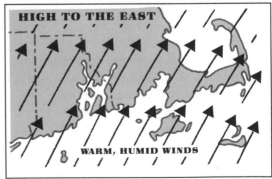

HIGH TO THE EAST

WARM, HUMID WINDS

SOURCE: SULLIVAN, ROBERT J. AND WRIGHT, MARIAN I. *THE RHODE ISLAND ATLAS*. RHODE ISLAND PUBLICATION SOCIETY, PROVIDENCE, 1982.

as much as 45° to 90°, which can cause some confusion.

Some good rules of thumb to remember are: Warm, wet, winds from the southeast mean a low pressure area lies to the west. Cold, wet winds from the northeast signal a low pressure to the east of Narragansett Bay. Warm, humid winds from the southwest mean a high sits to the east of the area; and, finally, cold, dry winds from the northwest mean a high pressure area is approaching from the west.

Tides and Currents

On average, the tidal range in Narragansett Bay is 3 to 4 feet, with spring tides about a foot higher. At the head of the bay, tide range is slightly higher. Expect tides from 4 to 5 feet in the Upper Bay, and 3 to 4½ feet in the Lower Bay. It is important to note that winds can affect the tides here, also. In a strong southerly, water "piles up" at the head of the bay, increasing tide height; in a strong northerly, water is pushed out of the bay mouth into Rhode Island Sound, decreasing the height of the tide—something to keep in mind when navigating at mean low water (MLW) using charted depths. (See Appendix for tidal current charts.)

In general, currents in the bay are less than one knot, but almost universally increase in narrow passages, rivers, or cove entrances. The Breachway at Point Judith boasts a significant tide rip, as do an old stone bridge and passages through the open railroad bridge on the Sakonnet River, where the current can run at 2½ knots and create turbulence that is easy to mistake for a shoal. Other places in the bay where the current runs a knot or more include: the east and west sides of Dutch Island; the west side of Rose Island; off Fort Wetherill and The Dumplings on Conanicut Island, and off Castle Hill near the opposite shore; in between the north tip of Patience Island and Warwick Light; and west of Coaster's Harbor Island. The entrance to the Kickamuit River is notorious for a significant

current, as is the head of the Barrington River, where some locals claim it reaches 3 to 4 knots. Tide and current tables, such as those printed in *Eldridge Tide And Pilot*, should be consulted when navigating the bay's many narrow passes.

Shipping and

Other Navigational

Hazards

The Port of Providence is the third largest in New England after Boston and Portland, Maine, and is the only port of entry on the bay besides Newport. Consequently, vast numbers of commercial ships ply the waters of Narragansett Bay. The bay is also home port for several U.S. Navy frigates. In addition, you will likely encounter large tankers, car carriers, tugs, barges, and an occasional cruise liner bound for Newport in the 40-foot-deep dredged ship channel that wends its way up the East Passage to Providence, Quonset Point, and Fall River. Large ships are rarely seen in the shallow waters of Greenwich Bay or the Sakonnet River, and infrequently in the West Passage, except north of Prudence Island en route to Quonset Point.

Recreational boats should give plenty of sea room to ships in every instance. These vessels are difficult to maneuver in restricted areas, and usually travel at 10 to 15 knots, even inside the bay. Whenever possible, stay away from the dead center of ship channels—there is plenty of water on either side for recreational craft.

Unlike large ships, commercial fishing boats are visible in almost every area of the bay. Expect to encounter fishing fleets on any summer day, particularly in early morning as they head out to fish offshore, and again in late afternoon as they return. Often, these boats are fishing as they steam to or from port and should be given a wide berth when passed abeam or astern. A basket (often a plastic laundry basket) hung in the rigging sig-

Commercial Ship Traffic

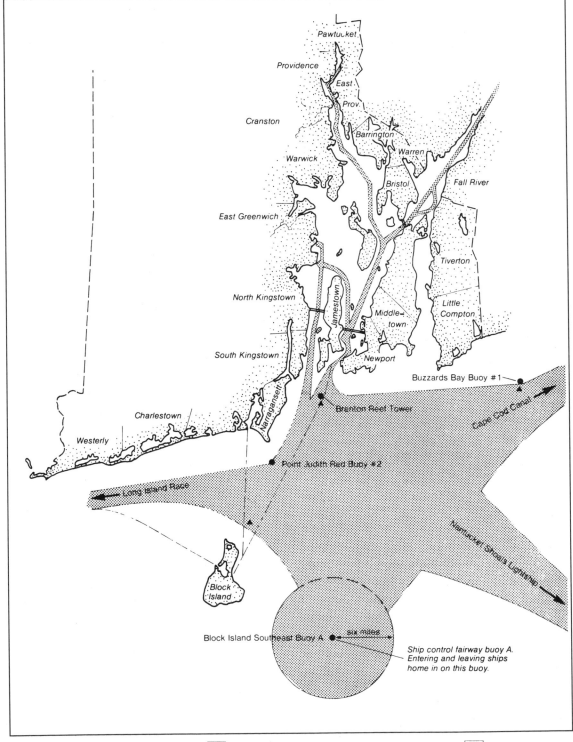

Pawtucket

Providence

East Prov.

Cranston

Barrington

Warren

Warwick

Bristol

Fall River

East Greenwich

Tiverton

North Kingstown

Jamestown

Middletown

Little Compton

South Kingstown

Newport

Narragansett

Buzzards Bay Buoy #1

Branton Reef Tower

Cape Cod Canal

Charlestown

Point Judith Red Buoy #2

Westerly

Long Island Race

Nantucket Shoals Lightship

Block Island

Block Island Southeast Buoy A

six miles

Ship control fairway buoy A. Entering and leaving ships home in on this buoy.

- - - **Block Island ferry routes**   ▓ **Area of ship traffic in Rhode Island**   ▲ **Pilot station**

SOURCE: MARINE ADVISORY SERVICE NOAA/SEA GRANT, UNIVERSITY OF RHODE ISLAND MARINE MEMORANDUM 51

nals that a vessel is fishing. However, the baskets seem to get hoisted aloft and stay there regardless of whether the boat is underway. (We have frequently seen them on boats at the dock.) To be on the safe side, alter course if necessary to give the fishing boats plenty of sea room. Watch for nets trolled astern while the boat is underway, which can often extend for considerable distance. Leave room!

In addition to fishermen, quahoggers—diggers of large clams indigenous to New England—are plentiful on the bay. These shellfishermen work from small skiffs, either by digging with long rakes, or by scuba diving. In some areas, such as Greenwich Bay and the waters between Patience Island and Rocky Point, there are so many quahog skiffs out on a summer's day that from a distance they seem to stretch across the water like a stone quay, a startling mirage if you aren't expecting it. One local fisherman estimated their number in the latter locale to be upwards of 500 per day, and we wouldn't doubt it. This makes for crowding in a few areas, but it is not only rude but dangerous to try to thread through the fleet. These boats are anchored, and their skippers fully occupied at the task of fishing for a living. Should you encounter a pocket of

Quahoggers work from small skiffs, and dig for the clams standing up using long rakes. Give these fellows plenty of room should you encounter them on a cruise of the bay. STEVEN KROUS PHOTO.

quahoggers, as you most certainly will on a cruise of the bay, take an extra few minutes and go around them.

Other Hazards

Any New England cruising ground is peppered with lobster pots, and Narragansett Bay has its fair share. They are usually well marked with white or orange floats so their owners can find them and retrieve their catch. In the flat waters within the bay, the floats are fairly easy to see and to avoid.

A larger and more annoying problem is fish traps, which are threaded like spider webs waiting to snare unwary boats in some parts of the bay. At the mouth of Sakonnet Harbor and along the coast between Brenton Reef and Sakonnet Point lies a series of virtually invisible, connected traps that extends for hundreds of feet in all directions. Once your propeller or rudder is snagged on one of these bothersome hazards to navigation, only a sharp knife will set you free. Most traps are marked—and we use the term loosely—by barrel floats that in some areas are blue or white rather than orange. They are difficult, if not impossible, to see in even the smallest chop, let alone the swells that are usually present outside the bay. Keep well offshore when sailing or powering between Brenton light and Sakonnet, and even then, keep a sharp lookout ahead for barrels.

Another potentially hazardous area has been created by the new Jamestown Bridge, under construction in the West Passage just north of the existing span. This work has created a flotilla of flotsam that is difficult to see in anything but a flat calm. Huge steel mooring balls, anchored barges, and menacing pilings jut haphazardly from the water near the site. At this writing, the construction is enmeshed in legal red tape and progressing at a clam's pace, so uncharted obstacles will likely remain for the foreseeable future. Be cautious in the West Passage when navigating in the waters near the bridge. Unless you are ex-

Cruise liners are not uncommon on the bay in the summertime,
particularly near Newport. Give monsters like this plenty of room.

tremely familiar with the area, do not sail or power through here at night.

Ferries to and from Block Island and Prudence Island share the waters of the bay with commercial and pleasure craft, and the ferry-size tour ship *Bay Queen* and similar tour boats steam the bay daily during the summer at a healthy clip, particularly near Newport. These ferries, like large ships, almost always have the right-of-way. If in doubt about a commercial ship's intentions, try contacting the captain or pilot on VHF Channels 13 or 16. Usually, commercial traffic monitors these channels—but don't count on it. In general, it's best to steer clear and remember the old saying, "Might is right."

Because of heavy shipping and the possibility of fog, carry a good radar reflector when cruising in these waters.

Supplies

Provisions and marine supplies are readily available and accessible in most ports on the bay, as noted at the head of each port description. Pro-

pane is a bit more difficult to find, but is available at Newport County Bottled Gas on Underwood Lane in Middletown, and at U-Haul and Company on Connell Highway in Middletown.

In Rhode Island, no alcoholic beverages of any type are sold in grocery or convenience stores, and cruisers seeking to restock their liquor locker with beer, wine, or spirits must do so at a designated privately owned liquor store. These retail outlets are closed Sundays.

For further information on the availability of marine supplies and repair services, consult individual port listings and the marina directory in the Appendix.

The telephone area code for the entire state of Rhode Island is 401.

Rhode Island State

Guest Moorings

The State of Rhode Island Division of Fish and Wildlife each season sets and maintains a certain number of guest moorings in various harbors around the bay. The mooring buoys are white with a blue lateral stripe, and are prominently marked "State of Rhode Island Guest Mooring." The weight of the ground tackle for each is also prominently marked on the mooring buoy. Refer to the table that follows to determine if a mooring is strong enough to hold your boat securely. Moorings are serviced annually by the state Division of Fish and Wildlife.

The state asks that visitors not occupy moorings longer than 12 hours. Note also that rafting to state moorings is prohibited. If you observe a state mooring being abused, stolen, or occupied for too long, write Dick Sisson at the Division of Fish and Wildlife, 150 Fowler Street, Wickford, RI 02852.

Moorings are set in water ranging from 9 to 25 feet deep around the bay in various harbors. The following table gives coordinates for these moorings, but sites may vary slightly from year to year.

LOWER BAY

Point Judith Harbor of Refuge:

3 moorings. Set in 20 to 25 feet near

A Rhode Island State Guest Mooring, white with blue lateral stripe and prominently marked. LYNDA CHILDRESS PHOTO.

center breakwater, north of the sandbar at the midsection.

Coordinates:

One at 41° 21' 25" N, 71° 30' 59" W
One at 41° 21' 23", 71° 30' 54"
One at 41° 21' 28", 71° 30' 63"

Point Judith Pond:

1 mooring. Set in 6 feet between The Narrows and nun "24" to starboard of the channel (heading north).

Coordinates:

41° 25' 17" N, 71° 29' 44" W

Dutch Harbor:

6 moorings. Set in 9 to 15 feet east of Beaverhead Pier at Fort Getty.

Coordinates:

One at 41° 29' 57" N, 71° 23' 71" W
One at 41° 29' 59", 71° 23' 68"
One at 41° 29' 58", 71° 23' 65"
One at 41° 29' 58", 71° 23' 60"
One at 41° 29' 58", 71° 23' 55"
One at 41° 29' 59", 71° 23' 63"

MIDDLE BAY

Wickford Harbor:

3 moorings. Set in 12 to 14 feet; 2 east of nun "8"; 1 east of can "7."

Coordinates:

One at 41° 34' 43" N, 71° 26' 61" W
One at 41° 34' 43", 71° 26' 63"
One at 41° 34' 39", 71° 26' 65"

Goddard Park Beach:

6 moorings. Set in 10 feet between Long Point and Sally Rock Point.

Coordinates:

One at 41° 40' 11" N, 71° 26' 12" W
One at 41° 40' 11", 71° 26' 23"
One at 41° 40' 07", 71° 26' 27"
One at 41° 40' 08", 71° 26' 34"
One at 41° 40' 18", 71° 26' 03"
One at 41° 40' 17", 71° 26' 08"

Potter Cove (Prudence Island):

3 moorings. Set in 10 feet north of nun "6."

Coordinates:

One at 41° 38′ 50″ N, 71° 20′ 53″ w
One at 41° 38′ 54″, 71° 20′ 44″
One at 41° 38′ 53″, 71° 20′ 55″

UPPER BAY:

Bristol Harbor:

2 moorings. Set in 9 to 11 feet northeast
of Bristol Yacht Club.

Coordinates:

One at 41° 40′ 70″ N, 71° 17′ 19″ w
One at 41° 40′ 72″, 71° 17′ 19″

SOURCE: Rhode Island Department of Fish and
Wildlife, Wickford.

DETERMINING PROPER
MOORING WEIGHT

Boat		Mooring (Mushroom)
Displacement	*Length*	*Weight*
To: 5,000 lbs.	To: 25 ft.	250 lbs.
15,000 lbs.	35 ft.	350 lbs.
35,000 lbs.	45 ft.	450 lbs.
60,000 lbs.	55 ft.	550 lbs.

SOURCE: Burke, Katy. "Home Is Where You Hang Your
Hook." *Cruising World*, November 1980.

Through the Ages: Bay History

When Columbus sailed westward and discovered outlying islands upon the coast of America he achieved lasting and deserved fame, though it occurs to the thoughtful to enquire whether it would not have been a more astonishing feat to have missed them. But to the Norsemen, Verrazano, or whoever discovered Narragansett Bay and grounded the prows of their boats on the pebbly shores, the world owes an unpaid debt.

Forty thousand years ago, Narragansett Bay lay buried under a miles-thick layer of continental ice. As millennia passed and the ice sheet advanced and retreated, glaciers ground away the earth to shape valleys and hills. Occasionally, the ice sheets halted before moving on again, leaving piles of rubble called terminal moraines in their wake. These formed the bay islands and Block Island, which once may have sat at the mouth of the bay like a cork in a very long bottle.

Narragansett Bay is a drowned river valley at the crossroads of two ancient mountain ranges. Eight thousand years ago the bay's deep- and shallow-water passages were valleys between peaks and hills that are present day islands and coastline. As time passed, glacial ice receded and the Atlantic Ocean began to filter into the valleys. Five thousand years ago the water had risen almost to its present level, and the valleys were transformed into the deepwater passages of Narragansett Bay.

Early Discoverers

There are conflicting views about who first sighted Narragansett Bay from seaward. Some believe that Norseman Leif Erikson led an expedition here from Iceland around the year 1000 and that Rhode Island was the "Vinland" referred to in his descriptions of the area. Mysterious rock inscriptions have been found near Mount Hope, where it is believed the Norsemen made camp. Hope may be the "Hop" in Viking sagas, and some think Newport's controversial stone tower was built by these early explorers. Poet Henry Wadsworth Longfellow paid tribute to the riddle of the tower in his poem "The Skeleton in Armor." Local legend has it there is a Viking ship entombed in the silt bottom of a salt pond northeast of Brenton Point, which then must have been a sheltered anchorage with a passage to the sea.

Although it has never been proved, the irresistible magic of the Viking legend permeates the area to this day. Local high school sports teams

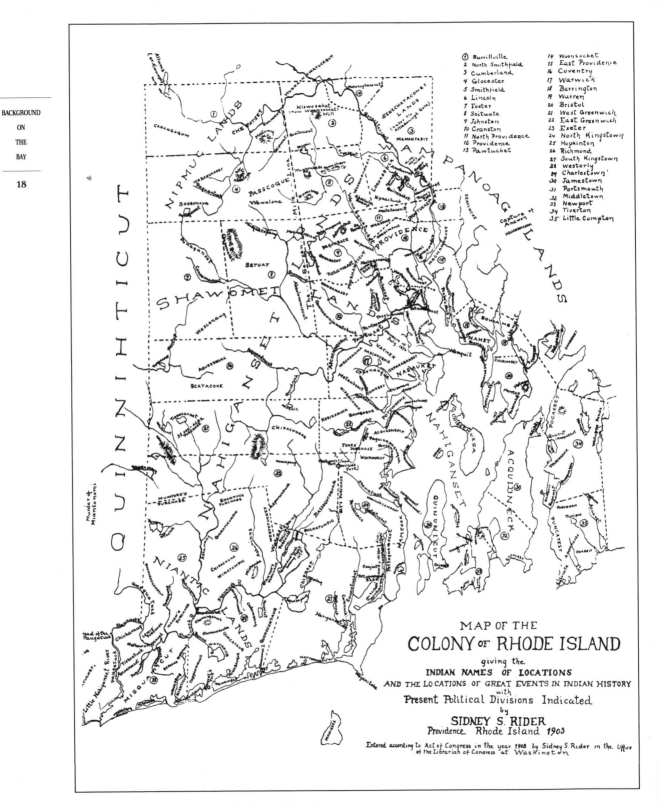

proudly use the title; the telephone exchange for Aquidneck Island is "VIking," and numerous local businesses, including a well-known tour company, have adopted the name.

Another explorer who almost certainly visited here, but who left no written record, is Portuguese explorer Miguel Corte-Real. Corte-Real sailed up the bay as far as the present-day Taunton River, where he allegedly left his mark on Dighton Rock, now on display at a museum near the river's head.

It's fun to speculate about these undocumented early visitors, but the first voyager who obliged posterity by leaving a detailed written and charted account of his visit earned the honor of being the discoverer of record. In 1524 Florentine adventurer Giovanni da Verrazano sailed here in search of a much-coveted passage through North America to the Orient at the request of France's King Francis I. Needless to say, he didn't find one, and instead returned to the king bearing glowing reports of one of the passages he did discover: Narragansett Bay.

After landing at what is now Cape Fear, North Carolina, Verrazano sailed north up the coast, eventually reaching what is now New York City. He anchored at The Narrows, beneath the spot where the bridge bearing his name now spans the Hudson River. From New York he sailed east and came upon an island he described as being "in size like the island of Rhodes." He christened the outcropping "Luisa," for the French king's mother. Today we call it Block Island, after Dutch explorer Adrian Block, who stumbled upon it years after Verrazano and immodestly named it for himself.

Verrazano sailed on, eventually dropping anchor outside Narragansett Bay. He was met by dugout canoes bearing friendly Indians, who escorted his ship to an excellent, protected anchorage—latterday Newport Harbor. Verrazano remained for 15 days, exploring both the bay and the nearby coast. Later, he enthusiastically described the bay as a sheltered anchorage studded with islands among which he felt certain boats could safely ride out any tempest.

The bay that sheltered Verrazano and his crew was surrounded by heavily forested land that had numerous clearings ideal for farming. Verrazano describes seeing bears, wolves, fox, and lynx in great numbers.

The Indians of the Bay

When Verrazano made landfall here, he found the bay populated by several thousand handsome and friendly Indians. The Narragansetts, a rich and powerful tribe, inhabited the lands to the west of the bay. Their rivals, the Wampanoags, lived to the north and east. All were members of the Algonquin Indian family, whose numbers stretched from present-day Canada to the Carolinas.

The bay provided the Indians with a rich livelihood. They hunted deer and wolf, caught blackfish and bass, and trapped beaver and muskrat. They gathered clams, oysters, lobsters, and quahogs, which they cooked in beds of hot stones and seaweed in trenches near the shore, thus inventing the Rhode Island clambake. We can also thank the Indians for naming the quahog. The term is a descendant of "poquauhock," the name the Indians gave the large hard-shell clam.

Quahogs served the Indians not only as food, but as ceremonial ornaments and currency—"wampum" was made by chiseling the purple-streaked shells into beads, which they polished to a high gloss and strung. The abundance of quahogs helped make the Narragansetts one of the richest and most powerful of the northeastern Algonquin tribes.

Unfortunately, their power did not last. What started as a friendly association with the colonists, who began to settle the area in 1636, eventually deteriorated into outright war. In 1676, a vicious attack launched by all the New England colonies except Rhode Island nearly wiped out the Indian population here. About 300 Indians survived the attack, and today a small tribe of

Rhode Island's native sons and daughters still lives in the area.

Colonial Days

One of the first colonial settlers on the bay—Roger Williams—was close to the Indians, sharing with them not only friendship but mutual respect. Williams, a dissident minister who firmly and vocally espoused freedom of religion, also strongly believed that Indians should be paid fairly for their lands. Unfortunately, his fellow Pilgrims did not agree, and banished him from Massachusetts in 1636. In the middle of a frigid New England winter, he set off on foot with a handful of like-minded comrades toward Narragansett Bay, eventually crossing the Seekonk River. Waiting to greet him were his friends the Indians, who promised him food and shelter and welcomed him with the words, "Wha cher, Natop" ("Welcome, friend"). Understandably relieved at having arrived safely in non-hostile territory, Williams declared he had been "delivered from a terrible fate by merciful Providence"—and so he named the city.

As the years progressed, Providence, led by Williams, became renowned for its free-thinking politics. More and more colonists seeking religious freedom flocked to the area. Settlement spread south along the mainland coast and down the bay to Aquidneck, which its first residents renamed Rhode Island in the mistaken belief that this was the island Verrazano had compared to the Isle of Rhodes.

Life on the bay thrived. Coastal areas, with the temperate climate near the bay ideal for a long growing season, proved lucrative for farming. Seaweed was an ideal fertilizer; after gathering the weed along the shore, farmers transported it by ox or horse-drawn cart to their fields, spreading it thickly over the soil before tilling it under. Some of the dirt roads leading to the bay's anchorages that can be seen today are remnants of colonial "seaweed paths." The fertilized soil produced bountiful crops, and the bay became a natural and efficient vehicle for profitable trade with

The Indians greet Roger Williams at Providence with the words, 'What cher, Natop,' or 'Welcome, friend.' COURTESY OF THE RHODE ISLAND HISTORICAL SOCIETY.

Newport Harbor in 1730. Lithograph by J.P. Newell, published
by J.H. Bufford, 1864. COURTESY OF THE RHODE ISLAND HISTORICAL SOCIETY.

Europe, Africa, South America, and the West Indies. Particularly lucrative was the notorious
"Triangle Trade": Molasses from the West Indies
was transformed into rum in Rhode Island, then
traded along the African coast for slaves.

Unable to find enough molasses among British
allies in the West Indies to convert to rum to
trade for slaves, colonists began trading with non-
British Caribbean islands. The Mother Country,
which had largely ignored the colonies up to this
point, suddenly took notice, sending ships to enforce trade restrictions and to levy what colonists
felt were unreasonable taxes. These acts planted
the seeds of discontent that prompted the Revolutionary War.

It was on Narragansett Bay—not in Boston as
many believe—that some of the first acts of colonial revolt occurred. Angry colonists burned
the British ship *Liberty* off Newport in 1769, four
years before the Boston Tea Party. A year before
the Boston uprising, they attacked and burned
Britain's *Gaspee* in 1772 off Warwick in the Upper
Bay.

During the course of the Revolutionary War,
the bay was heavily occupied by the British, who
succeeded in razing the beautiful forests described by Verrazano, using the lumber to build
shelters and for fires to keep warm. Bay residents
built massive stone forts, many of which still
stand, to defend themselves against the British.
British troops remained on the bay, burning and
pillaging, until shortly before the war's end in
1781. As the new nation emerged in the years
that followed, Rhode Island prospered, thanks
largely to the bay, which offered access to foreign
trade, and a temperate climate for crops and livestock.

Shipbuilding, fishing, and shellfishing were
major sources of economic growth. Oystering was
a prime industry, and Narragansett Bay oysters
achieved far-reaching fame for their superior
quality and flavor. The Herreshoff family of Bristol, who began building boats on the bay in 1863,
went on to produce a string of enduring designs
and lovely craft, including five America's Cup
defenders. The family still lives in Bristol, and

the yard is now open to the public as the Herreshoff Museum.

The Bay Flourishes

The 19th century also brought a new source of prosperity to Narragansett Bay, one that continues to thrive: tourism. After the Civil War, the bay became a summer playground. Newport achieved a reputation as a seasonal haven for the rich, but the Upper Bay, too, was a resort area in its own right. The area was renowned for its state-of-the-art amusement parks, beaches, and shorefront dining halls that served the famous Rhode Island shore dinner: clams, lobsters, fish, and corn, cooked on the shore, Indian fashion. Excursion boats carried crowds from New York and Connecticut past gilded Newport to enjoy the summer scene in the waters to the north. Today, Warwick's Rocky Point Park retains the atmosphere that must have prevailed in those days. The park is easy to reach by boat, and visitors can still enjoy the classic repast at the point's famous Shore Dinner Hall.

The breezes, sparkling blue water, and beaches of Newport lured some of the world's richest families. The Narragansett Bay sea air was said to have healing properties, and was even claimed by some wags to be an aphrodisiac. Wealthy summer residents spent millions of dollars building and furnishing extravagant "cottages" by the sea. Palaces by today's standards, these homes were lived in only six or seven weeks a year, and society women spent most of this time outdoing each other with gala balls (costs are estimated at upwards of $200,000 each) while the men commuted on luxury passenger boats from New York. Tales are told of partygoers digging in sandboxes for diamonds, rubies, and sapphires with sterling silver pails and shovels; of horses bedding down on fine linen sheets instead of hay; and of a wealthy eccentric who demanded that his gardeners duplicate the pattern of his expensive Persian rug —with flowers, on the lawn.

The Modern Bay

The bay also provided the power for industry, and by 1900 Providence and Fall River had become two of the most heavily industrialized cities in the nation. By-products of jewelry making and textile manufacture were heedlessly dumped into the bay, eventually polluting its prime oystering grounds and making the extreme Upper Bay unfit for fishing and swimming.

Today, thanks largely to the efforts of "Save The Bay," a determined environmental organization, pollution has been reduced greatly. While it is still unsafe to swim or fish near Providence, Somerset, or Fall River, the organization's goal is to restore these Upper Bay areas to their former levels of cleanliness and productivity. If its past record of success is any indication, Save the Bay is certain to achieve its objective.

The stock market crash of 1929 shattered the fortunes of many of Newport's regular summer patrons and the 1938 hurricane shattered the playgrounds of the regular folk. For a time, the bay's focus turned military. Narragansett Bay was home to the Navy's Atlantic cruiser-destroyer force and was populated heavily by the military during World War II, with most of the bay's islands used for ammunition depots or manufacturing torpedoes and other tools of war. The West Passage was blocked during the war by a floating boom with upended spikes that promised to tear the bottom out of any small boat attempting to cross it, and East Passage was guarded by a net, which could be opened and closed to admit vessels, that stretched across its entire entrance. The bay was also mined during this period. Quonset Naval Air Station was established north of Wickford, and a facility for overseas Navy base construction opened at nearby Davisville, home of the famous Seabees. The Newport Naval War College, established on Coaster's Harbor Island in 1884, continued to draw naval scholars and strategists.

The War College still remains, although the bulk of the fleet was moved to Norfolk, Virginia in 1973. While this move temporarily devastated the area's civilian economy, it provided an unexpected boon, especially for boaters. After the Navy pullout, the federal government found itself with a lot of surplus land—almost 500 acres of islands and coastline on Narragansett Bay. In 1979, it donated to the state several islands and other acreage surrounding abandoned military forts and outposts. The Bay Islands Park System, one of the prime attractions of a cruise on Narragansett Bay, was born and continues to expand.

The Navy presence, while much reduced, is still an integral part of life on the bay. Since the military cutback, the resurgence of tourism in Rhode Island has exceeded anyone's wildest dreams. Once again, the bay has become a playground not only for the rich and famous, but for all who choose to visit here.

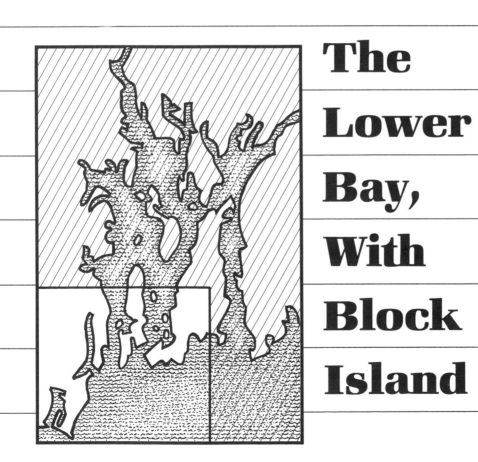

The Lower Bay, With Block Island

THE
LOWER
BAY,
WITH
BLOCK
ISLAND

26

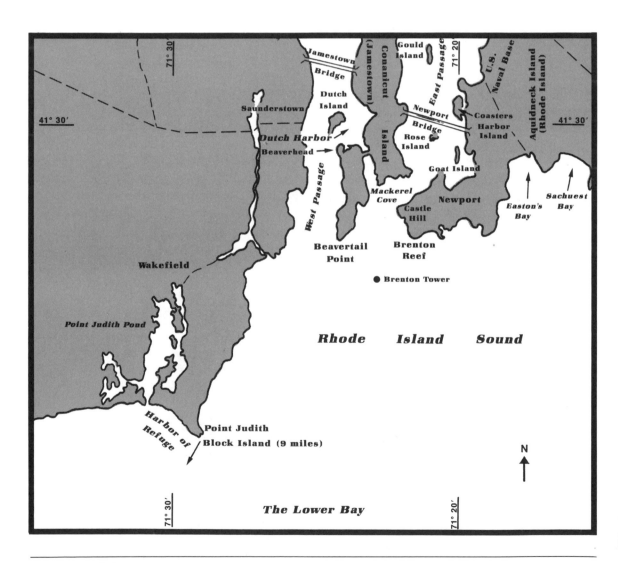

The Lower Bay

SCALE: 1″=**3.0** MILES

The Lower Bay

Nature seems to have planned here a great sanitorium, where the clean breezes of the ocean, tempered by the great heat storage of the bay, promise immunity from half the ills to which human flesh is heir. The frequent islands and rocks scattered broadcast through this part of the bay have each some claim to distinction. Between them moves an apparently endless chain of vessels of every sort and size. Sailboats and launches find their way amid this press with what seems like a marvelous immunity from harm, and add a touch of life to this panorama of wonderful beauty.

The lower end of Narragansett Bay facing Rhode Island Sound qualifies as one of the most scenic—and lively—places in the world to visit by water. The entrance to the bay is marked by Brenton Reef Light, an 87-foot-high Texas tower. At this writing, the light was still active, with a 10-second group flash visible for 25 miles. In early 1989, the Coast Guard stated its intention to replace the badly deteriorated tower with a 12-foot-high lighted buoy equipped with a flashing strobe visible at 8 to 9 miles and a steady passing light visible at 6 miles. Beavertail Light will be upgraded to cover the area now serviced by Brenton Reef Light, including the addition of a new radio beacon that will provide 14½ more miles of coverage than the present Brenton Reef beacon. The Guard's plans call for the new buoy to be operational—and the tower removed—by late 1990.

At its southern end, the bay is divided into two passages by its two largest islands, Conanicut (more commonly called Jamestown) and Aquidneck (called Rhode Island on nautical charts). In naming the respective waterways, bay cartographers seem to have taken the easy way out, labeling them "East Passage" and "West Passage" based on their relative positions.

Because they are close to Rhode Island Sound, Long Island Sound, and the routes of pleasure boaters plying the waters off the New England coast, ports in the Lower Bay are likely to be quite crowded, particularly those in East Passage. Sailing off Newport on a summer day among the large fleet of power and sailboats, ferries, tour ships, and commercial ships can be about as relaxing as driving on a Los Angeles freeway at rush hour—but no one can claim it isn't exciting.

Block Island, just nine miles off Point Judith and some 25 miles southwest of Newport, is a natural extension of a bay cruiser's itinerary. It is a popular and enticing destination, and at the height of the summer as many as 1,500 boats have been reported at the Great Salt Pond, Block Island's anchorage for most visiting yachts.

In spite of a tendency to be crowded, the clean waters of the Lower Bay offer some of the area's best swimming, diving, and fishing. The breeze

THE
LOWER
BAY,
WITH
BLOCK
ISLAND

28

Block Island

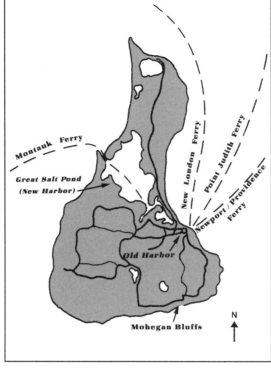

Montauk Ferry

New London Ferry

Point Judith Ferry

Newport / Providence Ferry

Great Salt Pond
(New Harbor)

Old Harbor

Mohegan Bluffs

N

SCALE: **1″ = 1.8** MILES

is always fresh, the sailing is superb, and the many ports of call cater to visiting mariners. Don't let the crowds keep you away.

East Passage

Threading between the rolling hills and rocky cliffs of Aquidneck to the east and the stony outcroppings of Jamestown to the west, East Passage is an unforgettable and impressive bay entrance. Northbound boats often pass close to the cliffs near Castle Hill, dressing ship for shorebound folks who flock there to lounge in the sunshine and watch the procession of yachts passing below them on the bay. For the sailor, the view of the eastern shore from mid-channel is equally impressive—a panorama of Newport's Ocean Drive, its stately mansions spaced at genteel dis-

tances among acres of wild beach roses, small sand beaches, green lawns, and cliffs. On the opposite shore, the surf meets Jamestown's rocky coast in explosions of white sea foam, the rolling green landscape above it a mirror image of the landscape across the bay.

Pilotage. East Passage is one of the deepest natural harbor entrances in the world, with average mid-channel depths of more than 100 feet well up the bay to Prudence Island. To either side of the East Passage are two well-marked but treacherous areas, both of which have caused ships and yachts to come to grief.

The most notorious area to avoid when entering the East Passage is Brenton Reef, which extends well south and east of Brenton Point on Newport Neck. The outer edges of the reef are marked by a series of red nun buoys. You may see recreational traffic cutting just inside the southernmost buoys, R "2" and "2A," where depths are 12 to 40 feet, but it is not advisable for pleasure boaters to try to pass inside R"4" or R"6," which mark shoal and potentially dangerous fingers of the reef.

Currents in this area swirl fast and furious off the cliffs; monitor your set and drift carefully here to avoid being set off course.

Just to the north of buoy R"6" marking Butter Ball Rock is Castle Hill Light, which has served as a beacon to guide mariners safely into the East Passage since 1890. The 40-foot, whitewashed stone light flashes a distinctive red that is visible for 12 miles. There is also a foghorn on the light. Castle Hill Light is a Narragansett Bay landmark, and seems almost a part of the rocky cliffs as it squats low on the hillside. Now automatic, the light was once tended by a keeper, whose dwelling was in Castle Hill Cove just northeast of the light. All but hidden from view from both land and water, this private cove is now home to the U.S. Coast Guard Station Castle Hill, an active search-and-rescue station. During the busy summer, you'll see Coast Guard boats of all sizes buzzing in and out of this secluded spot like bees entering and exiting a hidden hive. As a rule, recreational boats are not permitted in Castle Hill Cove. Legend once had it that a ghost haunted this cove, but the spirit was eventually identified as a keeper's restless wife, fond of taking nocturnal walks dressed in white.

On the opposite shore, at the southern tip of Jamestown, Beavertail Light marks the way for both East and West Passage–bound boaters. Standing alone on Beavertail Point, the light looks quite dramatic, its angular lines projecting an image of Yankee stoicism as it faces the sea.

Beavertail Light is the State of Rhode Island's oldest, dating to 1749. The 64-foot light is still active, flashing white and visible for 15 miles. There is a foghorn on the light as well. The lighthouse is also home to a maritime museum.

A look at the chart reveals the origin of the light's name. Indeed, the southernmost peninsula of Conanicut does resemble a beaver, and a glance to the north on the chart will produce the other end of the rodent's torso—Beaverhead, near Fox Hill.

As you proceed north past Castle Hill, the East Passage offers good water and few navigational hazards. You'll have clear sailing all the way past Fort Adams to the marked channel west of Rose Island. Since the island is surrounded by a shoal, the red nuns should be kept well to starboard. Although the East Passage is dotted with islands, it is well marked and offers more than generous depths for recreational boats as well as shipping. Keep this in mind when sailing or powering through here, and keep an eye out for commercial traffic in both good weather and bad. (See the chapter, "Cruising Conditions," for more information on shipping in the bay.)

The west side of the East Passage holds two potentially hazardous navigational areas that, while less dramatic than Brenton Reef, still manage to

A sloop ghosts past The Dumplings in the East Passage on a misty morning. The rocky outcropping was once the site of a military fort, but now is home to a private residence called "Clingstone." STEVEN KROUS PHOTO.

THE
LOWER
BAY,
WITH
BLOCK
ISLAND

30

snare their share of boats each summer. Kettle Bottom Rock, off Jamestown's Southwest Point, is one of these. Gong "7," which marks the shoal, tempts more sailors than the siren song of the sea, and boats attempting to cut it—if they draw 4 feet or more—are usually sorry they did. There *is* a 21- to 42-foot pass between the shoal and land that locals sometimes negotiate, but it is unmarked, as is the 4-foot-deep shallow area near the rock. Don't try to cut this one without the benefit of local knowledge or you may find yourself high and dry until the tide comes in.

Cruisers should note that currents along the shore of Jamestown from Beavertail to Fort Weatherill run strong, and should be taken into account when sailing near shore.

North of Kettle Bottom, the water past Bull Point is mined with unmarked, submerged rocks, especially near The Dumplings and Clingstone, a prominent rock formation with a house on top. Don't negotiate this pass without local knowledge or a local navigator aboard. The water between the point and The Dumplings is deceptive at a glance because there are plenty of moored boats and even a boatyard tucked back in here. Locals know their way through, but it's not advisable for strangers. A look at the chart will show how potentially hazardous this area is.

Verrazano made note of this unusual rock outcropping when he sailed into Newport in 1524, and the rock itself seems relatively unchanged since his time. The structure atop the rocks, now a private residence (appropriately named "Clingstone") once was a military fort. Fort Brown was built here during America's post-Revolutionary War conflict with the French. After the War of 1812, the fort was no longer used. It was demolished at the end of the 19th century.

The most obvious landmark in the East Passage is the Newport Bridge, which towers over the waters north of Newport and Jamestown Harbors and is visible for a considerable distance out to sea. Mariners approaching the bay in daylight should be careful not to confuse this span with its smaller cousin to the west, the Jamestown Bridge, which spans the West Passage of the bay. The center span of the Newport Bridge offers a horizontal clearance of 1,500 feet and a vertical clearance of 194 feet. A privately maintained siren on the bridge sounds in poor visibility. One of the world's largest suspension bridges, the span was completed in 1969 at a cost of $61 million. The bridge represented quite a change for residents of Aquidneck Island and Jamestown, who up until that time had relied on the Jamestown Ferry for the commute. The bridge's more than two-mile span is one of the longest in the United States and is the longest in New England.

History. East Passage was called Anchor Bay by early Dutch explorers, who also called Brenton Point the Cape of Anchor Bay, believing that the north end was attached to the continent. Some think that later Dutch visitors may have coined the name "Rhode Island," since they are believed to have called Aquidneck the "Red Island," or "Roode Eyelandt." The more widely held belief is that Rhode Island had already been named by colonists when the Dutch name for it was born.

Aquidneck (Rhode Island), the bay's largest island, was the first to be settled by colonists. The island encompasses more than 27,000 acres, or about 42 square miles. Its Indian name is said to mean either "Longest Island" or "Isle of Peace." Certainly its founders, religious dissidents all, found on Aquidneck the peace that came from worshiping as they chose. The settlers reportedly bought the island from the Indians for a substantial sum of wampum plus 10 coats and 20 hoes.

After settling in Portsmouth on the island's north end in 1638, a dispute erupted and the group split. Several well-to-do colonists set off for the opposite end of the island and in 1639 founded a settlement they named Newport after the capital of England's Isle of Wight. The names of the island's early founders linger today in place names around the bay: Anne Hutchinson, William Dyer, John Coggeshall, Nicholas Easton, John Clarke, William Coddington, Thomas Hazard, and William Brenton, after whom the reefs, tower and point of land on the east side of the East Passage and the cove in Newport Harbor are named.

Conanicut Island, the bay's second largest, has

a land area of almost 10 square miles, and is named for the Narragansett Indian chief Conanicus. Today it is more often called Jamestown, a name the island's first settlers gave to its only town in honor of British King James II.

West Passage

As a passageway up or down the bay, West Passage is the road less traveled by both ships and recreational traffic. Winding its way between the west coast of Conanicut Island and the Rhode Island mainland towns of Narragansett and North Kingstown, this waterway offers mid-channel depths ranging from 22 feet to 88 feet.

Pilotage. Boats entering the West Passage should leave Brenton Tower (or the Brenton Reef buoy) to starboard and proceed between the red-and-black buoy off Beavertail Point, keeping it to starboard, and the gong marking Whale Rock, keeping it to port.

Whale Rock, surrounded by deep water save for the submerged 4-foot shoal to its north, seems to rise up out of nowhere at the passage's entrance. A lighthouse once marked this shoal, and its stone foundation is still visible today. Perhaps the rock's abrupt appearance from the depths, not unlike a sounding whale's back, is how it got its name. Because of its isolated position, the rock can be an unexpected "close encounter" for mariners not tracking their progress on a chart. It is sometimes hard to see in one's path if there is a swell running, which there usually is in this part of the bay.

Proceeding north in the West Passage, there are unmarked shoals off the west and north coasts of Dutch Island, so boats with any significant draft should not stray in too close here.

The span of the Jamestown Bridge, as well as a new bridge under construction just north of the existing structure, bisects the West Passage. The original Jamestown Bridge, completed in 1940, also replaced a ferry. It is slightly more than a

mile long and offers horizontal clearance of 600 feet and vertical clearance of 134 feet. Check with locals for updates on progress of the new bridge.

Although it is relatively deep, West Passage is not well marked compared with the East Passage. We don't recommend navigating through here in poor visibility or at night if you are unfamiliar with the area. Even in daylight, keep track of your position on the chart to avoid unmarked rocks, particularly near the coast of the mainland and off Fox Island and Rome Point just north of the bridge.

Construction of the new Jamestown Bridge was begun in 1985 with completion slated for 1988. But a series of construction blunders and governmental red tape left the project stalled and severely behind schedule. At this writing, unmarked pilings, construction barges and steel mooring balls are strewn over the water north of the old bridge, making this passage somewhat unappealing, albeit temporarily. In limited visibility or at night, you'd be better off taking the East Passage north to your destination in the bay.

NEWPORT

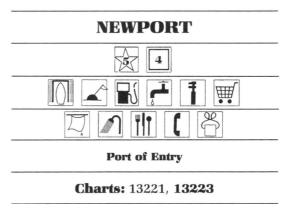

Port of Entry

Charts: 13221, **13223**

The City by the Sea has long been Narragansett Bay's most popular port of call for visiting yachtsmen, an honor that eventually earned it the title, "Yachting Capital of the World." Although the America's Cup yacht races are no longer held here, Newport is still a cosmopolitan and glamorous port and a city whose orientation is decidedly nautical. In few other places will you see

Newport Harbor Anchorages

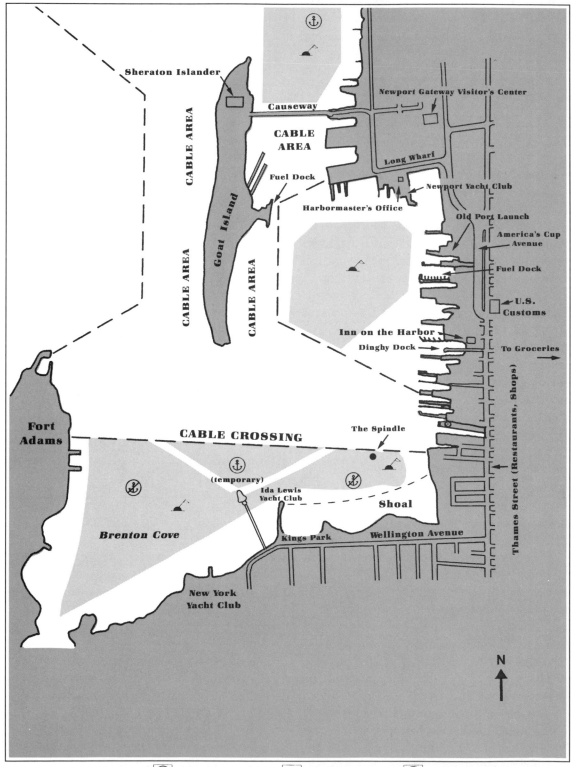

Sheraton Islander

Causeway

CABLE AREA

CABLE
AREA

Fuel Dock

Harbormaster's Office

Goat Island

CABLE AREA

CABLE AREA

Newport Gateway Visitor's Center

Long Wharf

Newport Yacht Club

Old Port Launch

America's Cup Avenue

Fuel Dock

U.S. Customs

Inn on the Harbor

Dinghy Dock

To Groceries

Fort Adams

CABLE CROSSING

The Spindle

(temporary)

Ida Lewis Yacht Club

Shoal

Brenton Cove

Kings Park

Wellington Avenue

Thames Street (Restaurants, Shops)

New York Yacht Club

N

SCALE: 1″=1,200 FT.   ⚓ **Do not anchor**   ⚓ **Mooring area**   ⚓ **Good anchoring**

such a wide variety of boats—from working fishing vessels to famous multimillion-dollar yachts.

Approaches. The harbor entrance is marked by the unmistakable stone fortress of War of 1812–era Fort Adams to starboard and the contrasting cluster of modern condominiums on Goat Island to port. The entrance is well marked and easy to navigate, even at night. By day, its comparatively narrow expanse is often clogged with boat traffic entering and exiting, so observe the speed limit and negotiate carefully through here.

Entering the harbor you will pass the flashing red skeleton tower on the very tip of land off the fort. The water here is fairly deep—20 feet at mean low water—which allows boats to pass relatively close to the seawall. Keep in mind, however, that the spot is popular with line fishermen, who often cast out their lures quite far into the channel. Keep an eye out for flying lures when passing close to land on this side of the channel.

Newport is a deep harbor, with depths of 14 to 28 feet in most areas, except close to shore. Aside from shallow spots near shore, one part of the harbor to beware of is a shoal (offering just 2 feet at low tide) that extends east from the stone jetty at King's Park to the pile of rocks marked by a triangular daymark (known locally as "The Spindle") in the southeast corner of the harbor and beyond it to the south and east. Since the construction of condominiums with accompanying docks several years ago in the southeast corner of the harbor, a channel has been dredged that is marked by large white mooring buoys. These mark the perimeter of a shoal area that lies in their center. Should you have occasion to use this channel, keep the buoys to starboard when approaching the docks and to port when leaving. Although the docks are for private use only, and visitors should have little reason to venture in here, the inner area marked by the white buoys is a common grounding place for unwary skippers touring the harbor. Newcomers and even some locals have been fooled by the appearance of large sail and power yachts to the south and east of the shoal, in addition to moored sailboats in the area. On a mooring near The Spindle, we sat for several seasons and watched a parade of boats go aground here almost daily. To be on the safe side, don't venture south or very far east of the rocks marked by The Spindle.

Anchorages/Moorings/Dockage.

Newport is Narragansett Bay's only port of entry for foreign yachts—the other, Providence, is utilized as such mainly by commercial traffic. Boats making landfall here from foreign ports must hoist their "Q" flag and contact the customs officer, who can be reached at the U.S. Customs Office in Newport on the second floor of the U.S. Post Office building on Thames Street, or by calling 847-2744 (days) or 846-3187 (evenings). If you know your destination within Newport Harbor, you may wish to radio the Coast Guard or dockmaster to have them notify Customs of your pending arrival.

Moorings in the harbor are available from private mooring services as well as the three yacht clubs (Ida Lewis, Newport, and New York) that call this port home. There is plenty of slip space. Accommodations for pleasure boats in this booming yachting town are too many and varied to detail here. For specific information, refer to the comprehensive list of accommodations in the Appendix. In past years, Rhode Island State Guest Moorings have been set east of Fort Adams, but so many have been lost to theft and vandalism that none are planned for the future.

If private or yacht club moorings are full, try contacting the harbormaster, who may know of an empty mooring. It's been our observation that some visitors to Newport, seeing a fleet of empty moorings, simply pick up the first one and make themselves at home. Please don't take an empty mooring without first checking with the harbormaster, who monitors VHF Channel 16. Newport's fleet is active, and many mooring occupants go out for regular day or evening jaunts. A returning owner surely will not be pleased to find an uninvited visitor occupying his spot in the harbor.

In addition to slip and mooring facilities, Newport Harbor has two designated anchorage areas, and the harbormaster asks that visitors who drop

The northernmost anchorage area in Newport Harbor. Rose Island shoal is visible in the background. STEVEN KROUS PHOTO.

the hook do so in these places only. Yachts are encouraged to anchor in the northeast corner of Brenton Cove (formerly the entire cove was approved for anchoring, but now it is too crowded with moorings) or in the area north of the Goat Island causeway between it and the span of the Newport Bridge (anchorage areas are marked on the chart on page 32). While slightly exposed to the north, both these areas offer 15- to 25-foot depths at low water, and holding ground is good. Because of crowded conditions here, scope is restricted to three times the depth of the water in which you are anchored. Under no circumstances should visitors attempt to anchor in mooring areas, in the channel, or over the cable that crosses between Newport and Fort Adams and across to Jamestown. The cable crossing and prohibited anchorage area are clearly marked by signs ashore as well as on nautical charts.

Just to the south of the Brenton Cove anchorage area is Ida Lewis Yacht Club, formerly the site of Lime Rock Light. The club is named for the lighthouse keeper Ida Lewis, who earned recognition in the late 19th and early 20th centuries for her daring rescues of no fewer than 18 souls. She eventually became quite famous for her deeds, and was paid a visit at the light by President Ulysses Grant. Lime Rock Light was renamed for her, and stood on the rocks where the Ida Lewis Yacht Club now stands. You can see her home on Spring Street, a block south of St. Mary's Church, itself of historical importance as the site of the wedding of John F. Kennedy and Jacqueline Bouvier in 1953.

Getting Ashore. For boats anchored or moored in Newport Harbor, launches are available to shuttle crewmembers back and forth to shore on a regular basis, running from early morning through the wee hours during the summer months. You can reach Oldport Launch Service on Channel 68. If the launch is in view, summon it with three short blasts of the air horn. If they are not overloaded, Oldport's friendly launch drivers will make every effort to give you a lift ashore. Other private launches are available from Newport Launch Service, which also monitors VHF 68. It keeps a less regular and reliable schedule than does Oldport. The harbor's three yacht clubs also offer launch service along with guest moorings for members or club guests.

There is only one main dinghy dock for transients in the harbor. Anne Street Pier, just south of the highly visible Inn On The Harbor, is the best place to tie up when you go ashore in your tender. There is no charge for a couple of hours, but it will cost $5 if you're ashore for a full day. Long-term visitors can use the dock daily for a monthly fee of $30. A word of caution: this is a busy harbor, and it is best negotiated only by larger, stable tenders. If your dinghy is small and skittish, we'd recommend leaving it tied astern and taking the launch. When you go ashore in Newport, be sure to lock both your boat and its tender. While Anne Street has a guard on duty days and evenings, a strong lock is still the best insurance against theft in this city, where unfortunately dinghies are a favorite target for thieves.

Incidentally, resist the urge to tie up your tender at any handy looking spot, including most restaurants, fishing wharves, and condominium docks. The concept of private property is taken seriously in this crowded, high-rent resort, and trespassers will meet with hostility.

Things to Do. Long known as a summer resort, the City by the Sea has become an increasingly popular destination in recent years for weekenders and daytrippers both ashore and afloat. In addition to its fascinating history, there are so many things to see and do here a volume could be written on Newport alone.

To get to know the city and what it has to offer, we recommend that newcomers make a stop at the entertaining and informative Newport

Gateway visitor's center on America's Cup Avenue. Just north and east of the Marriott Hotel on Long Wharf, the center is an easy walk along the waterfront from the harbor. Here you can pore over a variety of brochures presenting options on what to do, where to eat, places to see, and events of interest. A huge map of the city spreads over one full wall of the building to help you get your bearings in the confusing maze of Colonial-era streets, whose layout has no apparent rhyme or reason. You can buy tickets to various attractions and activities here, and the staff is happy to answer questions. If you're scheduled to meet or send off crew, this is a good place to do so. The Newport bus station abuts the building and the Cozy Cab shuttle to Green State Airport is just a block south on America's Cup Avenue.

Newport's streets are lined with trendy stores peddling everything from designer clothing and jewelry to fudge and scrimshaw, and the city's streets take on an almost carnival atmosphere on summer afternoons and evenings. The city is without doubt a window-shopper's delight. But if you're the sort who likes to prowl and browse the back roads, try heading off the main drag and exploring some of the city's lesser traveled wharves, nooks and crannies. Bannister's Wharf and Bowen's Wharf, sites of the popular Black Pearl Restaurant and Clark Cooke House as well as a plethora of shops, are no less crowded than the city's main streets in the summer, but the other wharves are more peaceful. When you've had your fill of excitement, head south down Thames Street to quieter regions. The Armchair Sailor Bookstore on Lee's Wharf is worth an afternoon of browsing among the best collection of nautical lore in the city, as is the Corner Book Shop, chockablock full of used and rare volumes. You'll have to hike a bit to reach this one, on Spring Street a block up Dearborn Street from Amsterdam's restaurant on lower Thames. The shop is only open a few hours a day, so if you're a book lover willing to make the hike, calling ahead is a wise idea.

Newport is the host city to any number of yachting events and other fairs and festivals from May through October. For current listings, pick up a free copy of the paper *Newport This Week*, available at most locations around town. In addition to various annual races and boat shows, two favorite events among mariners are the annual August jazz and folk festivals on stage overlooking the harbor at Fort Adams. A flotilla of listeners on the water that is nearly as large as the land-bound audience takes in and enjoys the performances. The Newport music festivals usually feature big-name performers as well as up-and-coming talents in the music business. During the festivals, boats anchor off the tip of Fort Adams, and no one seems to begrudge them the few hours spent there, though it is not a legal anchorage area and boats should plan to move as soon as the show ends in late afternoon.

Where to Eat. If it's nightlife or fine restaurants you're seeking, Newport has its fair share—and more. In fact, it would be hard *not* to find a good restaurant while strolling along the waterfront; there is one on literally almost every corner. If Rhode Island has the most people per square mile, surely Newport can make the same claim for restaurants and bars. You can get a good meal at almost any of Newport's waterfront establishments, but here are some local favorites:

Puerini's, a block uphill on Memorial Boulevard, serves superb Italian cuisine (BYOB). Cafe Zelda on lower Thames Street has excellent fare ranging from the restaurant's famous Zelda Burger to well-executed continental fare. Try the mussels dijonnaise, featured in *Gourmet* magazine. The International Cafe, a long hike or short cab ride from the harbor on extreme lower Thames, serves a spicy selection of foods from various countries (BYOB). Muriel's, just north of Washington Square on Spring Street, away from the hustle and bustle of the waterfront, is also a hike, but worth it. Try the restaurant's award-winning seafood chowder, and BYOB. Last but not least, don't leave Newport without a stop for breakfast or lunch at the Handy Lunch on Thames Street. "The Handy" harkens back to Newport in less trendy times, and is a favorite among locals and the former haunt of the America's Cup crews, who breakfasted here daily during their tenure

in Newport. Monday is "turkey day" at the Handy, and Gary and his crew serve it up in deliciously homemade style at a bargain price for lunch.

History. In addition to streetside sights, Newport has much to offer the history buff. The city is one of the bay's oldest settlements, with homes and cobbled streets dating back to Colonial times. Founded in 1639 by William Coddington and John Clarke, among others, the town—like the whole colony—became a haven for settlers seeking religious freedom. Its natural harbor and good climate led Newport to become one of the most thriving seaports in colonial America. The city, as were many ports on the bay, was active in the Triangle Trade (Caribbean sugar cane, Rhode Island rum, African slaves; see Bay history discussion, page 21), and until 1900, it was one of Rhode Island's two capital cities (the other was Providence). During the Revolutionary War, the city was occupied by the British. Recently, submerged wrecks of several Revolutionary War-era vessels were discovered in the harbor. Experts theorize the ships were deliberately scuttled in the late summer of 1778, when the British realized they had lost the naval war to the colonists' French allies, who were descending on the bay in their superior ships. Don't miss Fort Adams, a Newport relic from that era. It sits on the southwest side of the harbor in what is now a state park of the same name. The site is accessible from the water by launch. In addition to the fort, the park is the site of the Eisenhower summer White House, a Victorian mansion perched on a hill overlooking the bay, and the Museum of Yachting, a fine collection of maritime exhibits and restoration projects that is well worth seeing. Yachts can obtain water to fill their tanks at a spigot on a stone quay here, but are not allowed to tie up for more than a few minutes at a time.

Without a doubt, Fort Adams prevails over the corner of the harbor taken up by the park, as well it should, for it was one of the largest forts in the defense system in the early to mid-1800s. The fort was designed to repel attacks from the sea and land, but like most forts of its time it had an open top, since attacks from the air were as yet unheard of. The fort was one of a series of coastal fortifications pushed through Congress by President James Monroe. It was not completed until 1842, though work on it was begun some 18 years earlier. The fort was built primarily by Irish immigrant workers, and if it had been used during wartime (which it never was) it would have required more than 2,000 men to operate.

When you tire of the colonial era, try taking a peek into the Gilded Age, which had its beginnings after the end of the Revolutionary War and persisted through the early 20th century, when Newport became a world-class resort and attracted the rich who built their summer "cottages" along its breezy cliffs. Via taxi or tour bus, try visiting one or two of the city's famous mansions. (Many tour packages offer combinations of three houses—take it from us, this is one too many at one time!) Mrs. John Jacob Astor's "Beechwood" is one worth seeing as a first stop. Here, the butler receives guests' tickets at the mansion's front entrance, pretending they are invitations to tea. Allegedly because Mrs. Astor is late for her date with you, tours through the house are conducted by her staff, who are dressed in period costume, full of Bellevue Avenue gossip and not afraid to whisper behind their mistress's back. A slide show presented before the servants and guests embark on their tour is invaluable in describing life during the era of luxury and wealth on Bellevue Avenue.

Don't miss touring the Vanderbilts' "Breakers." A more apt description of this mansion might be "palace." Its grandeur is breathtaking. Not on Bellevue Avenue but worth the price of admission is Hammersmith Farm on Ocean Drive, summer White House of President John F. Kennedy. These grounds were the estate of one of Newport's founders, William Brenton, who named the farm after the one he'd left behind in England. You can enjoy it not only for its historical significance but for its beautiful gardens and stunning vistas of the bay.

Several blocks north of the mansions on Bellevue Avenue stands a structure that speaks of another era and remains cloaked in mystery and

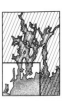
conjecture today: the so-called Viking Tower in Touro Park. Though it is likely the structure was built in the 17th century and probably was a windmill, the legend surrounding the tower refuses to die. According to local lore, the tower was built around the year 1000 by wandering Vikings, possibly led by Leif Erickson. The Vikings are said to have discovered the bay long before any European sailors did and to have sailed as far north as Mount Hope Bay, where it is believed they made camp for a winter while they explored surrounding terrain. Whether it was a windmill or was left here by Leif the Lucky, the tower is a sight to see—and standing near its damp stone walls, one can't help but sense the presence of people and times past.

Provisioning. For trips either short in duration or long on budget, Newport is a provisioner's dream. But supplies here tend to be more expensive than they are at supermarkets elsewhere on the island you can reach by taxicab. If you have a large amount of shopping to do for a long passage, the cab fare out to Middletown's Super Stop & Shop on West Main Road is probably worth it. The store sells everything from groceries to books, and is really a first-class and reasonable supermarket and department store rolled into one.

Much closer, but a bit too far to reach on foot is Crest Farm, popular for its excellent (but expensive) selection of fresh produce, gourmet food and other grocery items.

Fortunately, there are plenty of supplies available within an easy walk of Newport Harbor, too. Along the waterfront, there are several small variety stores (as well as the Thames Street Laundry) and liquor stores. Gourmet and specialty foods are available along the water, too. For the best fresh pasta you've ever had, pay a visit to Pastabilities on Spring Wharf. If you need fresh fish to accompany it, the Seaside Lobster Market on the corner of Spring Wharf and Thames, run by an elderly woman who handpaints the daily special signs taped to her window, is a Newport institution. For lobster, though, hike down to Bowen's Wharf and visit Aquidneck Lobster Com-

Newport Region Anchorages

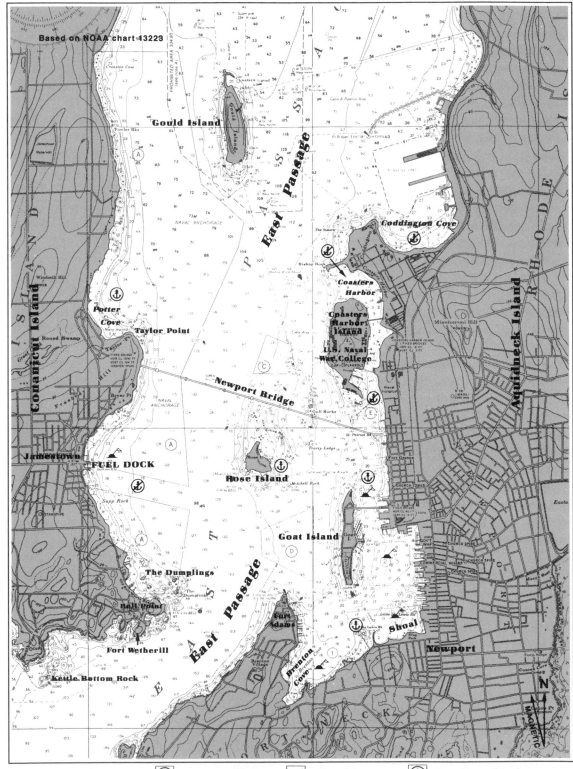

Based on NOAA chart 13223

Gould Island

East Passage

Coddington Cove

Coasters Harbor

Coasters Harbor Island

U.S. Naval War College

Potter Cove

Taylor Point

Newport Bridge

Jamestown

FUEL DOCK

Rose Island

Goat Island

The Dumplings

Bull Point

Fort Adams

Fort Wetherill

Shoal

Newport

Brenton Cove

Kettle Bottom Rock

East Passage

Conanicut Island

Aquidneck Island

RHODE ISLAND

N

MAGNETIC

SCALE: **1″=.62** NAUT. MI.   **Do not anchor**   **Mooring area**   **Good anchoring**

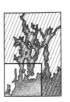

pany, where you can watch live crustaceans loaded into tanks for sale right from lobster boats at the adjoining piers. Even if you don't buy any shellfish, this market is interesting to see.

On Waite's Wharf on lower Thames is Anthony's, which sells excellent seafood as well as a few other gourmet and everyday foods. Waite's Wharf is also the site of the Newport Shore Dinner Hall, as well as the S.S. Newport, the city's only floating restaurant. At this writing, plans were underway for a dinghy dock at Waite's Wharf for patrons, and after it is installed this may be the most convenient place for transient yachts with dinghys to pick up odds and ends.

Two blocks uphill from Anne Street dinghy dock is Almac's Supermarket, which stocks everything you'll need for major provisioning but is a bit pricey and short on fresh produce. Also in this shopping complex are a drugstore, bookstore, card and gift shop and other retail stores, with more just across Bellevue Avenue south of the International Tennis Hall of Fame and Museum. Nearby are a liquor store and the excellent Cappuccino's bakery/restaurant.

Ice is widely available along the waterfront at various marinas, but by far the best deal in town is at the Eastern Ice Company on Brown and Howard Wharf. If you happen to arrive toting your ice bag after hours, not to worry—you can put quarters into a machine and the ice slides neatly and noisily down a chute and either into your waiting bag or onto your waiting feet.

Marine Supplies and Repairs. While Newport is a city that caters to yachtsmen and women, it is also, unfortunately, a city that has lost several important shipyards to the developers' wrecking ball. Famous shipyards, such as Williams and Manchester and Newport Offshore, have been moved off the Thames Street waterfront by construction of resort condominiums; the former moved out of state and the latter is in a precarious position on land at the north end of the harbor. For major repairs, Newport Offshore can handle the job, but most visiting pleasure or charter yachts head up the bay to one of several excellent repair facilities—Little Harbor

Marine, in Portsmouth, or East Passage Yachting Center just north of there. Farther up, Cove Haven Marina in Barrington is also a good spot for major repairs.

Yachts with rigging problems should give Jim Miller of Portsmouth's Rigging Company a call (683-1525); and one of the best electronics experts and troubleshooters in the area is Rick Viggiano, owner of Pro-Tech Marine (683-9172). You can often see Pro-Tech's Mako 23 in the bay, and Viggiano monitors VHF Channel 78A when he's out on the water.

For small, do-it-yourself repairs and supplies, everything you need can be found at JT's Ship's Chandlery on Thames Street in the heart of downtown. A smaller, less well-stocked marine store is Mayday's on Mill Street, about 10 blocks south along Thames.

As we said earlier, Newport has so much to offer that books could (and have) been written on this one port alone. We've shared what we think are some of the best things to do in this bustling seaport, and will leave you to discover the city's other merits on your own!

GOAT ISLAND

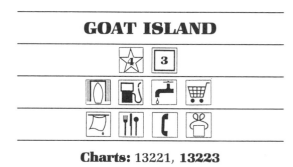

Charts: 13221, **13223**

Approaches. Goat Island, a little more than a half-mile long, stretches north to south on the west side of Newport Harbor and in effect forms the harbor's western boundary. The island is attached to the mainland by a causeway with a minimum vertical clearance of just 14 feet. Marina facilities are south of the causeway, but to reach the harbor's northern mooring/anchorage area, yachts must go around the west side of the island, passing between it and Rose Island.

On the northern tip of Goat stands the 33-foot Goat Island Light, which flashes a green signal visible for 11 miles. The light is not the original, which was built around 1820. The current lighthouse has stood in that spot since 1865.

Anchorages/Moorings. To the north of the causeway is a mooring area and designated anchorage for transients. Most boats can reach this spot only by sailing out of Newport Harbor and around the west coast of Goat Island due to the limited clearance under the bridge. This area is a bit remote and tends to be exposed in a northerly, but holding ground is good and launch service is available.

Traffic-wise, you'll find this anchorage more peaceful than the one in the harbor's midst. It may take you a bit longer to get back and forth to town, but the calm may be worth it—and there's no better spot to watch the sun set the sky ablaze behind the towers of the Newport Bridge.

Where to Eat. Just above the fuel dock is the Marina Pub Restaurant (also the unofficial home of the Goat Island Yacht Club). This is a pleasant place to visit for lunch, dinner, or cock-

Goat Island, Newport, as it looked during World War II, when a torpedo station dominated the island. NAVAL HISTORICAL COLLECTION, NAVAL WAR COLLEGE, NEWPORT.

tails, particularly when an ocean race is going on, when it is abuzz with international press corps, racers, and support crews. Photographs of ocean racers adorn the walls here and the atmosphere is always festive.

Fuel/Provisions. Fuel is readily available at the dock on the east side of the island, and there is a laundromat a short walk from the docks. Ice is available at the fuel dock, and a short walk away is a liquor store next to a small, somewhat scantily stocked grocery.

History. Like Hog Island farther up the bay, Goat Island gets its name from the livestock that once roamed here—early settlers used it as a goat pasture. The island's Indian name was Nomsussmuc and it was purchased from the Indians by colonists in 1723.

One of the first Colonial forts, built in 1700, once stood on Goat Island. Originally named Fort Anne, it was later known by a successive string of names, including George, Liberty and, later, Fort Washington. In 1869, the Navy purchased the island and established a massive torpedo station that remained operational through World War II, when it manufactured 80 percent of the torpedoes used by the Navy.

Today the island is home to the large and well-equipped Goat Island Marina as well as private residences and the tall, angular, and highly visible Sheraton Islander hotel and conference center. Although it is an island, Goat is generally considered to be part of Newport Harbor. In addition to providing shelter from the west-north-west for moored boats in the harbor, the island is a popular site for transients, and during the summer it is home to some of Newport Harbor's most spectacular visiting yachts from around the world. During the several long-distance ocean races that begin or end in Newport, the fleet was housed at Goat Island Marina.

ROSE ISLAND

No facilities

Charts: 13221, **13223**

Just outside the entrance to Newport Harbor to the west of Goat Island lies another of the bay's smaller islands. Tiny Rose Island, unlike Goat, has remained free of development and at this writing the State of Rhode Island plans to buy part of it to preserve its publicly accessible open space.

Anchorages. Unfortunately for larger cruising boats, the 14-acre island is surrounded by shoals, and is not a good anchoring spot for any but the most shoal-draft boats. A strong current runs in the waters surrounding the island and may be the basis for the island's name. Originally, it was called Race Island and Rose is most likely a corruption of that.

Beware of a rocky sandbar that extends about 4/10-mile north-northeast of the island. It is almost totally submerged at high tide, but is exposed at low water. The shoal itself is unbuoyed, though the red nun marking the channel lies to the southwest of it. Avoid going near the north end of Rose to be on the safe side. Small boats may be anchored or beached on the east-southeast side. The shoal at one time was a grassy cow pasture, but a gale around the turn of the century reduced it to the tidal flats that are there today.

Things to Do. In recent years the island's ownership has been juggled between government and private interests, but it always has been an excellent place for a day's outing by small boat. If you go ashore here, avoid hiking too extensively around the interior during gull nesting season since gulls have been known to become hostile toward intruders.

Scuba diving around the island, particularly

on the west side, is excellent, and local divers report the rocky ledges of the shoal are excellent lobstering grounds.

Until the status of Rose Island is settled, visitors should probably check with local authorities before going ashore here. With luck, Rose will continue to sit placidly amid the noise and haste of Newport Harbor, and will remain an oasis for all to enjoy.

History. The island's Indian name was Conockonoquit ("place of the long point"). Indeed, the island originally did have a long point on the north end (now the shoal), but its shape, once compared with a teardrop, today has been described as more like a pork chop.

The distinctive Rose Island Light, once badly deteriorated, is being restored by the Rose Island Lighthouse Foundation, a group of concerned citizens. When work is complete, it will be cared for by a live-in lighthouse keeper as it was in the days of old. It will also be the site of a public museum. The light dates back to 1870 and guided mariners into Newport Harbor until construction of the bridge was completed in 1971. The light's foundation rests on remains of the stone bulwarks of Fort Hamilton, which was built in 1798. During World War II, the island was used by the

Navy as a storage depot for torpedoes built on nearby Goat.

CODDINGTON
COVE—
COASTERS HARBOR
ISLAND

No rating/Off-limits to private yachts

Charts: 13221, **13223**

Coaster's Harbor Island and Coddington Cove are part of the U.S. Navy base and are off-limits to civilians, including those on boats. Nevertheless, both are conspicuous sites on the bay, and we include them for the sake of information rather than accessibility.

History. Coaster's Harbor Island is the home of the U.S. Naval War College, the large and very visible stone building complex just north of the Newport Bridge. After the founders of Newport

Newport Naval Training Station, as it appeared in 1890. The building still stands facing the bay, north of Newport Bridge, on Coaster's Harbor Island. NAVAL HISTORICAL COLLECTION, NAVAL WAR COLLEGE, NEWPORT.

left Portsmouth (then called Pocasset) in 1639 and headed to the island's south end to begin a new settlement, they sought overnight refuge on the island before proceeding into Newport Harbor. The island's Indian name is Woonachaset. After the Indians sold the island in 1822, it was the site of an asylum for the poor. In 1884 the same building, still standing today, was transformed into the Naval War College, an obvious landmark north of the Newport Bridge. It is the oldest such college in the world.

Coddington Cove, named for Newport founder William Coddington, is home to several navy ships and is protected from all directions except due west. A large stone jetty built by the navy as well as several resident destroyer-type ships mark this site just north of the War College. The cove is also the site of Derektor Shipyard, builders of large commercial and government craft.

As mentioned, this sheltered spot is off-limits to transient craft, and visitors should look elsewhere for a place to drop the hook.

JAMESTOWN

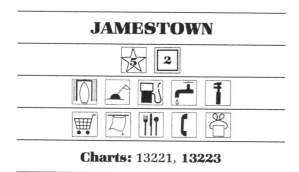

Charts: 13221, **13223**

Jamestown Harbor, a bight on the east side of Conanicut Island, is a pleasant, if somewhat exposed, port on the west side of East Passage in the lower bay.

Jamestown is an attractive waterfront village and a pleasant respite from life in the fast lane in Newport across the bay. Despite some renovations and the addition in recent years of a few conspicuous condominiums, trendy shops, and restaurants, the town has managed to retain a slow-paced and friendly small-town charm.

Anchorages/Moorings. Because of the large numbers of moored boats here, there isn't much of an anchorage area. The harbormaster reports that the outer (eastern) row of moored boats lies in 60 feet of water, and that transients wishing to anchor must do so to the east of these vessels. The depths in this area, combined with an eelgrass bottom, result in poor holding ground, and a tidal back eddy makes anchoring inadvisable.

Fortunately, Conanicut marina in town has 20 guest moorings and several permanent transient slips, and there are three additional guest moorings available from both Jamestown and Clark boatyards (see listings on page 188).

Things to Do. The water in Jamestown Harbor is clean enough to swim in, but people generally don't. If you can arrange a ride, (the town has no taxis) we recommend highly a visit to Fort Wetherill State Park, about a mile farther south along the island's east coast. Here, the swimming is fine and the snorkeling and scuba diving even better, all in the vicinity of the historic fort. The remnants of the building that stand today were built just after the turn of the 19th century, but the land was purchased by the government more than 100 years earlier. During the Revolutionary War, cannons were installed here to help guard Newport against attack by the British. Today, the sprawling state park on the site overlooks one of the best views to be had of Narragansett Bay. The terrain is half wooded and half grassy hills, and picnicking and hiking around the old fort and grounds and climbing the cliffs are favorite activities here.

Farther along the coast is Beavertail, visible as you enter either East or West Passage by boat and about five miles by car from Jamestown Harbor. Nowhere will you find more commanding vistas than on this 153-acre tract of land, which also is now a state park. The fishing, hiking, picnicking and scenery here are unsurpassed anywhere in the bay.

Where to Eat. Ken's East Landing Restaurant, on Narragansett Avenue, serves excellent seafood, and Pezzulli's Cafe and bakery, not far from Ken's, serves Italian food that is a favorite among locals.

The Islander is a good beer and sandwich spot, while the upscale Bay Voyage is quite chic and expensive.

Provisions. Within a few blocks of the harbor you'll find adequate, if not wide-ranging, conveniences. In the town's main square are Pitcher's Liquors, a bank with an automatic-teller machine, and a small marine supply store, as well as assorted other shops and eateries. On Narragansett Avenue, which runs east to west almost directly opposite the harbor, you'll find additional sundries. Jamestown Distributors is a well-stocked marine supply store with some of the most competitive prices we've seen anywhere—but note that they close at noon on Saturdays, even in the summer. Farther up you'll find a laundry (not a laundromat); hardware store, gift and clothing stores, and a convenience store at a Sunoco gas station which carries basic grocery items. A few blocks west of here are a pharmacy and post office, though the latter is a bit of a hike.

The island's only supermarket, McQuades, is less than a mile from the harborfront, but is a bit far to walk if you plan to provision extensively. Should you wish to walk to the market, continue heading west on Narragansett until you reach a four-way intersection with a flashing red light. A post office is on the corner. Turn left here, and you'll find McQuade's ahead on your left.

History. As early as 1667 there is said to have been a watchtower and fire beacon on the point where the Beavertail Light now stands. The lighthouse that is there today was built in 1749, and is one of the East Coast's oldest such structures.

Jamestown, named after England's King James II, is Conanicut Island's only town. Its first settlers, like most who first made the bay islands their homes, were fleeing the religious restrictions of Plymouth Colony and came to Conanicut in search of religious freedom.

The island is home to one of the more fascinating Narragansett Bay legends, which says that the notorious pirate Captain Kidd buried a treasure somewhere on the island, perhaps near The Dumplings. His ghost is said to haunt Beavertail. As related by Edgar Bacon in his 1904 book on Narragansett Bay, the story goes like this:

> Over on the end of Conanicut, just above the Beavertail, a strange adventure befell Ben Gladding, a fisherman and quahogger. Ben had mended nets all day, and when a full August moon arose, he decided to dig some clams. Shouldering clam rake and basket, he started for the cove now called Austin Hollow, on the west side of Beavertail. After digging here awhile, Ben beheld a vision that made him rub his eyes in disbelief. A strange vessel unlike any craft he'd ever seen hove into view. She had a high stern, crossyards on her bowsprit, and strangely fashioned sails. The vessel sailed towards him at a rapid clip, but even odder than her strange appearance was the fact that she seemed to have passed over a shoal where no ship could have come. Not only that, she was sailing swiftly *into* the wind, yards square and sails full! She sailed, goes the story, within "a biscuit's toss" of poor Ben, heading straight for shore just south of him, and he fully expected to witness her destruction on the rocks. But she crossed the land as easily as she had sliced through the water, and the last Ben saw of her she was sailing away unharmed. In the moonlight, he caught a glimpse of the flag flying from her mainmast: On it was the outline of a skull and crossbones. The pilot, of course, was said to be none other than the restless soul of Kidd, returning, perhaps, in search of his lost treasure.

Legends such as this one are not the only thing visitors will find fascinating about Jamestown. As a Lower Bay port, it has for many years been overshadowed by its larger sister to the east. But the breezes are equally fair and the sunshine equally bright on this side of the East Passage. Jamestown has come into its own as a stop for visiting yachts, and we recommend a stop at this homey New England town.

POTTER COVE

(JAMESTOWN)

No facilities

Charts: 13221, **13223**

Narragansett Bay has several spots that have duplicate names, and Jamestown's Potter Cove is one of them. Don't confuse this cove, an inlet just north of the Newport Bridge on Jamestown's eastern shore, with Potter Cove on the north tip of Prudence Island farther up the bay.

Anchorages/Moorings. This Potter Cove has been popular for years among locals as a spot to drop the hook for lunch and a swim, but is becoming increasingly popular with visitors as an overnight anchorage. The cove is protected from the southwest by Freebody Hill and Taylor Point, and is a suitable overnight anchorage if winds remain southwesterly. However, waves break in the cove in a strong north or east wind, so be sure of the forecast before dropping anchor here for the night.

The center of the cove is deep, though the rock-and-sand bottom stays shoal quite a way out from shore, and the transition from deep to shallow water is a sudden one. As long as you stay well off the beach to the west and the rocky ledges to the south, Potter Cove offers depths of at least 20 feet, with good holding ground.

In prevailing southwesterly winds, this is a good anchorage whose only drawback is a bit of noise from traffic on the nearby Newport Bridge and an occasional swell from waterskiers or larger traffic out on the bay.

Things to Do. The cove is excellent for swimming and the ledges of rocks along the southern shore offer perches for sunbathers. This is a particularly good spot for beginning board-

sailors, with usually flat water and enough wind for a good sail.

MACKEREL COVE

No facilities

Charts: 13221, **13223**

Mackerel Cove lies sandwiched between Jamestown's Beaver Neck and the opposing shore of Conanicut, and like Potter Cove, is a popular spot for day-trippers as long as prevailing summer southwesterlies blow. If the wind backs south or southeast, however, the swells are considerable and the friendly sand beach becomes a lee shore. Avoid it if a wind shift is predicted and weigh anchor and head elsewhere if you're caught here in winds from the south-southeast.

Approaches. Mackerel offers good depths almost all the way in to the sandy beach at its northern end, but beware of rocks near the northwest shore. Depths range from 38 feet in the south end of the cove to 2 to 5 feet just off the beach.

Anchorages. The best spot to anchor here is at the northwest end, since even when the wind is southwest a slight swell runs in here, and the farther you are from open water, the better. Anchor in 7 to 11 feet and sit back and enjoy the scenery, or dinghy ashore for a walk along the beach.

The cove most likely gets its name from the abundance of fish that could once be caught here. It is a perfect destination for an afternoon daysail from Newport or Jamestown, but if the wind begins to kick up a noticeable swell, be on your way. Because of exposure to the south-southeast, we don't recommend staying here overnight.

Jamestown Region Anchorages

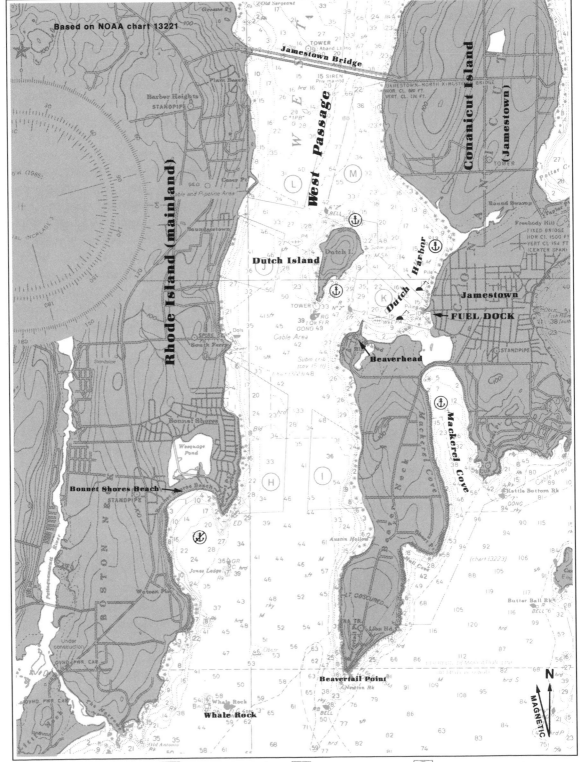

Based on NOAA chart 13221

Jamestown Bridge

West Passage

Conanicut Island (Jamestown)

Rhode Island (mainland)

Dutch Island

Dutch Harbor

Jamestown

FUEL DOCK

Beaverhead

Mackerel Cove

Bonnet Shores Beach

Beavertail Point

Whale Rock

MAGNETIC

SCALE: 1"=.76 NAUT. MI.   Do not anchor   Mooring area   Good anchoring

DUTCH ISLAND

No facilities

Charts: 13221, **13223**

Dutch Island is one of our personal favorite destinations in Narragansett Bay. It's a peaceful retreat that, though popular, is not overly crowded even on summer weekends. Don't miss this one—but remember to set a good, strong anchor, use plenty of scope, and keep an ear out for the forecast when anchoring here overnight.

Anchorages. Dutch Island, a small spot of land in the West Passage of the lower bay, is bordered on its west side by a shoal and foul water. But in the prevailing southwesterly winds of this area, the water to the north and northeast of the island is a popular overnight or weekend anchorage. With plenty of scope, holding ground here is fairly good, but be sure your anchor is securely set, since currents swirl around the island and your boat is likely to swing to both current and wind here.

Despite the crowds that frequent the northeast

Dutch Island Light is a prominent landmark when approaching the island from the south. The light was built in 1826, and is no longer active. LYNDA CHILDRESS PHOTO.

anchorage, it is no place to be in a strong northerly wind, although holding ground is good. Caught in an unpredicted northerly gale here during the wee hours one summer morning, we weighed anchor and moved around to the small cove on the southeast side of the island. There we sounded our way in and anchored in 28 feet with all 200 feet of rope-and-chain rode out. Despite the depth, the anchor held well, and though we spent the night standing anchor watches, all was well. We don't recommend the southeast cove as an anchorage except as a last resort should you find yourself bobbing in the swells on the north side of the island. If you sound your way in at night or in poor visibility, keep in mind the land is extremely steep-to and depths of 28 feet prevail right up to shore.

In the northeast anchorage, sailors can find depths of at least 15 feet. You should be aware of a 29-foot-deep trough that runs through shallower depths in this area. The shoal along the island's west edge snakes around the northwest side of the island to the western edge of the anchorage area, and is marked by red nun buoy "2." There is some shoaling east of the buoy, particularly between it and Conanicut's Beaverhead, so stay well to the east of it.

Things to Do. Swimming at Dutch Island is excellent, but watch the current if you jump overboard. Especially on a flood tide, it can sweep you astern with startling swiftness, and in such a situation you may wish to trail a line for swimmers to hold.

Don't leave Dutch without a hike to the south end and a visit to the lighthouse that stands on the rocks there. The light, which has stood in the spot since 1826, is no longer active. The point was also once the site of a keeper's house, which was torn down when the light was automated in the 1940s. The light was deactivated in 1979 and is now owned by the state.

History. Eighty-one-acre Dutch Island gets its name from the early Dutch explorers who established a fur trading post here in the 1600s. Dutchmen traded their native goods with the In-

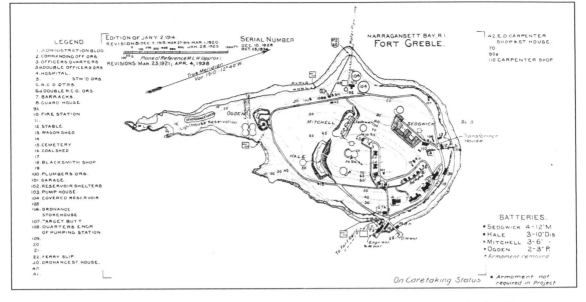

LEGEND

EDITION OF JAN'Y 2 1914
REVISIONS:DEC 7,1915, MAR 27,1916, MAR 1,1920
JAN 28,1925
OCT 23,1934
SERIAL NUMBER
DEC 10,1926
REVISIONS:MAR 23,1921; APR 4,1938
Plane of Reference M.L.W.(approx.)
True Meridian
Var 1910-12°40'W.

1. ADMINISTRATION BLDG
2. COMMANDING OFF QRS
3. OFFICERS QUARTERS
3d. DOUBLE OFFICERS QRS
4. HOSPITAL
5. STW'D QRS
6. N.C.O QTRS
6d. DOUBLE N.C.O. QRS
7. BARRACKS
8. GUARD HOUSE
9.
10. FIRE STATION
12. STABLE
13. WAGON SHED
14.
15. CEMETERY
16. COAL SHED
17.
18. BLACKSMITH SHOP
19.
100. PLUMBERS QRS
101. GARAGE
102. RESERVOIR SHELTERS
103. PUMP HOUSE
104. COVERED RESERVOIR
105.
106. ORDNANCE
STOREHOUSE
107. TARGET BUTT
108. QUARTERS ENGR
OF PUMPING STATION
109.
20.
21.
22. FERRY SLIP.
30. ORDNANCE ST. HOUSE.
40.
41.

NARRAGANSETT BAY, R.I.
FORT GREBLE.

42.E.D.CARPENTER
SHOP & ST. HOUSE.
70
90s
110 CARPENTER SHOP

BATTERIES.

• SEDGWICK 4-12"M
• HALE   3-10"Dis
× MITCHELL   3-6"
• OGDEN   2-3" P.
× Armament removed

On Caretaking Status   • Armament not
required in Project

Dutch Island was the site of Fort Greble, a turn-of-the-century military outpost built at the outbreak of the Spanish-American War. The fort was reactivated in World War I. Now, the island belongs to the state, but some of the buildings remain. Use this to help identify old buildings as you hike around the island. NATIONAL ARCHIVES.

dians in exchange for furs, fish, and venison. The island was purchased from the Indians in 1650.

Uninhabited, the island is part of the Bay Islands Park System, and offers excellent hiking on terrain ranging from flat flowering meadows to hillocks peppered with pine and cedar. Today the island is a wildlife refuge, but once it harbored troops in Fort Greble, parts of which still stand on the island today, awaiting exploration.

Greble was a turn-of-the-century military outpost built in 1898 at the outbreak of the Spanish-American War. After the war the fort was dormant until World War I, when it was reactivated to aid in the defense of Narragansett Bay. A net was stretched from the island across the channel west of the fort, closing the passage to traffic. In the 1940s it was used as a rifle range and later was sold to the state as one of the first parcels in the Bay Islands Park System. One of the island's Indian names apparently was Quotenis, but another, Aquidnesuc, occasionally appears, and may have meant "Little Island."

DUTCH HARBOR

(JAMESTOWN)

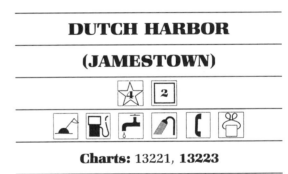

Charts: 13221, **13223**

Just to the east of Dutch Island is Dutch Harbor, sheltered in all but northerly or westerly winds. This pretty cove on Jamestown's western shore is a popular place with both residents and transients, and has grown quite thick with moorings in the past several years.

Dutch Harbor is a better overnight anchorage than Dutch Island, though it is still a bit exposed, and the island is close enough to be reached by auxiliary powered tender. If you anchor off Dutch Island by day, you may wish to retreat the short distance east to this cove to spend the night. Whatever the case, this area is one of the bay's most enjoyable stops.

Approaches. Dutch Island Light, which once marked the rocky tip of the island and the western harbor entrance, was replaced in 1979 by a quick-flashing red and green gong just south of the light. Approaching from the south, pass between it and red nun "2," keeping the latter to starboard. Nun "2" marks an extensive shoal off Beaverhead, where there are depths as shallow as 2 feet.

Anchorages/Moorings. The south end of the harbor beyond the moored boats, due east of the dock at Fort Getty, is the choice anchoring spot in Dutch Harbor. But at this writing it was well on its way to being declared a wildlife sanctuary, where anchoring would be forbidden.

The north end of the harbor, beyond the mooring area, offers sufficient depth for anchoring at 8 to 17 feet and holding ground is good, but the area is marginally more exposed in the prevailing southwesterlies that funnel between Dutch Island and Beaverhead.

There are 6 State of Rhode Island Guest Moorings at the south end of Dutch, set in 9 to 15 feet of water just east of the pier off Beaverhead. (See "Cruising Conditions," page 14, for coordinates, rules and regulations.)

Marine Repairs. Dutch Harbor Shipyard in the southeast corner of the cove is a full-service yard offering repairs and moorings with launch service. (See marina listings in the Appendix for more specific information.)

Provisions. There are no provisions within an easy walk of this harbor, but if you're in the mood for exercise, McQuade's Market is roughly 3/4 mile away on foot, along with a post office, laundromat and convenience store.

History. Fort Getty, now a 31-acre park and popular campsite, is at the south end of the harbor on Fox Hill (or Beaverhead). During the Revolutionary War, this area was used to keep watch over ship movements in and out of West Passage. It was permanently fortified around 1900. More than 75 years later, this historic landmark was buried to make way for the park, and only remnants of it can be seen today.

GOULD ISLAND

⭐2 🅇

No facilities

Charts: 13221, **13223**

Two miles north of Rose Island in East Passage is Gould Island, one of the two islands bearing that name in the bay. (The other is in the Sakonnet River.) Formerly entirely Navy-owned, several acres on the south end of this island are now part of the Bay Islands Park System, but lack of a secure anchorage makes this island relatively inaccessible for cruising boats.

The island is a nesting area for birds and is off-limits from April 1 through August 15, but visitors may go ashore before or after those dates. There is reportedly an old seaplane ramp and a beach on which to ground small or shoal-draft boats on the south end of the island.

This Gould Island gets its name from Thomas Gould, who purchased it in the mid-17th century from the Indians, who called the island "Aquo-pimokuk." In 1919 the Navy bought the island to expand its torpedo-making facilities, already in full swing on Goat Island to the south.

Part of the island is still owned by the military, but there is the possibility of additional land being acquired by the state.

If you have a small, beachable boat, Gould is worth exploring on a calm day—but please, don't visit here between the first of April and August 15.

POINT JUDITH

HARBOR OF REFUGE

Chart: 13219

On the southwest shore of the Rhode Island mainland, and considered by some to be outside the boundaries of Narragansett Bay, Point Judith is a popular stopping point for boats on their way to and from the bay, or for traffic en route to Block Island just offshore.

The Harbor of Refuge, just to the southwest of Point Judith itself, is a sheltered deep-water anchorage protected on three sides by breakwaters and on one side by land. It is less a destination than a stopping point for recreational boaters when the weather turns or the fog rolls in over Rhode Island Sound.

Approaches. Point Judith is prominently marked by a 65-foot-high lighthouse with foghorn and radio beacon. The flashing light has a charted visibility of 16 miles.

We count ourselves among the faction of bay residents who consider the light (and the point) to mark the western boundary of Narragansett Bay. The light was erected in 1810, and marks the site of the Point Judith Coast Guard station, a full search-and-rescue facility, which sits just to the north.

To the southwest of the light, the breakwater forms a large three-sided shelter for yachts. Shelter from the north is provided by Sand Hill Cove Beach at Galilee. More than a million tons of rocks are in the three sections. Construction was begun in 1896, and the breakwater was completed in 1902. Since then, it has served as a shelter for boats in stormy weather, and fishermen enjoy excellent angling along its walls, snaring bluefish, bass, cod, and flounder, and trapping lobster.

The east entrance to the harbor through the breakwater, called "East Gap," is marked by skeleton towers on either side. To port as you enter East Gap is a 39-foot-high tower that flashes green. It is visible for 5 miles, and bears the number "3." A square, green daymark is also on the tower. To starboard, the 31-foot-high structure flashes red and can be seen from a distance of 5 miles in good visibility, and is numbered "2." Depths in the entrance and approaches are more than adequate for pleasure yachts at 24 to 35 feet, but watch for lobster pots. And give Point Judith itself a wide berth, because it is surrounded by fish traps, shoals and foul ground.

Point Judith Harbor of Refuge Anchorages

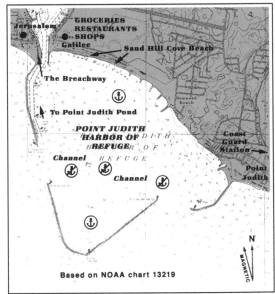

Based on NOAA chart 13219

SCALE: **1″=.61** NAUT. MI.

Mooring area

Do not anchor

Good anchoring

The western entrance to the Harbor of Refuge, called "West Gap," is also well marked. To port, you'll find a 35-foot-high flashing-green tower bearing the number "3." It has a foghorn and is visible for a distance of 7 miles. On the starboard side of the gap, mark number "2," also bearing a triangular red daymark, stands 35 feet tall and flashes red. According to the *Atlantic Coast Pilot*, the East and West breakwater entrances are 400 and 500 yards wide, respectively.

At the apex of the V-shaped outer breakwater facing Rhode Island Sound is yet another skeleton tower. It stands 33 feet tall and emits a white flash that is visible for a distance of 7 miles.

Anchorages/Moorings. Within the Harbor of Refuge, the best area to anchor in prevailing southerlies is within the apex of the "V" of the outermost breakwater, where the bottom is soft and the holding ground is good. Stay well off the rocks of the breakwater to avoid a reported sand bar that has appeared there in recent years, and to avoid being blown down onto the rocks should a windshift occur. In this area the depth is 20 feet or more at mean low water, except for one small patch where depth is 18 feet. Three State of Rhode Island Guest Moorings are set here in 20 to 25 feet. (See "Cruising Conditions," page 14, for exact coordinates, rules and regulations.)

Toward the middle of the harbor, swells can make the anchorage uncomfortable because they push through the stones in the breakwater. The area is too near the channel used by traffic entering and exiting Point Judith Pond along the northwestern breakwater's wall. Do not anchor in the channel or approaches, because the commercial and ferry traffic here is fast, furious, and of considerable size. If you desire to go ashore in the Harbor of Refuge, you can find temporary anchorage off the northwest end of Sand Hill Cove Beach, though there's lots of traffic in this area due to the proximity of the channel leading into Point Judith Pond. At this excellent swimming beach you'll also find a selection of gift shops, a fast-food seafood restaurant and bar, and just beyond them, the bustling village of Galilee.

The Harbor of Refuge is an adequate stop for emergency shelter or as a quick-entrance, easy-exit overnight stop on the way to or from Block Island, but if you stop here, be prepared to feel the swell of the sea. And bring a good book, because there's not much else to do in this isolated anchorage. For better shelter, facilities, and scenery, shoal- and medium-draft boats might

wish to head north to enjoy the peace and protection of Point Judith Pond.

History. The Indians called Point Judith "Weyanitoke." Its English name may be biblical in origin (early maps show the names Judah or Judeah), or it may have been named for the wife or mother of one of the area's early settlers, John Hull. But the legend surrounding the point's naming is infinitely more fun. This version of the story, told by Edgar Bacon in the 1904 edition of his book, *Narragansett Bay*, is our favorite:

> "Once upon a time, an old sea captain of Nantucket took his wife with him on a voyage along the coast, and being enveloped in fog he made her lookout. After awhile, the woman piped out: 'Land!'
>
> " 'Whar away?' bellowed her husband.
>
> " 'Why, right over there, just the other side of those ropes,' she answered excitedly.
>
> " 'T'other side o'fiddlesticks!' roared the captain. 'Can't you tell me in straight talk, whar away?'
>
> "Now it happened that the captain's wife was unacquainted with nautical terms, and while she could do many useful things, she could no more have boxed the compass than she could have flown, so presently another order came from the impatient steersman.
>
> " 'Pint, Judy, pint,' he bellowed, whereupon Judy 'pinted,' and the shore she had discovered and indicated was ever afterwards known as 'Pint Judy'."

POINT JUDITH

POND

☆5 5

Chart: 13219

Along the northwest jetty in the Harbor of Refuge is the buoyed entrance channel leading to The Breachway at the mouth of Point Judith Pond. Although it is quite shallow, the pond offers some of the bay's best cruising, and no one should stop at the Harbor of Refuge without exploring the waters to the north, if draft allows.

Approaches. The narrow, buoyed channel known as The Breachway calls to mind the proverbial camel attempting to pass through the eye of a needle. Its eastern boundary is marked by a red daymark on a jetty that juts out from Galilee Town Beach. Locals say the current runs 4 to 5 knots through here, which from our own observations seems accurate, so it's a good idea to enter and exit here with a fair tide. Sailboats unfamiliar with the area should only attempt this entrance under power; Galilee is a thriving commercial port and the traffic through here, consisting of fishing vessels, ferries, charter vessels, and recreational craft, runs as briskly as the current. On any summer day, the rocks of the breakwater to either side of the channel are lined with tourists who congregate to watch the excitement.

Entering the pond, be sure to stay within the dredged channel to avoid shoals to either side. Once past The Breachway, the waterway widens though the channel remains narrow, and the current lessens considerably. The dredged channel heading north in the pond cuts through fairly dramatic shoal areas, so be certain to keep within the buoys at all points here. Proceed carefully, particularly near nuns "2" and "2A," since shoals encroach to either side of the channel. Farther up, you'll be treated to flocks of egrets and herons nonchalantly stalking the shallows for prey to either side of you.

Locals advise hugging the port side of the marked channel heading north between cans "9" and "11," and report recent uncharted shoaling near nun "10" just inside the buoy. Once past this point, there is 7 to 9 feet at mid-channel until you reach can "15," which sits on a 5-foot-deep shoal area. If you are of deeper draft, leave this well to port but take care to keep clear of another shoal to starboard, with 0 to 5 feet MLW, marked by a stake. As you approach The Narrows, channel markers reappear and depths are 5 to 8 feet until you reach the dredged channel leading

Current is strong and traffic is heavy in 'The Breachway' at the entrance to Point Judith Pond. LYNDA CHILDRESS PHOTO.

Point Judith Pond Anchorages

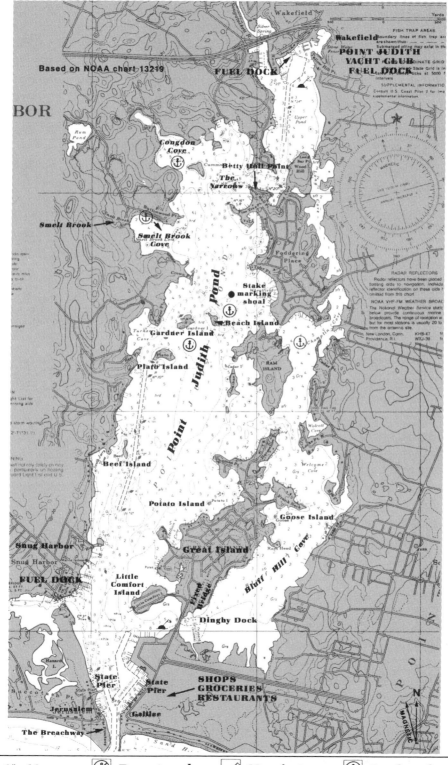

Based on NOAA chart 13219

HAR BOR

Wakefield

Silver Spring

FUEL DOCK

Wakefield

POINT JUDITH YACHT CLUB FuEL DOCK

Rum Pond

Upper Pond

Congdon Cove

Betty Hull Point

The Narrows

Smelt Brook

Smelt Brook Cove

Foddering Place

Stake marking shoal

Beach Island

Gardner Island

Plato Island

RAM ISLAND

Walcott Cove

Beel Island

Welcome Cove

Potato Island

Goose Island

Snug Harbor

Snug Harbor

FUEL DOCK

Great Island

Little Comfort Island

Bluff Hill Cove

Dinghy Dock

State Pier

State Pier

SHOPS GROCERIES RESTAURANTS

Jerusalem

Galilee

The Breachway

N
MAGNETIC

SCALE: **1″=.44** NAUT. MI.   ⚓ **Do not anchor**   ◤ **Mooring area**   ⚓ **Good anchoring**

to Wakefield, which has minimum depths of 5 to 5½ feet at MLW.

At the northern terminus of Point Judith Pond, Wakefield is marked by another cluster of marinas and accessible through a dredged channel. Approaching Wakefield, use caution nearing The Narrows, particularly near nun "18," which marks a shoal locals call "Gilligan's Island." A shoal area also exists off Betty Hull Point; hug the port side of the channel here. Just before the turn north into the channel to Wakefield, take a glance over your shoulder to starboard into Spring Cove. Here you'll see a strange boat a-building that has stood in the spot so long locals call it "Noah's Ark." Indeed, it's not hard to imagine a biblical menagerie lining up by twos to board this unusual looking craft.

The fishing village of Galilee sits at the south end of the pond, to starboard of The Breachway. On the opposing shore is the hamlet of Jerusalem. Galilee is the heart of the East Coast commercial fishing industry, and the large fleet that calls this port home provides seafood for the East Coast from Maine to South Carolina. Galilee is second only to New Bedford, Massachusetts, as an Eastern Seaboard producer. Galilee is also a popular port for sportfishermen and fishing charters. The U.S. Atlantic Tuna Tournament has been held here for almost 50 years. Giant bluefin tuna, swordfish and marlin migrate to nearby waters of Rhode Island Sound in late summer and early fall.

Fishing is the lifeblood of this area. Galilee and Jerusalem were settled by fishermen from Nova Scotia, who gave them their biblical names. Today, the fishing fleet is ubiquitous at the south end of the pond. Rows of working craft and circling hordes of voracious gulls make an immediate impression on the senses.

Anchorages/Moorings. There are no overnight facilities for transient yachts in Galilee, but visitors may tie up for up to two hours to a bulkhead at the state pier just north of the ferry dock. Limited slip space for transients is available on the Jerusalem side of the channel at Point Judith Marina, which caters to sailors, or Snug Harbor Marina, which caters to powerboats due to limited depths at its docks. (See marina listings, page 189, for specific information.) Visitors with capable auxiliary-powered tenders can berth in Jerusalem and dinghy across to Galilee, where there is a dinghy dock and launching ramp just east of the fixed bridge between Galilee and Great Island. If you tie up here, be sure to do so in a way that does not restrict boats entering and exiting the water on the ramp.

In the waters north of Galilee and Jerusalem, depths in the pond are shoal for large, deep-draft cruising boats, ranging from 4 to 10 feet in viable anchorage areas and in the channel. For small to medium-size cruising boats, however, upper Point Judith Pond is one of Narragansett Bay's greatest undiscovered cruising grounds. Almost a minibay itself, it is largely devoid of the masses of recreational boaters who congregate in some of the bay's more popular anchorages on summer weekends.

Within the pond's northern reaches, anchoring is permitted anywhere a wily skipper can find a place to tuck in for the night, except in channels and mooring areas. Visitors are permitted to go ashore—with respect for nature and property—on all islands but Plato (called Conrad's Island locally), which is owned by a gentleman who values the privacy of his island retreat. Please don't disturb him by going ashore here.

Holding ground in the upper pond is reported to be excellent, and, as mentioned, visitors can anchor anywhere they find appropriate. Some of the better anchorage areas include Smelt Brook Cove, Beach Island and Gardner Island. Approaching Smelt Brook Cove, beware of a cluster of rocks at the northeast edge, and proceed carefully to anchor in 4 to 5 feet. This is a sheltered, pastoral place surrounded by woods and marshes. Here you're likely to see osprey and herons, egrets, fishing cormorants, and ducks. A more peaceful place is hard to imagine, and chances are you'll have the place largely to yourself.

Other good spots to drop the hook can be found east of Beach Island, or between it and

Gardner Island. Both places offer 7-foot depths at low tide. Near this area you'll notice a cute little tugboat tethered to her anchor. This is the *Firefly*, one of the last steam-powered tugboats on the Eastern Seaboard.

To the west of Gardner Island is Camp Fuller, an oceanside retreat for inner city children. You may encounter them should you go ashore on Gardner since it is a favorite place for cookouts and campouts for the children.

For the most part, the islands in the pond get their names from either past or present owners, or from the animals or provisions that were once corralled or stowed there. A glance at the chart will reveal several such titles: Ram, Goose, Beef and Potato, to mention a few.

Three Wakefield marinas offer slips and moorings for visitors (see marina listings) as does the Point Judith Yacht Club, which has one transient dock. Billington Cove Marina and Silver Springs Cove cater only to powerboats, while Ram Point Marina has full facilities for sailboats, with 7 feet at its docks. Anchoring in Wakefield is not advised —it is the only place in the pond with poor holding ground.

Provisions/Things to Do.
There is no town on the bay quite like Galilee. The tangy scent of salt water pierces the air along with the aroma from the day's catch. Once ashore here, you'll find a charming village bustling with activity, all of it centered around commercial fishing. Along the state pier, boats bearing fish by the bucket and basketful come and go, unloading their wares directly to dockside restaurants, seafood markets, and fleets of waiting refrigerated trucks. On the opposite side of the only main street, tourist-oriented shops sell tee shirts, sou-

venirs, bumper stickers bearing fishermanly slogans, and of course, salt water taffy.

We'd be willing to bet Galilee is unmatched anywhere for its multitude of fresh seafood, which can be sampled in any number of shoreside eateries in massive quantities for reasonable prices. Restaurants run the gamut from the fried-clams-and-beer variety to more formal settings, though nothing in this shoreside town is remotely stodgy. Handrigan's Market, south of the ferry dock, sells excellent sea fare for cooking aboard your boat, and locals claim the food at George's of Galilee is among the best to be had in town. Across the way in Jerusalem, Jim's Restaurant also receives rave reviews from locals for good, home-cooked food. The original speedboat driven by Don Johnson on early episodes of the TV series, "Miami Vice" sits at Jim's dock and is an attraction quickly pointed out to visitors by locals. On Galilee's main street you'll find ice, groceries at the small Galilee Market, and several pay phones among the shops and eateries that line the street.

In Wakefield, fuel, ice, and limited supplies are available and there is a small marine store at Ram's Point. But for provisioning you'll have to take a taxi to the center of town a couple of miles away. If you're hankering for a restaurant meal, the Marina Bay serves good fare, and several other good restaurants are available by taxi.

Perhaps the commercial nature of the south end of the pond, combined with its overall shallowness, have kept visiting cruisers from exploring. Whatever the reason, it remains an unspoiled and interesting port of call for shoal to medium draft boats. Once you're tucked away in the scenic and peaceful reaches of the Upper Pond, we guarantee you'll find it hard to tear yourself away.

Block Island

THE
LOWER
BAY,
WITH
BLOCK
ISLAND

56

Just 9 miles from Point Judith is a small, pork-chop-shaped island that is a logical next stop after a visit to Point Judith Pond. Block Island is to southern New England sailors what Catalina Island is to Southern Californians: an offshore mecca close enough to be attainable in a weekend but far enough away to provide a certain amount of intrigue. Unlike California sailors, southern New Englanders have plenty of other options for weekend cruises, but Block Island remains one of the favored destinations for Narragansett Bay cruisers.

Block Island stands proudly alone nearly 25 miles southwest of Newport off the Rhode Island and Connecticut coasts, situated east-northeast of Montauk Point on Long Island and lapped continually by the waters of the open Atlantic to the south. To the west is Block Island Sound, and, separating the isle from Narragansett Bay, is the wide expanse of Rhode Island Sound.

The small, high island, which measures about 7 miles long by 3½ miles wide, is a "terminal moraine," land left in the wake of the glaciers and deposited where it sits today. At one time, it may have sat at the mouth of Narragansett Bay, blocking the ocean's access to the sheltered estuary.

Block Island's proximity to scores of mainland mariners in Rhode Island, Connecticut and Long Island make it a crowded port of call on summer weekends from Memorial Day to Labor Day, and at the height of the season as many as 1,500 boats have been reported at the Great Salt Pond, the only viable anchorage for most visiting yachts. Until around the turn of the century, the pond was precisely that, and was totally landlocked until a channel was opened through the west-facing beach to the sea. Described by one early resident as "big enough to contain the whole British army," the pond spreads over hundreds of acres, and fortunately is large enough to hold the armies of a different sort who converge on the spot today. The pond is home to a Coast Guard search-and-rescue station.

Block Island Anchorages

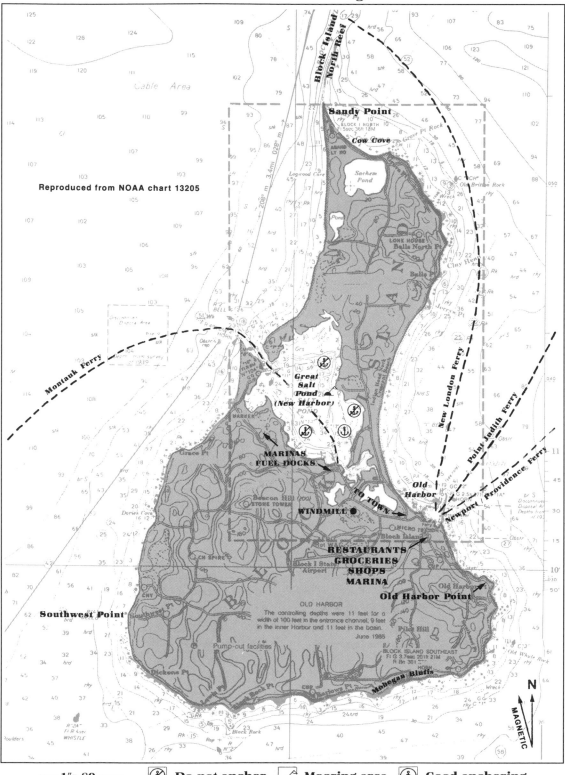

Reproduced from NOAA chart 13205

SCALE: **1″=.80** NAUT. MI.   **Do not anchor** ⛵ **Mooring area** ⚓ **Good anchoring**

GREAT SALT POND

Chart: 13217

Approaches. Before setting off on a passage to Block Island, be certain both boat and crew are prepared for conditions in the open waters of Rhode Island Sound, where mild swells can build quickly to significant waves in strong winds. Both water and air temperatures are cooler this far offshore, and cooler ocean water means a much higher incidence of fog, so be sure your navigational abilities and equipment are up to speed before leaving protected waters. Fog can set in with little warning, and often you will find yourself sailing in and out of fogbanks, so keep track of your position carefully.

Approaching the Great Salt Pond from Narragansett Bay or Point Judith, keep well off the north tip of the island to avoid a mean shoal called North Reef. The shoal lies between the north tip of the island, marked by North Light on Sandy Point, and bell buoy "1BI," which marks its end. North Light was the first light erected on the island, and though it is not the original structure, the present light was built in 1867. The light flashes a white signal, stands 36 feet above water, and has a charted visibility of 13 miles. Buoy "1BI" is lit as well, flashing white. To be on the safe side, stay outside this buoy when approaching Block Island; though there is deep water between it and the end of the reef, the tide rip off the north end is severe. You may see other boats sailing close in toward shore or cutting the buoy, but prudent mariners will opt for the safer course outside the mark.

From buoy "1BI" it is just over 3 miles to the entrance to Great Salt Pond. On any summer afternoon, you'll be sailing in company with flotillas of boats like ducks in a row converging on the 150-foot-wide entrance channel. In spite of all the boats with their bows pointed in its direction, the entrance is difficult to pick out visually until you are quite close; it almost looks like a pass between separate islands. On approach, watch for red bell buoy "2," which marks the outer channel entrance. A 49-foot-tall tower that flashes red and has an easily discernable horn stands on the end of the stone jetty marking the starboard side of the channel. Proceed with caution, giving other entering and exiting boats plenty of room. The channel was once dredged to a depth of 17 feet, but it frequently silts over, and groundings in soft bottom are not uncommon when deep-draft boats stray too close to either edge.

Anchorages/Moorings. Once inside the pond, there is plenty of room, and in many places, depths ranging from 12 to 50 feet are almost too generous for comfortable holding. Don't skimp on scope when anchoring here, and put out plenty of fenders whether or not you're expecting a rafted guest; looking unseamanlike will be worth it when the boats that have anchored on a shoestring drag down on you. At Block Island, the "unpredicted nocturnal squall" is a phenomenon well known to sailors who frequent the island, and one which has built to legendary status. Particularly prone to strike on crowded holiday weekends, this fast-moving combination of rain and winds inevitably causes poorly anchored boats to fall upon each other like dancing dominoes. When sleeping crews become conscious of events outside, they discover decks all around them full of scantily clad, flashlit crews, whose oaths can often be heard quite clearly above the shrieking wind. Fortunately, the mysterious squalls usually sweep through in relatively short order, and before long all is calm again and crews retire, though some boats inevitably return home from a weekend at Block with a few bruises to show for the experience. In addition to significant depth in the anchorage, matters are made worse by notoriously poor holding ground in soft mud and sand loaded with eelgrass.

Most boats (and raft-ups) favor the southeast

corner of the pond, which provides the best shelter in summer southwesterlies. The size of the pond gives it considerable fetch, but if conditions permit and you're not feeling especially social, try tucking into quieter realms where it is quite peaceful and pleasant and where swimming in the cold, crystal clear water is wonderfully refreshing.

At this writing, there is talk of restricting anchorage in the pond to preserve shellfish beds; ask locally for updates. You are restricted from anchoring in the southeast portion of the harbor near the marked channel that is the path of the daily ferry from Montauk, and you are required to use your onboard holding tank during your stay at the pond.

Fortunately for those not fond of midnight traverses through the anchored fleet, there are many town guest moorings available in the pond on a first-come, first-served basis. However, you may be hard-pressed to arrive in time to snag one on a summer weekend. The moorings are red-orange, and vacant ones can be picked up at will; the harbormaster will be by to collect his fee later. There are also four excellent marinas on the Salt Pond (see listings on page 190), and launch service is available both from the town and from Oldport Marine, the Newport-based company that sends a fleet of launches to the island for summer duty. Both monitor VHF Channel 68.

Old Harbor, formed by dual breakwaters on the east side of the island, is chock full of local boats and sportfishing boats and is the spot where ferries from Newport and Point Judith steam in and out several times daily, disgorging full loads of daytripping tourists. There is a town dock where transients can tie up, but space is limited and most transients choose to put into the Great Salt Pond.

Provisions/Things to Do. Ashore on Block Island, there is plenty to keep you occupied, whether you're seeking the bustling action of a summer resort, the solitude of a nature walk complete with deer and exotic birds, or the magnificent splendor of an unobstructed ocean view from high above the sea.

Within walking distance of the pond (also called New Harbor) are several restaurants, delis and bars, as well as readily available marine supplies, gift shops, drug stores, and groceries. There are two liquor stores on the island as well as a pair of laundromats.

Shuttle service to town, on the east side of the island overland from the Salt Pond, is available from marinas onshore, and Block Island Boat Basin rents mopeds, bikes, and cars, but the walk

The clay cliffs of Block Island rise steeply from the sea as a racing fleet sails downwind flying spinnakers off the southwest side of the isle. STEVEN KROUS PHOTO.

to Old Harbor is an easy and pleasant half to three-quarters of a mile. In town and along the road leading to it you'll find plenty to explore, including restaurants, gift shops, bicycle rentals, and all the other accoutrements of a summer island. The main street of New Shoreham offers spectacular ocean views and is lined with handsome old hotels venerably facing the sea, their verandas lined with rows of inviting rocking chairs.

Don't leave Block Island without renting a bicycle or moped or hiring a taxi to explore the less populated regions south of town. Many local taxi drivers provide guided tours of the island, and away from town you'll be inundated with the scents of honeysuckle, wild beach rose, and fresh salt air as you ride toward the south end. Here lies the island's most spectacular and popular natural wonder, Mohegan Bluffs. The multi-colored clay ledges rise dramatically from the foaming sea far below them, and you will certainly feel you've been transported farther than a few miles when you catch your first breathtaking glimpse of them. A turn-of-the-century historian wrote of the bluffs: "To gain a full impression of their power, a visitor must stand on their brows and gaze far out to sea; then also at their feet by the water's edge and look up . . ." We have found this to be well-found advice.

If you're in the mood for a hike in the woods instead of along the bluffs, try a trip to "The Maze," a series of forested trails that are a great spot for an afternoon of exploring.

Block Island has an abundance of wildlife, including deer, and unusual bird species not often seen elsewhere in southern New England often are spotted on the island, particularly in spring and fall, when birds are migrating; apparently the spot is as convenient a resting point for birds as it is for wayward mariners. Strolling the beaches, you may notice the sand has a black cast—this is due to the large percentage of iron it contains, which also makes it too heavy to easily be blown about. The island has a pond for every day of the year (yes, 365) and more than 300 miles of stone walls. Some are said to have been the result of the labor of slaves, who were offered their free-

dom if they could build a wall across the entire width of the island. If this is the case, only two ambitious souls ever managed to complete the task to receive their just reward.

History. Block Island's first residents, the Manisses Indians, called it "Manisses," which means "Island of Little God." The sachem of Manisses was subordinate to the Great Sachem on the mainland; in essence, he was the "little god," hence the name.

In 1524, when Giovanni da Verrazano sighted the island while exploring the coast, he noted campfires burning along the coast. Recently, archaeologists have established evidence that indicates the Manisseans may have lived on Block Island year round as early as the year 500. Originally, it was believed the island was only a seasonal habitat, but experts now believe Indians lived along the shores of the Great Salt Pond, depending largely on the sea for survival. Remains of seal bones, dolphin bones, fish hooks, net sinkers, spear points, and knives have been found to support the theory.

The bluffs and surrounding moors were the site of a rather grisly bit of history from which they derive their name. When the island was the sole domain of the Manisses Indians, Mohegan Indians arrived from nearby Connecticut and western Rhode Island by boat under cover of darkness and attacked the resident tribe. A battle ensued, and eventually the invaders were driven to the south end of the island near the bluffs. Here, the victorious Manisses exacted a grisly revenge by penning up the Mohegans and starving them before driving them over the cliffs to their deaths. The bluffs retain the name of the unfortunate Indians who died here.

Verrazano did not land on Block Island, but that didn't stop him from giving it a name; he called it "Luisa" after the mother of King Francis I of France, his benefactor. Nearly 100 years later, Dutch trader/explorer Adrian Block officially "discovered" the isle, and made the first recorded landing in 1614. After this date, it was noted on Dutch charts as "Adrian's Eyelandt," but in 1876 the name was changed to the explorer's surname and remains so to this day.

New Shoreham, the island's sole town, was named in 1672. The "new" refers to its place in the New World; "shore ham" signifies a home, or hamlet, near the shore.

The Manisses Indians, a branch of the Narragansett tribe, murdered a Boston trader who visited the island in 1636, creating an uproar that resulted in Massachusetts Bay Colony claiming the isle after sending a party to punish the Indians. They established the claim by virtue of their conquest, and their ownership was formally acknowledged by Narragansett Sachem Miantonomi.

Later, the island was transferred to a group of private individuals from Braintree, Massachusetts, who are thought to have reached the island from the Taunton River and Narragansett Bay. These first colonial settlers are said to have landed at Cow Cove, where the island's first bovine resident made its lumbering way ashore.

After a less than friendly start, the Manisseans and colonists coexisted peacefully on this small slab of land. In 1664, the island joined the colony of Rhode Island, and during the revolution, participated with the other colonies in protesting the British tea tax. This was a bold move for a tiny island with no means of protecting itself from attack, and it created a state of paranoia. Islanders were forbidden to leave the island unless they planned to depart permanently, for fear that commuters would become enemy spies. Neither could islanders communicate with off-islanders without fear of fine. After the revolution, such bans were lifted and life returned to normal on the island.

It has been suggested that the name Block Island might just as well have been derived from the fact that the land rising unexpectedly from the depths was indeed a frequent "stumbling block" in the path of unfortunate early vessels. Multitudes of ships have been wrecked on its shores, and books could probably be written about all of them, but the most famous Block Island shipwreck was the wreck of the *Palatine*. The original

story has grown into the stuff of legend best told by historian Edgar Bacon:

"Of all the tales that old wives tell and children remember when the wind howls at night, the most dreadful is that of the German vessel that sailed in the 1750s from the Palatines for Philadelphia with passengers and merchandise, and met her untimely end upon the shores of Manisses, or Block Island. Set out of her course by gales, the voyage was a chapter of misfortunes, to fill the measure of which the crew mutinied and killed the captain, driving the passengers to the cabin, where they were held prisoners and starved. What food they were able to procure from the wretches who had become their masters was doled out at exorbitant prices. A cup of water cost twenty guilders, and fifty six dollars paid for a single biscuit, so that presently the crew had all the ready money there was on board, and the passengers saved them the trouble of outright murder by obligingly dying of starvation.

"At last, when there seemed nothing more to be gained, when they had secured all the ready money on board, when they had looted whatever of value they could lay their hands upon, the mutineers took to the boats, leaving the few surviving passengers to their fate. That fate, merciless to the last, flung the *Palatine* upon the rocks of Block Island, where the wreckers soon found her and swarmed aboard, stripping the hull of whatever the crew had left and only rescuing the passengers to leave them robbed and penniless. Having got all they could, the shore sharks set fire to the hull, and the tide lifted and bore the blazing wreck away. It is told that one poor crazed woman, who had hidden on board, was driven by the fire to the stern of the ship, where she stood screaming and wringing her hands until flames enveloped her.

"Of course the story did not end here. Year after year the blazing ship came back and the people who had watched the tragedy saw it repeated each twelvemonth;

saw the flames rise from hull to rigging, and sweep along the side of the ship, each port a roaring tongue of fire; saw the maniac woman rush aft and wring her hands, and above all heard the screams of her despair."

Some residents claim they still see the strange light off Sandy Point, where the ship struck North Reef, and the story inspired poet John Greenleaf Whittier to write a poem, "The Wreck of The Palatine," about the strange ship.

The Wreck of the Palatine

BY JOHN GREENLEAF WHITTIER

Old wives spinning their webs of tow,
Or rocking weirdly to and fro,
In and out of peat's dull glow,

Nor looks nor tones a doubt betray;
'It is known to us all,' they quietly say;
'We too have seen it in our day.'

Is there, then, no death for a word once spoken?
Was never a deed but left its token
Written on tables never broken?

Do the elements subtle reflections give?
Do pictures of all the ages live
On Nature's infinite negative,

Which, half in sport, in malice half,
She shows at times, with shudder or laugh,
Phantom and shadow in photograph?

For still, on many a moonless night,
From Kingston Head and from Montauk Light
The spectre kindles and burns in sight.

Now low and dim, now clear and higher,
Leaps up the terrible Ghost of Fire,
Then, slowly sinking, the flames expire.

And the wise Sound skippers, though skies be fine,
Reef their sails when they see the sign
Of the blazing wreck of the *Palatine!*

And old men mending their nets of twine,
Talk together of dream and sign,
Talk of the lost ship *Palatine*,

The ship that, a hundred years before,
Freighted deep with its goodly store,
In the gales of the equinox went ashore.

The eager islanders one by one
Counted the shots of her signal gun,
And heard the crash when she drove right on!

Into the teeth of death she sped:
(May God forgive the hands that fed
The false lights over the rocky Head!)

O men and brothers! What sights were there!
White upturned faces, hands stretched in prayer!
Where waves had pity, could ye not spare?

Down swooped the wreckers, like birds of prey,
Tearing the heart of the ship away,
And the dead had never a word to say.

And then, with ghastly shimmer and shine
Over the rocks and seething brine,
They burned the wreck of the *Palatine*.

In their cruel hearts, as they homeward sped,
'The sea and the rocks are dumb,' they said:
'There'll be no reckoning with the dead.'

But the year went round, and when once more
Along their foam-white curves of shore
They heard the line-storm rave and roar,

Behold! again, with shimmer and shine,
Over the rocks and the seething brine,
The flaming wreck of the *Palatine!*

So, haply in fitter words than these,
Mending their nets on their patient knees
They tell the legend of Manissees.

Nor looks nor tones a doubt betray;
'It is known to us all,' they quietly say;
'We too have seen it in our day.'

Is there, then, no death for a word once spoken?
Was never a deed but left its token
Written on tables never broken?

Do the elements subtle reflections give?
Do pictures of all the ages live
On Nature's infinite negative,

Which, half in sport, in malice half,
She shows at times, with shudder or laugh,
Phantom and shadow in photograph?

For still, on many a moonless night,
From Kingston Head and from Montauk Light
The spectre kindles and burns in sight.

Now low and dim, now clear and higher,
Leaps up the terrible Ghost of Fire,
Then, slowly sinking, the flames expire.

And the wise Sound skippers, though skies be fine,
Reef their sails when they see the sign
Of the blazing wreck of the *Palatine!*

In spite of the crowds, and the increasingly resort-like atmosphere, Block Island is a special place, and one of the most appealing destinations near the bay for those who wish to point their bows southwest and set their course for landfall at an "offshore" port of call.

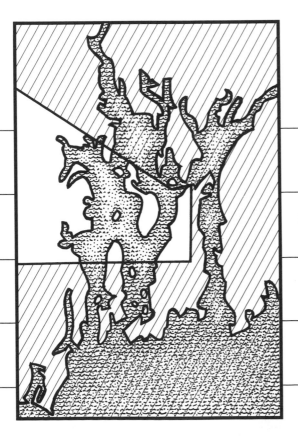

The Middle Bay

The Middle Bay

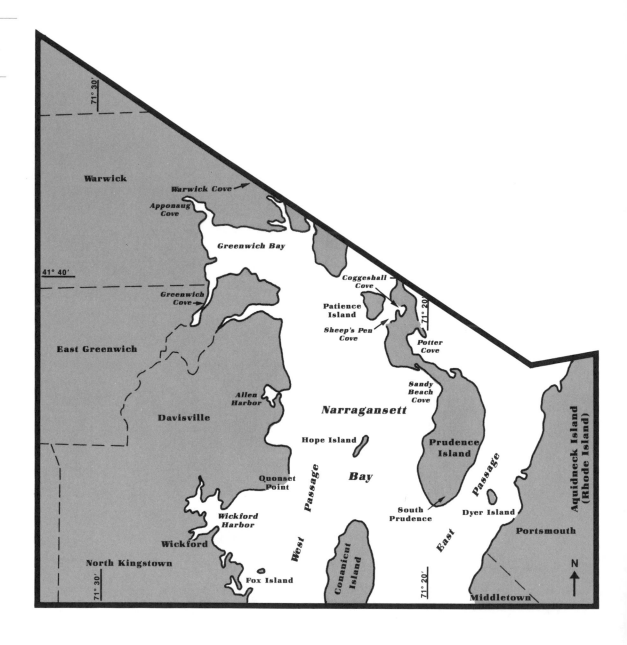

Serene

and

Inviting

All evidence points to the fact that the shores and islands of this unsurpassed body of water were in past times more densely wooded than they are at present. From the groves that remain we may judge the beauty of those that have been removed.

The middle portion of Narragansett Bay, sandwiched between the hustle and bustle of the Lower Bay and the predominantly urban areas to the north, is one of the most delightful areas in these waters to explore. Here, the remnants of once-luxuriant pine and cedar forests speak of less populous times. The northern reaches of East and West Passages are separated by the greenery of Prudence Island and, to the northwest, the inviting expanse of Greenwich Bay with its border of pine trees awaits exploration by cruisers.

Pilotage. Generally speaking, waters here are shallower than the generous depths in the Lower Bay, with 20- to 40-foot depths prevailing. The water is for the most part clean and the breezes are fair, and the abundance of coves and islands can provide endless enjoyable hours of relaxed gunkholing.

In the Middle Bay you'll find the press of recreational traffic significantly less than in regions to the south, though the area is an extremely popular local cruising ground. On weekends, you can expect to share the waterways as well as your anchorage with other weekending cruisers from around the bay. Shipping traffic does steam through here, particularly near Quonset Point and in the ship's channel east of Prudence Island heading north to Providence, so keep an eye out for large, fast-moving traffic while sailing here.

As with other parts of the bay, harbor approaches, channels and shoals are generally well-marked. Visitors should be aware from a look at the chart that Greenwich Bay and approaches are significantly shallower than other areas in the Middle Bay, and should use caution from Allen Harbor northward, staying well off the coast to avoid thin water just 2 to 5 feet deep at low tide. Be especially careful to leave buoy "1" near Round Rock to port on approaching Greenwich Bay, as well as the marks just beyond it, cans "3" and "5," which mark both the northern edge of the shoal and submerged rocks.

Currents in the Middle Bay are generally less than 1 knot, except in constricted entrance channels and in the relatively narrow pass between the northwest tip of Patience Island and Warwick

Point on the opposite shore, where a tide rip can often be seen as well as felt.

Like most destinations within Narragansett Bay beyond the reaches of ports near Rhode Island Sound, the Middle Bay remains relatively undiscovered by visiting yachtsmen. Whether you sail up the bay to poke around the historic village of Wickford or anchor in a secluded island cove, the push up the bay to new horizons is worthwhile.

FOX ISLAND

No rating/private

Charts: 13221, **13223**

In the West Passage of Narragansett Bay, just north of the Jamestown Bridge, lies one of the bay's more mysterious islands. Rocks on the south and west sides guard against unwanted intruders, yet the white sand beach, dock and private residences among the trees on this 4½-acre oasis prompt endless speculation.

As you sail this vicinity of the bay, you can't help but wonder about this offshore retreat. While it is a private island and inaccessible to cruising boats, we include it here to solve its mystery and enlighten those, like us, who have spent years wondering about its history.

The island has four known Indian names, Azoiquaneset, Sowonexet, Nonequasut and Azorquanset, but it appeared on maps as "Fox" as early as 1777, perhaps because of quarry that made its way across the bay ice to the shelter of the offshore woods. In 1659 it was purchased from the Indians by the town of Warwick. Today, the island is the property of a Narragansett dentist.

Seals have been sighted on the rocks near the island during fall and winter, and its isolation provides a habitat for any number of Narragansett Bay shore birds and small mammals.

Many years ago, Fox Island is said to have been connected to the mainland, perhaps at Rome Point (note the rocky shoal that reaches toward the island at low tide). Even now, it is only about ½ mile offshore.

The first house to be built on the island was erected sometime in the 1870s, but the building visible today was built by a Providence businessman in the 1930s.

Throughout its history, the island has had a string of private owners. In 1908, it was valued at $100. In 1985, Fox was on the market for over half a million dollars.

A book was written about Fox Island in 1889 by a Reverend William Pendleton Chipman, *Budd Boyd's Triumph, or The Boy-Firm of Fox Island*. The tale told of two brothers who lived in an abandoned house on the island and earned a living by chartering their sloop *Sea Witch* and selling clams and fish. According to the story, the boys helped capture the perpetrators of a jewel robbery in a nearby village, the reward no doubt adding to their livelihood.

During the war years, the island was rumored to be a haven for enemy spies, though this later proved to be untrue.

Although Fox Island's present owner at one time put this spectacular spot in Narragansett Bay on the market, he has gone on record as saying he is opposed to the site being transformed into condominiums, and eventually took down the "for sale" sign. Thanks to his good conscience, it remains unspoiled for all to enjoy—if from a distance.

WICKFORD

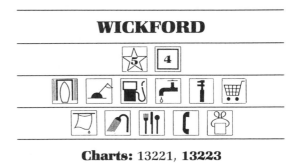

Charts: 13221, **13223**

Without a doubt, Wickford is one of the prettiest and most interesting harbors on Narragansett Bay. The quaint New England town actually has

Wickford

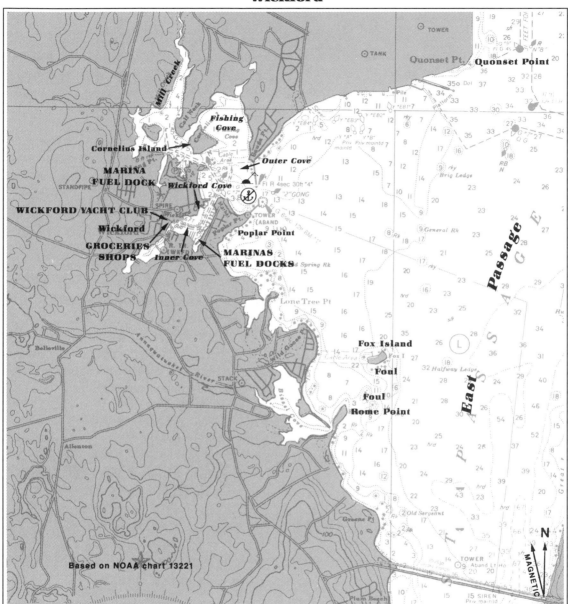

SCALE: **1″=.67** NAUT. MI.   Ⓐ **Do not anchor**   ⚓ **Mooring area**   Ⓐ **Good anchoring**

two harbors. The outer harbor, west of the breakwater, is filled with moorings. To the south, a dredged 6-foot-deep channel bypasses several marinas offering slip space as well as local boats moored to pilings fore and aft, which line the channel until you reach town.

Approaches. Approach from either East or West Passage is trouble-free, and the entrance is well marked. Visible on the port side of the harbor entrance is an abandoned lighthouse (now a private residence) on Poplar Point, as well as a 12-foot tower numbered "1" that flashes a green signal. The starboard (northern) entrance is

Ubiquitous military Quonset huts, manufactured at Quonset Point north of Wickford, were named after their place of origin. LYNDA CHILDRESS PHOTO.

marked by a breakwater on the end of which is a 30-foot tower numbered "4," which flashes red.

On approach to Wickford from the East Passage, keep in mind the ship's channel leading to Quonset Point/Davisville off the northern tip of Conanicut Island. Boats approaching from this direction will also notice a small and picturesque red lighthouse on the north tip of Jamestown. The Conanicut Island Light marks the division of East and West Passages, but is no longer in commission. Now a private home, it dates to 1886.

When sailing in this area on approach to Wickford, don't be surprised to look astern and see a military transport plane in full camouflage trailing low behind you. Quonset State Airport, once a large military installation, today is still home to a considerable number of military planes, which can be seen taking off and landing here frequently.

During World War II, Quonset was the primary manufacturing site for the popular inverted-U-shaped metal huts that, ever since, have borne the name of their port of creation.

Dockage/Moorings: Outer Harbor.

Once past the breakwater in Wickford, be sure to stay within the marked channel, whether you head west in the outer harbor or turn towards town. Shoals are prevalent in this harbor and even mooring areas are laced with thin water. Due to unmarked shoals outside virtually all

mooring areas in this picturesque harbor, locals advise against anchoring here, but transient slips and moorings are widely available (see marina listings on page 190).

Wickford's outer harbor area is a delightful and peaceful place. Despite the fleet of moored boats, an aura of relaxation prevails. As you head westward in the marked channel, the Wickford Yacht Club is to port, marked by docks lined with pretty overturned sailing dinks. The yacht club has two to three guest moorings that are available free of charge on a first come, first served basis, although you may call ahead to reserve one. Located to starboard of the entrance channel just west of the breakwater, these moorings are marked by white barrel floats with the numerals "222." If you arrive late in the day and find one unoccupied, pick it up, but check with the club to be sure the space has not been reserved.

In addition to the yacht club moorings, Wickford's outer harbor has three Rhode Island State Guest Moorings; two east of nun "8" and one east of can "7" (see "Cruising Conditions, page 14, for exact coordinates, rules and regulations).

Provisions: Outer Harbor.

Just to the west of Wickford Yacht Club on the same side of the channel is a marina that lives up to its namesake: the Pleasant Street Wharf, which offers fuel, ice and a small ship's store, but no transient slips or moorings on a regular basis. The wharf is run by a congenial older couple who are willing to share local knowledge with visitors who stop for fuel or supplies. The wharf also has a good selection of live local lobsters for sale at reasonable prices.

History.

The gem of Wickford's outer harbor is Cornelius Island, an uninhabited 18-acre oasis whose partially wooded expanse is a habitat for deer, foxes and other small mammals as well as egrets, herons, swans and other shore birds. According to locals, the island was willed to the town as a public right of way, although a portion of it is now privately owned. Still, visitors are free to roam ashore and enjoy the island's sandy beach, marshes and woods. Just to the south of

Cornelius is its smaller cousin, Rabbit Island, which consists mostly of salt marsh.

Like most of Narragansett Bay's islands, Cornelius has a fascinating history. One of the island's first residents was a sea captain named Ezekiel Gardiner, who built the island's stone house in the mid-18th century. Later, the house was used as a menhaden (pogy) smokehouse and at one time was the headquarters of Wickford Yacht Club. As a result of weather and neglect, the house is now in a sorry state, but still stands stoically off the beach, half-hidden by trees on the island's west end, a brooding backdrop to stalking egrets and herons.

Evidence of even earlier inhabitants of Cornelius was found in the form of hand-hewn oak beams buried underground near the house, believed to date back to the 1700s. Then, the island was owned by the Smith-Updike family, who purchased the site from the Narragansett Indians.

How the island acquired its name remains a mystery, although some believe it was the first name of a pre-Colonial Dutch trader. Roger Williams, the state's founder, is believed to have operated a trading house at the head of Mill Cove just west of the island. The site was purchased from Williams by a Richard Smith, and is now called Smith's Castle. The castle is open to the public most weekdays and weekends during the summer season, though shallow water prevents access by dinghy except at high tide.

At one time, the 1881 America's Cup defense candidate *Pocahontas* was beached on the island, where it deteriorated and finally was burned on July 4, 1936. Today, locals express hope that the privately owned portion of Cornelius can be bought by the Audubon Society or some other like-minded group to preserve its natural beauty and history in its entirety.

Wickford's outer harbor is a peaceful spot surrounded by natural beauty, and is an excellent place for an overnight visit—or longer.

Dockage/Moorings: Inner Harbor.

To port as you pass through the breakwater entering Wickford you'll see a channel leading south

At Wickford's inner cove, boats are moored to dolphins to conserve space. This photo shows the approach to the Wickford town dock. LYNDA CHILDRESS PHOTO.

and then west. Lined with marinas that welcome transients, this dredged 6-foot channel is also marked by row upon row of resident boats moored to pilings on either side.

At the head of the cove is the whitewashed, tree-lined village of Wickford, where visitors can tie up for as long as two hours at the town dock, which has 4-foot depths at MLW. The dock is a stone's throw from Wickford's main street, on which can be found any supplies you're likely to need with the exception of chandlery items.

Provisions/Repairs: Inner Harbor.

Ryan's Market across Main Street is easily accessible from the town dock. The market has an excellent selection of groceries, and a well-stocked drugstore and a liquor store are within easy reach. Take time out to look over the bridge crossing an arm of the cove in the center of town, a favorite spot for flocks of ducks and geese, which cluster here to be fed by locals.

If you're in need of repairs while cruising the Middle Bay, the port of Wickford offers some of the bay's best full-service yards, including Johnson's Boat Yard, Wickford Cove Marina and Wickford Shipyard, all equipped to service both small and large boats.

Things to Do: Inner Harbor.

Don't leave Wickford Cove without taking time to stroll the old streets and admire the 18th century architecture, or browse in shops selling items from antiques to dried flower arrangements and books. A historic site not to be missed here is the Old Narragansett Church and cemetery on Church Street (just off Main). Built in 1707 and moved to its present site in 1800, it is said to be the oldest Episcopal Church north of the Mason-Dixon Line. It is open to visitors during the month of August.

You may wish to time your visit to coincide with Wickford's annual art festival in July. The festival is one of the largest and most well attended in the vicinity, and artists display their works in the crisp backdrop of the town's pleasant, shady sidewalks.

Another notable annual Wickford event is the International Quahog Festival, held in August, featuring a host of colorful events in honor of the State Shellfish.

History. The village of Wickford was the inspiration for John Updike's best-selling novel, *The Witches Of Eastwick*, and you may find it an amusing read while visiting here.

Settled in 1663, Wickford was originally christened "Updike's Newtown" after an early settler. Later, it was renamed for Wickford, England, and still later incorporated as Kings Towne. Eventually, the town divided into present-day North and South Kingstown. Wickford presently is a village in the confines of North Kingstown.

In the 19th century, the town was one of the bay's leading seaports and shipbuilding towns, and the homes of early sea captains still line Wickford Cove today.

On Poplar Point, where the abandoned light now stands, a company of colonial soldiers were surprised and captured by raiding British soldiers. The light, built in 1831, is one of the oldest lighthouses in Rhode Island still standing where it was originally built. It was deactivated in 1882.

Whether you're in the mood for a quiet natural setting or the pleasures of visiting a picture-postcard New England village, Wickford is a satisfying port of call for visitors to Narragansett Bay.

ALLEN HARBOR

No facilities

Charts: 13221, **13223**

Allen Harbor, a sheltered and picturesque anchorage, is nonetheless almost never visited by transient yachts, perhaps because there are no facilities and little to do ashore except stroll the deserted beach, dig for clams off the east-facing shore or watch seabirds on the wing in adjacent fields.

Allen Harbor Anchorages

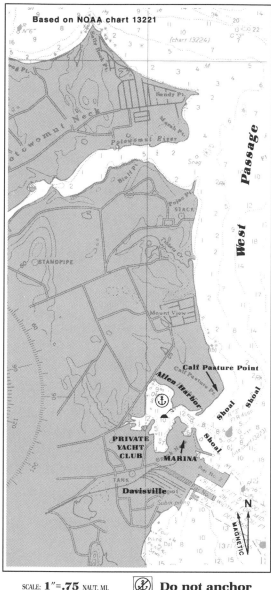

Based on NOAA chart 13221

SCALE: 1"=.75 NAUT. MI.

🚫⚓ **Do not anchor**

🛟 **Mooring area**   ⚓ **Good anchoring**

bered "3," we saw no such distinction. Don't be surprised to see swimmers and clamdiggers wading in knee-deep water off the point in areas where the senses dictate shallow water should not be; keep both chart and depth finder close by when entering here, and if possible, do so at high tide.

Entrance to the channel is made by passing between can "1" and nun "2," with not much room to spare. Beyond, the channel is unmarked until you reach the basin, and passage through the narrow inlet can cause some hair-raising moments. Due to uncharted shoaling, it's probably a good idea to post a bow lookout when threading through here, in addition to monitoring depth electronically if you're a deep draft vessel. On a visit in the summer of 1988 we found depths considerably less than those charted, with 4½ to 8 feet at the channel entrance. Depths continued to be less than charted in the channel, with 4½ feet to 9 feet dead-center. Once inside the harbor, comfortable depths of 9 to 11 feet prevail.

Anchorages. There are no moorings here, but there's plenty of room to anchor in depths of 9 to 11 feet in the harbor's north end, outside the mooring area. Soft mud holding ground is excellent, and the harbor provides shelter from every direction but due east. Even from this direction, the anchorage is somewhat protected by a low sandbar through which the narrow entrance channel threads.

Things to Do. When we visited here on a recent weekday, there were only one or two other transient boats and not much activity in the harbor. Although Allen Harbor Marina has slips and moorings for local boats, there are no facilities for transients and no supplies of any kind. All we found in the way of provisions was a Coke machine, and a local told us the nearest place to get ice was Wickford. On the south end of the harbor is the Navy Yacht Club, which a local boat owner said was a "very private" club whose members "don't like to be disturbed."

Fortunately, the anchorage in the north end of this harbor is the most pleasant area by far. A

Approaches. The approach to Allen Harbor is surrounded by shoals, particularly off Calf Pasture Point, where depths of 1 to 5 feet extend well offshore. A green can marks the shoal's eastern edge, but due to reported recent uncharted shoaling here, we don't recommend passing inside it. Although the chart says this buoy is num-

sunken barge and some abandoned pilings are the only inhabitants of this area other than the birds, and the harbor's northern extremity is surrounded by woods and fields. We spotted snowy egrets and cormorants, and a red-tailed hawk while anchored here.

The anchorage is also within dinghying distance of the sandy beach that lines the north edge of the channel and winds around the corner to the east shore facing the approach to Greenwich Bay. Pull up the dink on the beach and dig for clams, or hike the scenic empty shoreline strewn with scallop, oyster, razor clam, mussel and steamer shells. Neither shellfishing nor swimming are permitted within the anchorage, but both are excellent in the waters outside to the north of the entrance channel. To the south, waters are off-limits due to their proximity to Quonset/Davisville.

Allen Harbor once was under the jurisdiction of the military. Today, it is a study in contrasts, with the red-checkered watertower and buildings of Davisville to the south and scenic woods and marshlands to the north. Davisville has been home of the Atlantic Seabees since 1942. Just to the south, former Quonset Naval Air Station is now a state airport and industrial complex.

Despite the industry to the south, the north end of Allen Harbor is a pleasant, peaceful and well-protected anchorage in the Middle Bay, as good a place as any for an overnight stop if you don't require shoreside amenities. One word of caution, however: If you overnight here, bring plenty of insect repellent—no-see-ums and mosquitoes are fierce.

GREENWICH BAY

⭐5 3·5

🚽 ⛵ ⛽ 🚰 ⛴ 🛒

🛏 🚿 🍴 📞 🍞

Charts: 13221, 13223, **13224**

Once a port whose focus was commercial shell-fishing, East Greenwich in recent years has undergone a surge of popularity both ashore and afloat. Now, the once-quiet waterfront bustles with resident and transient traffic, and rates five stars as one of the most diversified destinations on Narragansett Bay.

Approaches. As a whole, Greenwich Bay is more shoal than the rest of Narragansett Bay, with prevailing depths less than 12 feet. Approaching Greenwich Cove, stay outside buoys marking the entrance, beginning with can "5," which marks Sally Rock and Potowomut Rocks, an area of foul ground just south of it. Further west, keep nun "6" to starboard, as the buoy marks the edge of an extensive shoal off Chepiwanoxet. Can "7" should be kept to port on entering to avoid yet another shoal off Long Point.

Anchorages/Moorings. Once inside the cove, you'll find depths of 7 to 11 feet MLW until you reach its southern end, where depths shoal to 1 to 6 feet MLW. The southernmost end of the cove is the only area where there is room for transients to anchor—and there's not much of it at that due to shallow water. However, this is an excellent place to tuck into for shelter in bad weather, and while locals say it can be buggy here, it certainly is peaceful.

In actuality, Greenwich Cove is located half in the city of Warwick and half in the town of East Greenwich. Divison Street, just north of Norton's Shipyard, marks the boundary line onshore. On the water, the imaginary town/city line runs in an east-west direction down the center of the cove. Warwick (and the Warwick harbormaster) has jurisdiction over the eastern half, where most of the boats are moored. He can be reached on VHF Channels 8 or 16.

Most visitors to Greenwich Cove either pick up a mooring or take a slip for the night. The friendly folks at East Greenwich Yacht Club are happy to provide a mooring or slip if one is available. Fuel, ice and showers are available for guests. If the club is crowded, they enforce the yacht club reciprocity rule, otherwise, if they have room,

Greenwich Bay Anchorages

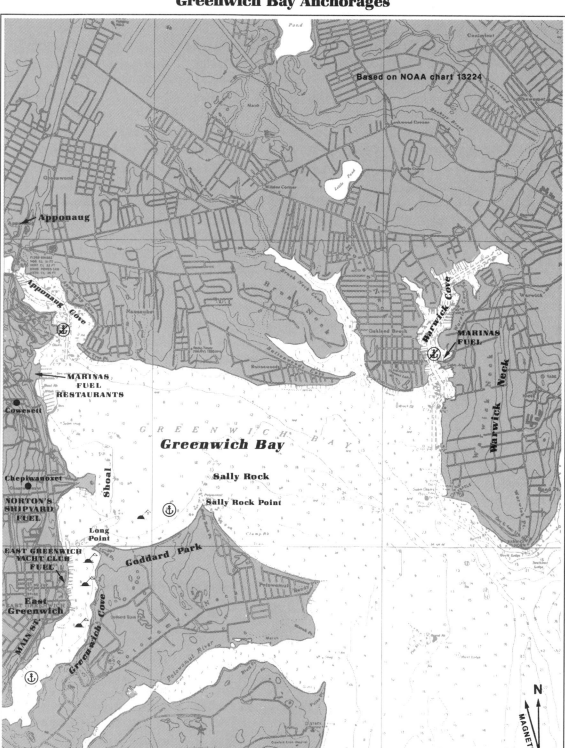

Based on NOAA chart 13224

Apponaug

Apponaug Cove

MARINAS
FUEL
RESTAURANTS

Cowesett

G R E E N W I C H   B A Y

Greenwich Bay

Chepiwanoxet

NORTON'S
SHIPYARD
FUEL

Shoal

Sally Rock

Sally Rock Point

Long
Point

Goddard Park

EAST GREENWICH
YACHT CLUB
FUEL

East
Greenwich

MAIN ST.

Greenwich Cove

Warwick Cove

MARINAS
FUEL

Warwick Neck

Potowomut River

N

MAGNETIC

SCALE: **1″=.63** NAUT. ML.   ⚓ **Do not anchor**   ⛵ **Mooring area**   ⚓ **Good anchoring**

they will provide any cruising person with a slip or mooring for the night, with launch service available. The club dock is on the starboard side of the cover as you enter, past Norton's Shipyard. Your best bet is to pull up to the fuel dock and inquire about accommodations. On the club's front porch beyond the docks, rows of inviting wicker rockers and pots of bright petunias await the sea-weary visitor.

Norton's Shipyard and Marina, which can be reached on VHF Channel 16, also has transient slips and moorings available (see listings on page 192) as well as a well-stocked ship's store, fuel, showers, and launch service. Norton's has been in business for more than 40 years, and is an excellent full-service yard capable of handling any repair job you might need while visiting here.

Provisions. West of the waterfront area sprawls the town of East Greenwich, which can be reached by hiking up steep King Street. At the top of the hill you'll find Main Street, which has every type of supply and service you're likely to need during a visit here. Heading north along Main, you'll find a bakery, post office, liquor store and movie theater. In the other direction, after a considerable hike you'll find a convenience store and an Almac's Supermarket a bit further down. We walked to Almac's and back from the yacht club, and the trip back with a canvas tote full of groceries was taxing on a hot summer day. If you need to buy in quantity, we'd advise finding a ride. Near the grocery store is a camera store, another bakery, theater and hardware store as well as two pharmacies.

Where to Eat. Near the marina ashore is the popular Meritime Restaurant. Here guests are greeted with the slogan, "Welcome to the Mer-itime Restaurant, where pretension and formality are replaced by good food, friendly service, and a restful atmosphere." Indeed, here one gets the feeling everyone knows everyone else, and it is a pleasant place to linger over a cup of coffee and a hearty meal. Restaurant owners Dennis and Bette serve up excellent fare for breakfast and lunch, and offer a complete provisioning service,

with dockside or mooring delivery available. You can reach them on VHF Channel 9.

South of Norton's and the yacht club, the waterfront is bustling with several excellent restaurants that cater to yachtsmen, many offering temporary dockage for diners. On any summer evening, both docks and tables are full, and while you wait for a table you can enjoy cocktails outside on any one of several open-air, umbrellaed patios overlooking the cove. 20 Water Street serves excellent continental fare, and has dinner dock space for boats ranging from "rubber rafts to large yachts." Harborside Lobstermania also offers slips to diners, and specializes in good, basic steak-and-seafood fare. Between these two establishments is yet another restaurant, the Inn Between, which in addition to steak and seafood offers live music on occasion. Transient dock space is available here as well, though most of the boats that dock here seem to be of the small, shoal draft variety. The restaurant monitors VHF Channel 16 should you wish to make a dinner or dock reservation.

Things to Do. Greenwich Cove is a very active harbor, even in midweek, with an active sailing fleet, shellfishermen buzzing by in quahog skiffs, and large and small power and sailboats arriving at restaurant docks for dinner. The cove sits near the railroad tracks, and occasionally an Amtrak will clatter by to add to the action, but the noise is fleeting and not bothersome. Green State Airport is not far from here, and in early morning and late afternoon you'll see and hear jets taking off overhead. This is not particularly bothersome, either, and East Greenwich is an excellent place to pick up or drop off crew due to its proximity to air transportation.

Despite all the activity here, East Greenwich offers a quiet side, too. In contrast to the west side of the cove, the entire eastern perimeter is bordered by the forested acres of Goddard State Park. Greenwich Bay was called Cowesett Bay at one time, an Indian name meaning "place of pine trees," and it's easy to understand the name's origin when you gaze at the forests of Goddard. Egrets stalk this quieter shore, fishermen cast

The tall shade trees in Goddard Park frame the anchorage on Greenwich Bay, and provide cool shade for sailors on a hot summer day. LYNDA CHILDRESS PHOTO.

9 feet off the beach until you near shore, where depths shoal to 2 and 3 feet and submerged rocks abound. Swimming is excellent, both off the boat or off the beach, in beautiful surroundings.

Provisions/Where to Eat. Heading clockwise around Greenwich Bay, there are several full-service marinas that cater mainly to resident boats, including Brewer's Marina and the Masthead Marina. Both of these locations have ship's stores and excellent restaurants nearby, but are mostly inaccessible to visiting yachts. If space is available and you call ahead, they will try to accomodate you, however. Masthead Marina monitors VHF 16 or can be reached from a shoreside telephone at 884-1810. Contact Brewer's by phone at 884-0544.

The site where Brewer's now stands was a prime coal landing point from the 19th century through World War II. It was kown as "Folly's Landing" —a name that survives today as the moniker of the excellent restaurant above the marina. At Folly's you can enjoy one of the best vistas of Greenwich Bay to be had, as well as a fine meal and entertainment at its outside bar.

their lines from along the grassy banks and laughing gulls soar overhead. The wooded expanse of the western shore provides a peaceful buffer from the activity on the opposite side of the cove.

Alternative Anchorage. Outside the confines of the cove, just off the white sand beach bordered by thick woods that is also part of Goddard Park, is the area's other designated anchorage. Boats may anchor anywhere off the beach in the lee of Sally Rock Point. If you don't wish to anchor, there are six Rhode Island State Guest Moorings here, strung in an arc off the beach (see "Cruising Conditions," page 14, for exact locations, rules and regulations).

While the inner cove is fun for a night or two, this excellent anchorage is preferable for longer-term enjoyment of the area in prevailing winds (it is somewhat exposed to the north). Holding ground is good in soft mud, with depths of 7 to

Things to Do. In addition to the beach, Goddard Park has miles of hiking trails that wind their way through thick, pine-scented woods, as well as an ongoing series of naturalist and historical programs each summer. Going ashore on the east side of the cove you'll find a boardwalk leading to buildings housing park rangers, where information on the park and its programs can be obtained. Also located in this complex are snack bars, rest rooms with showers, and telephones, as well as some small exhibits on area fish and wildlife. Picnic tables set up under the trees provide a pleasant place for lunch ashore—but bring plenty of repellent—the mosquitoes can be bothersome.

Aside from an occasional swell from traffic entering and exiting Greenwich Cove, the only detriment to this peaceful spot are bevies of beer-swilling waterskiers who emerge after the workday ends, and careen through the anchored fleet, endangering both themselves and others despite the efforts of both the East Greenwich and War-wick harbormasters to control them. If you get a hankering for a swim off the stern before supper, keep an eye out for these revellers, who make a great case for mandatory boat operator licensing.

History. East Greenwich joins Newport in the distinction of having once been a capital of Rhode Island. The town was settled in 1677 by a group of men who had been granted 5,000 acres of land as payment for fighting in the war between colonists and Indians that later became known as King Philip's War. The town is named for Greenwich, England, and was a booming seaport and shipbuilding center in the late 1770s.

Later, the shallow waters of Greenwich Bay became one of Narragansett Bay's prime scalloping grounds, and one area of the waterfront near town was once known as "Scallop Town." Today, the primary catch here is quahogs and clams, but Greenwich Bay remains one of the state's leading shellfish producers. Greenwich Bay Clam is a testament to the area's productivity; located at the south end of the cove, this commercial enterprise bustles with activity. The company's large boats can be seen daily out on Greenwich Bay purchasing the day's catch fresh from individual quahoggers.

This area is the largest boating center north of Newport, but it hasn't yet been ruined by excessive crowds. It would be easy to spend a week or more enjoying its attributes. Although the spot is in the process of being "discovered," it remains a worthwhile stop on any cruise of Narragansett Bay, and rates as one of the area's most diverse and pleasurable destinations.

APPONAUG COVE

No facilities for transients

Charts: 13221, 13223, **13224**

Once a pleasant stop for visiting yachtsmen, Apponaug Cove has become so full of local boats there is no longer any room for visitors to anchor, moor or dock for the night—which is a shame, since it ranks among Narragansett Bay's most sheltered and scenic coves. Inquiring about slip space before visiting here recently, we were told by more than one person, "We don't get visitors here. There's nothing here for transients." On a jaunt up the channel by dinghy, we found this to be true.

Approaches. The channel entrance is shoal, offering 4½ feet (and, in places, less) with the head of the cove shoaling to a scant 1 to 3 feet outside the channel.

Should you care to poke your nose in here for exploration's sake, stay between the buoys in the narrow channel and be mindful of the general lack of depth here. There is a town dock at which small boats can tie up for brief forays ashore; it is located near the top of the cove on the port side of the channel.

Provisions. Surrounded by marshlands and trees, the cove is pretty enough, with an abundance of egrets, ducks and other shore birds. The Crow's Nest restaurant offers only small-boat dockage for patrons, and a fuel dock, bait shop, ice machine and phone are located at Ponaug Marina at the head of the cove, which caters primarily to small and mid-sized local powerboats due to limited depth at its docks.

Apponaug Cove is part of the city of Warwick, and is under the jurisdiction of the Warwick Harbormaster, who monitors VHF 16.

Due to Apponaug's limited access and facilities, we would suggest nearby East Greenwich as a much better cruising stop. Although there used to be both slips and moorings available here, it is no longer a destination easily accessible to visiting yachts. The cove's shallowness, added to its lack of transient facilities, will see that it is left largely for the enjoyment of locals who keep their boats here.

History. The name Apponaug is a direct descendant of the Indian term for the area, and means "place of many shells" or "place of oysters." It is reputed to have been a favorite place for Narragansett Indians to gather to roast the succulent shellfish, and its shores are said to have once been lined with piles of oyster shells.

WARWICK COVE

Charts: 13221, 13223, **13224**

Like Apponaug, Warwick Cove once was a well-visited harbor that has recently become clogged with local boats. The entire area has a congested, run-down feel to it, and although there are facilities for transients, we truthfully cannot see much attraction here for visiting yachts.

The entrance channel to Warwick Cove is extremely hard to pick out along the north shore of Greenwich Bay and, once you point your bows toward the channel, you can count on fleets of large powerboats roaring past you through the pass at dangerously high speeds, creating equally dangerous wakes for all involved.

Approaches. The entrance channel hugs the shore on the northeastern edge of Greenwich Bay. Proceed through can "1" and nun "2," then head northward, keeping within the 6-foot-deep channel to avoid extensive shoals close by to either side.

Anchorages. Unlike Apponaug, Warwick Cove does provide some facilities for transients, as well as a small anchorage area in 5½ feet on the west side of the channel at the entrance to the cove. Despite a breakwater, the area is exposed to prevailing summer southerlies. Farther up inside the cove, however, the shelter is excellent.

There are no public or rental moorings available here, but several marinas accommodate transients (see Appendix). According to locals there are two good restaurants within walking distance: Cherrystones and The Beachcomber.

This cove is one of several under the auspices of the city of Warwick, though it is the only one that bears the city's name. In our opinion, it is one of the least appealing harbors the area has to offer for visiting yachts. Most of the city's other coves are as pleasant as any on the bay.

When we visited Warwick Cove, we arrived intending to stay the night, and were so put off by the poor seamanship we observed, as well as the general downtrodden air, that we canceled our slip reservation and headed north to Occupessatuxet—also one of Warwick's coves, but infinitely more pleasant.

History. Warwick was the first West Bay settlement, and was founded in 1642 by Samuel Gorton. Originally, it was called "Shawomet," but on early Indian maps it appears as "Nasauket," and later was named Warwick for Robert, Earl of Warwick, England. The Earl allegedly supported Samuel Gorton's attempt to gain protection by legal charter against encroachment on the territory by Plymouth Colony.

PATIENCE ISLAND

No facilities

Charts: 13221, 13223, **13224**

Although there are no anchorages on Patience per se, it rates five stars as one of the bay's last untamed wilderness areas. It is part of the Bay Islands Park System, as is its nearby neighbor, Prudence, which offers coves that are close enough to Patience to allow exploration by visiting boats.

Approaches. The only place on Patience Island for small boats to beach or anchor off in 1

Patience and Prudence Islands Anchorages

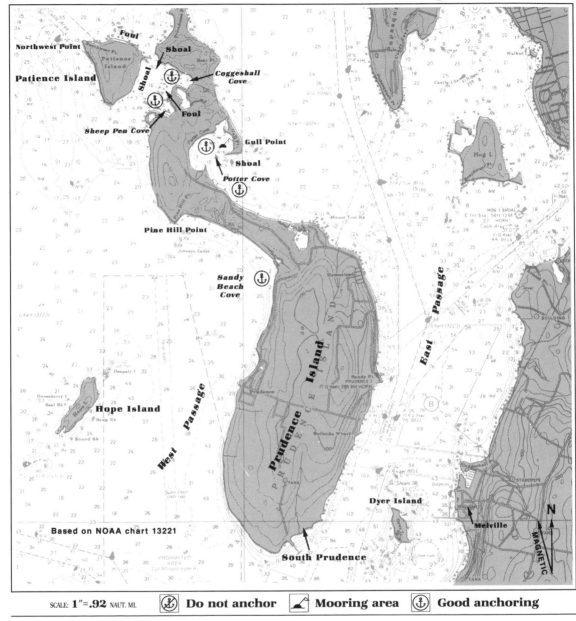

SCALE: **1"=.92** NAUT. MI.   ⚓ **Do not anchor**   ⚓ **Mooring area**   ⚓ **Good anchoring**

to 3 feet is on the island's east coast, just south of the remains of an old dock.

Reaching the beach on Patience's east side from the north requires threading through the narrow, unmarked pass between the two islands. This is one of the only unmarked areas of Narragansett Bay, but it is possible to negotiate, using caution, by keeping to the dead center of the passage, and is best done at high tide. Although there is a deep area with 15 to 18 feet between islands, the line between deep and shallow water is a fine one, and extreme caution should be exercised when navigating this unbuoyed area. If you're a shoal-draft boat heading for the beach, give the area just south of the old dock a wide berth before turning in toward Patience Island.

Anchorages. Although most of the island is thick with woods and underbrush and hard to negotiate unless you plan to bushwhack your way through, the area near shore is clear enough to provide space for picnicking and/or camping out, and is well-populated on weekends.

Larger boats sometimes anchor north of the island inside Northwest Point, where there is a small, pebbly beach, but a strong current around the point combined with lumpy seas from traffic between Greenwich Bay and the Upper Bay make it rolly and uncomfortable, and its exposure to the north is considerable.

Beyond the small beach at Northwest Point, boats should keep well offshore, as the area near shore is fouled by numerous rocks and a wreck marked by a Coast Guard buoy.

History. Patience was named by Roger Williams, its first owner, who purchased it from the Indians in 1637. Williams bestowed such virtuous names on several islands in the bay, including Hope, Despair and Prudence. In 1664, Patience Island became part of the town of Portsmouth, but now is maintained by the state. At one time the island was used as farmland, but now has returned to a completely wild state.

As a destination, Patience is limited to the small-boat explorer. For yachtsmen with larger boats, it merits a visit by dinghy when anchored in another cove nearby.

COGGESHALL COVE

(PRUDENCE ISLAND)

No facilities

Charts: 13221, 13224

Directly across from the landing place at Patience is Prudence Island's Coggeshall Cove, a wonderful anchorage for boats drawing less than 4 feet

and a popular summer weekend small-boat anchorage.

Coggeshall is a beautiful little cove surrounded by wild woods and salt marshes. In the heart of Prudence Island's Estuarine Sanctuary, it is abundant with birdlife, and on a quiet dinghy trip to the marsh at the cove's south end at high tide, you are almost guaranteed to spot more herons and egrets than you've probably ever seen before. On one early morning visit, we sighted five great egrets stalking the shallows here at one time, with a sixth roosting regally in a nearby tree—a spectacular sight. Great and little blue herons as well as other bird and wildlife, including deer, abound in this unpopulated place.

Approaches. Approaching from the north, use care when threading your way through the narrow pass between Patience and Prudence. The 16-foot-deep center is bordered by 1-foot-deep shoals to either side, and the passage is unmarked, leaving mariners to con their way through with chart and depth sounder close at hand. Keep to the center of the pass, and proceed with extreme caution. A shoal area extends well off the shore to port as you turn to enter Coggeshall Cove, and unmarked rocks proliferate to the west of Long Point, so don't attempt to enter here without the aid of a NOAA chart. In the middle of the cove small boats will find safe 4 to 5-foot depths quite a ways in, but entering at high tide is an excellent idea here.

Anchorages. Although the cove is somewhat exposed to the southwest, holding ground is good in soft mud, with depths of 4 to 5 feet in the center of the outer cove at low tide.

Just south of Coggeshall is Sheep Pen Cove, which is considerably shallower and more exposed to the southwest, with unmarked rocks abounding. Although we have seen boats tuck in here when Coggeshall is full, Coggeshall is the better choice for overnight anchorage on Prudence's west coast. Sheep Pen Cove has been known as such since the early 18th century, and probably gets its name from the ruminant mammals who were once corralled near here.

Prudence Island

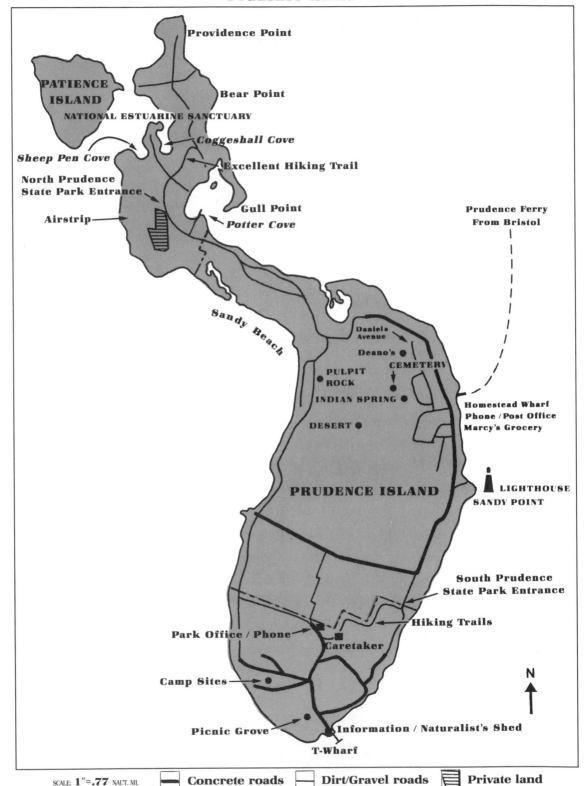

Providence Point

PATIENCE
ISLAND

Bear Point

NATIONAL ESTUARINE SANCTUARY

Coggeshall Cove

Sheep Pen Cove

Excellent Hiking Trail

North Prudence
State Park Entrance

Airstrip

Gull Point

Potter Cove

Prudence Ferry
From Bristol

Sandy Beach

Daniels
Avenue

Deano's

CEMETERY

PULPIT
ROCK

INDIAN SPRING

Homestead Wharf
Phone / Post Office
Marcy's Grocery

DESERT

PRUDENCE ISLAND

LIGHTHOUSE
SANDY POINT

South Prudence
State Park Entrance

Hiking Trails

Park Office / Phone

Caretaker

N

Camp Sites

Picnic Grove

Information / Naturalist's Shed

T-Wharf

SCALE: 1"=.77 NAUT. MI.   Concrete roads   Dirt/Gravel roads   Private land

History. Coggeshall Cove is probably named for John Coggeshall, who lived near the cove in 1840 before moving to Patience Island. Once, it was known as "Long Cove," named for the rabble-rousing gent named Richard Long, who lived on Prudence in the 1720s before being banished from the island for his misconduct.

For shoal draft boats, the west coast of Prudence offers an atmosphere that is sometimes elusive on the waters of the bay—when planning a visit here, don't forget to bring a good pair of binoculars and your camera, as you will certainly not want to miss the chance to observe the abundance of wildlife in its natural habitat.

SANDY BEACH COVE (PRUDENCE ISLAND)

No facilities

Charts: 13221, 13224

Locals call this cove east of Pine Hill Point "Sandy Beach," and at low tide there is indeed a wide expanse of deserted white sand shore here. At high water, however, the beach is virtually swallowed by the encroaching tide. In prevailing summer southwesterlies, exposure makes this cove an untenable overnight spot, but in late summer and early fall when occasional northerly breezes infiltrate summer's wind patterns, a prettier, more sheltered cove is hard to find.

Bordered to the north by the beach and Pine Hill Point and to the east by woods perched on rocky ledges, the cove is a pleasant place to drop the hook for lunch and a stroll along the deserted expanse of sand, as long as winds are light. Because it is a windward-facing shore, it is a beachcomber's delight, with all sorts of interesting driftwood and other natural flotsam washing up along its shores.

Anchorages. The best place to anchor here is in toward the trees on the eastern shore, in 11 to 20 feet. Whether you dinghy ashore to explore the beach and the mud flats or remain aboard to enjoy the scenery, you'll find this a pretty and uncrowded anchorage on an otherwise frequented island.

SOUTH PRUDENCE ISLAND

No other facilities

Chart: 13221

Marked by a T-shaped wharf, a small naturalist's shed, and a weathered but sturdy dock near a white sand beach, the cove at the southern tip of Prudence Island is a popular daytime anchorage for Narragansett Bay boaters.

Anchorages/Moorings. The dock accommodates dinghies for a 10-minute tie-up period as well as a small ferry that delivers hikers and campers from the mainland to the trails and campsites on the island's south end. The cove's southwestern landmass and the pier provide a fair bit of shelter from that direction, though on weekends boat wakes make this anchorage a rolly one, and in a due south or southeast wind, it is out of the question.

There are four guest moorings here, marked by metallic blue-green floats. Tie-up is limited to daylight hours only, which is fine, as this area is too exposed for a comfortable overnight stay.

Things to Do. Ashore, you'll find a fine sandy beach and picnic tables, with good swimming and miles of wooded hiking trails that are part of the Bay Islands Park System. Stop in at the naturalist's shed and pick up material for a self-guided nature walk along the trails, as well

At south Prudence, visitors can pick up guest moorings, but dockage is restricted to short-term tie-ups to leave space open for the ferry. LYNDA CHILDRESS PHOTO.

as other literature on marine life, birds and wildlife on the island.

Prudence has one of New England's densest herds of white-tailed deer, and although they are shy, they are so numerous it's hard to hike around the south end without sighting at least one. Most likely sighting times are early morning and late afternoon, when the deer emerge from the thickets in search of food.

Thanks to the deer, Prudence also has a large population of tiny ticks whose bite can cause Lyme Disease, or Lyme Arthritis, which can lead to serious long-term health problems. Lyme ticks are about the size of the head of a pin, and their bite causes a small red area on the skin, which sometimes expands to a diameter of five inches or more. Sometimes the bite is followed by fever, chills, and stiff neck, accompanied by muscle and joint aches. Since the tick is so small, it is easy to be bitten without being aware of it.

For this reason, when hiking around Prudence, even in the summertime, wear protective clothing and frequently check yourself for clinging ticks. Stick to trails and avoid walking through long grass or fields where the ticks proliferate.

This area of Prudence was once owned by the

Navy, and many whitewashed buildings still remain. Emerging from a woodsy trail to discover clusters of deserted buildings makes you feel as if you've stumbled upon some Pacific isle outpost, and exploring the old Navy haunts is nothing short of Nancy Drew/Hardy Boys fun.

You can easily spend a whole day exploring the delights of South Prudence, but before darkness falls, cruising visitors should plan to depart this lovely area and head north to the shelter of Potter Cove at the island's opposite end.

POTTER COVE
(PRUDENCE ISLAND)

5 | 4

Charts: 13221, **13224**

On the north end of Prudence Island is a sheltered cove formed by the arm of Gull Point. This scenic sanctuary is Potter Cove, without doubt one of Narragansett Bay's more magical destinations. Consequently, it is also one of the most popular, and the cove is inevitably filled with visiting cruising boats by late morning on any summer weekend day. Midweek visitors, however, are likely to have this beautiful anchorage largely to themselves. In fact, it would be easy to spend a week or more in this almost landlocked, uninhabited cove, for while there are no facilities here, there is plenty to keep visitors occupied.

Approaches. Approaching Potter Cove, keep nuns "4" and "6" to starboard. These mark a submerged 2-foot-deep shoal that inevitably snares those deeper draft boats that attempt to cut inside of them. On the port side of the entrance channel, there is good water up to the small dock, but only 3 feet to the southeast and southwest of it.

Anchorages. Within the cove, yachts are free to anchor anywhere there is sufficient space and depth. Although there is shelter from all directions, the favored anchoring area is in the north end of the cove, but beware of tiny Shell Island when searching out your spot here. At high tide, it is submerged and marked only by a stake with a red flag on it. At low tide, Shell Island is clearly visible, and it is easy to see how the islet came by its name. A wreck lies in 8 feet southwest of the island, and is marked by a Coast Guard buoy.

The southwest corner of the cove is the least appealing area to anchor, for while it is sheltered from prevailing winds, it is subject to considerable swell from boat wakes both in the channel and farther out in the bay, and you may find yourself rolling unmercifully while anchored here. This end of the cove also tends to be buggy due to its proximity to the woods.

When Potter Cove is full, an equally popular anchorage is available along the pebbly beach to the east of the cove, where shelter from southwesterlies is good, but again, swell can be a problem. This area is exposed to the north and east

as well, but fleets of boats anchor overnight here in prevailing winds with no problems.

Holding ground both within the cove and in the area outside is excellent, with a soft mud bottom prevailing. The state of Rhode Island maintains three guest moorings inside the cove. These are located south of Shell Island and west of Gull Point in 10 feet of water (see "Cruising Conditions," page 14, for coordinates, rules and regulations).

Don't be surprised when anchored at Potter to see a small private plane buzz out of the treetops or circle the anchorage before descending onto a small airstrip that parallels the south side of the cove. Occasionally, when the wind is right, you'll see or hear a larger jet pass overhead, but aside from other visiting boats, these are the only signs of civilization you're likely to see while anchored here.

Things to Do. Potter Cove is renowned for its excellent clamming, and visitors should try their hand at digging some succulent steamers or littlenecks to enjoy with cocktails at sunset. Safe shellfishing can be found on the east-facing side of Gull Point, where clams are plentiful despite the area's popularity. Heed the posted legal and illegal shellfishing areas, clearly marked by red and white triangular signs. The area on the red side of these signs is off-limits; the white side points to areas that are legal shellfishing grounds.

Potter Cove is surrounded by woods, marshlands, and trails that are part of the Narragansett Bay Estuarine Sanctuary, one of the first such national sanctuaries to be established in the Northeast. In addition to land on the north end of Prudence, both Hope and Patience Islands are now part of the sanctuary's 1,000-acre land trust.

Should you tire of relaxing at anchor, swimming, shellfishing, or strolling the beach, there are endless miles of excellent hiking to be had ashore. For the ambitious walker not afraid of distances, the island has much to offer in the way of both natural and historical sites.

Walking south along the dirt road that parallels the shoreline on the east coast of Prudence, there is an abandoned oyster farm, a haven for

Rhode Island Shore
Dinner In A Pot

For centuries, Rhode Island has been renowned for its superior clams, and this meal, made with steamer clams instead of quahogs, never fails to be impressive. It's easy to do aboard as it requires only one large pot, and is best served on deck, with plenty of napkins. Neat it isn't, but it's loads of fun. Serves 4.

>   2 1½-pound lobsters
>   2 quarts steamer clams
>   2 ears of fresh corn, shucked and broken in
>   half
>   2 to 3 large onions, quartered
>   2 to 3 potatoes, peeled and quartered
>   2 cups chourico sausage, sliced
>   6 cups water
>   ½ pound butter
>   2 lemons, sliced

In your largest pot, place cleaned clams in shells, corn, onions, potatoes, sausage, and water. Bring to a boil. Add live lobsters and cover tightly. Steam for approximately 20 minutes, until clam shells are uniformly open and lobster shells turn bright red. (Shellfish may cook before potatoes and corn; if so, remove shellfish and continue cooking vegetables for a few additional minutes.) Melt butter and pour into several small bowls. Serve the dinner directly from the pot with a slotted spoon, and briefly immerse each morsel of seafood in butter before popping into your mouth. Garnish with lemon wedges. It's a good idea to have a large bowl on hand for discarded shells. Also serve with mugs full of steaming clam broth ladled from the top portion of the liquid in the pot. (As you near the bottom, it inevitably becomes a bit sandy). Rhode Islanders drink the broth, which is heavenly, but this practice often elicits gasps of horror from those from other regions, who prefer to use the broth to primly dip their clams but eschew drinking the liquid. These nay-sayers will never know what they are missing, as there's nothing better to complement this feast, except perhaps an ice-cold Hope Lager beer.

rare wading birds including black-crowned night herons, cattle egrets, blue and green herons as well as finches, kingfishers, and other birds. The site is also full of fresh deer tracks. When hiking around Prudence, use caution to avoid tall grasses and fields and stick to trails and roads; the island has a booming population of tiny ticks whose bite can cause Lyme Disease (or Lyme Arthritis). Bites are characterized by red areas that sometimes spread to a diameter of five inches or more, and can cause joint pain and stiffness, fever and other symptoms. The ticks are not much bigger than fleas, and they are hard to spot on clothing and skin. If you suspect a bite, seek medical treatment immediately. Antibiotics are used to treat symptoms. Wear protective clothing when hiking here, and check yourself frequently for these small hitchhikers.

About two miles from the anchorage, west of the center of town, are an historic Indian cemetery as well as a natural spring locals call the "Indian Spring." Both sit on land believed to have been inhabited by the Narragansett Indians. In his excellent but hard-to-find book, *Paragraphs On Early Prudence Island*, Prudence resident Charles Maytum passes on a legend as to how the stone markers in the cemetery came to be broken. During the Revolutionary War, the story goes, the British came ashore on Prudence to get water at the Indian Spring. As they were relaxing, they were surprised by American troops, and in defense their ship anchored offshore began to fire on the area. Cannonballs hit the gravestones, it is said, breaking off their tops. According to Maytum, most islanders believe the cemetery was a burial ground primarily for slaves, not Indians, as true Indian burial grounds do not have headstones. Strolling through the shady woods toward the spring, one gets the distinct feeling that invisible eyes are watching from a vantage point hidden in the trees. At the spring, visitors can sample the cold, clean water, and fill jugs if they so desire. Libation of a different sort can be found nearby at Prudence Island Vineyards, where tours of the winery are available by appointment during the season.

In the same vicinity as the vineyards you'll

find an area known locally as "The Desert," a fascinating geographical locale that is believed to have been the winter camping ground for the Indians. The area is extremely sheltered in winter months, and in all seasons, for reasons no one can quite explain, it is one of the warmest spots on the island. In summer, unusually high temperatures of 100° or more have been recorded here, giving the area its name.

Another of Prudence's historic sites is Pulpit Rock, which is situated northwest of the Indian Spring and cemetery. It is believed to have been the throne of Narragansett chiefs Conanicus and Miantonomi, and is the site from which Roger Williams preached to the Indians in about 1637. Islanders say the rock is located about 200 feet in from the road, north of the center of the island, but on a recent exploration we could find no trace of it, and were reluctant to venture into the woods too far off the beaten path due to the heavy population of Lyme ticks. To search out this landmark, wear long pants and prepare to tackle heavy underbrush.

Provisions. On Daniels Road, about ¾ mile from Potter Cove, you'll find Deano's grocery and wildlife station. In this one-room market, which is part of a private home, you'll find bread, milk and other basic provisions as well as a good selection of fresh meats. The proprietor of Deano's, John Canario, is also the island's conservation officer, as the small neighborhood of birdhouses and other wildlife-oriented structures surrounding his house well attest. He is happy to chat with visitors and share local knowledge. A visit to this Prudence Island institution is a must.

At Homestead Wharf, site of the ferry dock and a small-boat pier where visitors may tie up at no charge, you'll find the island's other small grocery store, Marcy's. Marcy's carries a slightly larger selection of items than does Deano's, including ice. Here, too, is the island's tiny post office, which generally is only open when the ferry, which also picks up and delivers mail to and from the island, is expected.

Still farther south on Narragansett Avenue you'll find a small fresh produce stand opposite Sandy

Point Light. The lighthouse dates back to 1823, and its original location was on Newport's Goat Island. It was moved to Prudence in 1851, and had a keeper until 1939, when it was automated. Today, the light flashes a green signal and is equipped with a foghorn warning unsuspecting boats off the shoal that extends quite far east of the light. Sailing in the waters off the light, be sure to leave can "27" to port going north or starboard going south, as it sits right on the tip of the sandbar jutting out from the lighthouse and cannot be cut.

History. The Indian name for Prudence was "Chibachuwese," ("place of separation of the passage"). Like Patience, Prudence received its virtuous English name from Roger Williams, who purchased the isle from the Indians in 1637. Later, the island was known as "Sophy Manor" for a time before reverting to its present-day name. For a short time during this period the island had its own governor, and was the smallest republic in America. Early residents of Prudence were sheep and cattle farmers, and the fields on the island produced such crops as tobacco, peaches, plums, apples, pears and Indian corn.

During the Revolutionary War, all homes on the island were torched by the British. Residents fled in terror to the mainland, and the island was not inhabited again until it became a popular summering place, which it continues to be to this day. Fewer than 50 people reside on this isolated island in the busy bay during the winter months, but during the summer the population swells into the hundreds. During World War II, land on the south end of the island was owned and used by the Navy as a storage depot. Today, like much of the island, it is part of the Bay Islands Park System and is owned by the state.

The island itself, like Patience, belongs to the town of Portsmouth. It is the bay's third largest island, measuring about 7 miles long by 1⅓ miles wide, and is home to New England's densest population of white-tailed deer as well as other wildlife.

Potter Cove may have been the landing spot for Roger Williams on his first expedition to Prudence. Like many of the island's coves, Potter probably took its name from someone who lived nearby. As early as 1815, a man named Rowse Potter leased a large farm bordering the cove, and it is likely named for him.

On the west shore of the cove stands another Potter Cove residence, though this one was built around the turn of the century. The deserted mansion has a haunting quality, which is not surprising when one learns its history.

The mansion was the brainchild of a wealthy young millionaire named James Garland. Like many bay sailors over the years, he discovered Potter Cove while seeking shelter from a gale aboard his yacht *Barracuda* in the spring of 1904. With his wife and a crew of friends aboard, he departed Providence bound for Newport in a moderate southeast wind. As they headed south, the wind increased, eventually reaching gale force. They headed in to Potter Cove and dropped anchor to wait out the blow. From then on, Garland was a man obsessed with buying the surrounding land and building a secluded home in the cove.

Within a week, he had purchased 800 acres on the north end of the island, and built the home using stones unearthed as workers cleared the land. He had a channel dredged through the cove to accommodate his yacht, and built a pier so construction materials could be ferried back and forth from the mainland. While the palatial house took shape, Garland supervised from aboard *Barracuda* anchored in the cove. Obsessed with his privacy, he ordered a yacht club that had been built in the cove in 1890—one of the state's first—off the land.

Only the finest materials were used to finish the large, high-ceilinged house. No expense was spared on either the house or its grounds and outbuildings, which included a barn. But sadly and ironically, Garland was never to live in his dream house. He died shortly before it was ready for occupancy and the house was never lived in. It has stood empty since that time, and today overlooks the cove in brooding silence.

Hiking around Prudence, one is surrounded by the tranquility of a way of life not often still seen in these busy times. Scattered cedars, pines

and unchecked brambly undergrowth grow in abundance, sprinkled with honeysuckle, bittersweet, and wild beach rose. The aromatic mix of scents provides a perfume that is particularly pleasant to the sailor leaving ocean smells to come ashore.

Most islanders don't bother to register autos that never leave the island. They simply number them instead, and as you walk you'll be passed by jalopies of all kinds, bearing plates reading "149" or "202," and so on. A word of caution: cars tend to travel the dirt roads at a pretty good clip, so don't dawdle when moving out of the way of the occasional vehicle that passes you by.

On a recent summer weekend, we counted more than 100 boats in the cove, plus another 50 anchored outside. Despite the popularity of the water, not many people leave their boats to discover the delights ashore. Even on busy weekends, we always enjoy a solitary hike and never feel we've spent as much time as we'd like at this anachronistic haven in the midst of the busy bay.

If you can manage it, visit this cove during the week, when it is as deserted as the day James Garland first laid eyes on it in 1904. But even on a busy weekend, you'll enjoy yourself here in spite of the crowds, and we can't recommend it highly enough as a stop for visiting cruisers.

On Prudence Island, cars aren't registered— they're simply assigned a number. LYNDA CHILDRESS PHOTO.

Prudence Island Etiquette

Because of Prudence's isolation and wildlife population, the islanders ask visitors to observe a few simple rules to preserve the natural beauty of their island home. They are as follows:

- Please help keep Prudence clean. All trash must be taken off-island with you. Do not leave anything behind.

- There are no open fires allowed ashore.

- Please do not throw lit cigarettes or matches while hiking ashore. Both water and fire-fighting resources on the island are limited.

- No vehicles of any kind are allowed on the island's beaches.

- The islanders ask that you please enjoy, but do not disturb, the wildlife, especially the young. If you find a baby animal, please leave it alone. Its mother is likely to be nearby. Injured animals can be brought to the Animal First Aid Station at Deano's store on Daniels Avenue.

HOPE ISLAND

Off-limits April 1 to September 15

No Facilities

Charts: 13221, **13224**

Hope Island, a small, low dab of land west of Prudence Island, is part of the Bay Islands Park System. The island is a wildlife sanctuary and is home to hundreds of shore birds. For this reason, people are asked not to go ashore during nesting season between April 1 and September 15. Cruis-

ers are unlikely to be roaming the bay much before April 1 in New England waters, but there is ample good boating weather after September 15, when visitors are welcome to go ashore and hike around this deserted isle.

Approaches. When negotiating near the island, use care to avoid a 4-foot-deep shoal near Round Rock and the shoal area near the red-and-green buoy off the south end of the island, where some old pilings are visible as well. Several other rocky outcroppings surround the island, including Scup Rock and the cluster known as Despair Island to the east and north respectively, as well as cormorant-covered Gooseberry Island near Seal Rock on the island's west side.

Anchorages. Although there is not much protection in Hope's one and only cove, it is possible to anchor here if you pick your day carefully. It is wide open to the south, so visit here only on windless days or when a light northerly is blowing—neither of which is uncommon after September 15 in this area. Set your hook well before you go ashore, for the bottom is rockier here than in most areas of the bay, except very close to shore. Depths in the center of the cove are 14 feet even at low tide.

Hope was cleared at one time, and now is mostly open meadows dotted with wildflowers and shade trees interspersed with strangely out-of-place electric poles, remnants of the island's Navy past. Old overgrown roads still bisect the landscape here, and the island and its environs are rocky and fairly steep-to, looking more like it belongs in the Galapagos than Narragansett Bay.

History. The island was a gift from Narragansett Indian sachem Miantonomi to Roger Williams, who gave the island its name. During World War II it was owned and used by the Navy as an ammunition storage depot. In the early 1970s it was acquired by the state of Rhode Island as part of the Bay Islands Park System.

In the calm of a recent early morning, we anchored but did not go ashore, and enjoyed cof-

DYER
ISLAND

PORTSMOUTH
(MELVILLE
AND
COGGESHALL
POINT)

90

fee in the cockpit in the company of exotic-looking black-crowned night herons sunning on the rocks with the ubiquitous herring gulls. The peacefulness of the place is broken only by the cries of the birds, who wheel above the remnants of World War II ammo bunkers that sleep ashore under blankets of grass, wild roses and Queen Anne's lace.

If you time it right, a visit to deserted Hope is well worth the effort.

DYER ISLAND

No facilities

Chart: 13221

Dyer Island, an unassuming speck of uninhabited and undeveloped land smack in the middle of upper East Passage, lacks a suitable anchorage and is not a place for cruisers to stop. To local sailors, Dyer is probably most widely known as an obstacle surrounded by foul water to be avoided when sailing through the upper East Passage, with a rock painted emergency orange on the island's western shore its most notable landmark. Squat, low and brambly, Dyer is privately owned by a group calling themselves "Dyer Straits."

At this writing, the island was for sale, with the stipulation that its eventual use must not disturb the habitat or prove detrimental to the environment. Its present owners foresee a beach club on the island. With luck, it will eventually be purchased and preserved as open space.

History. The island is named for William Dyer, one of Aquidneck's founders, who received it in 1658 from a Narragansett sachem named Cachanaquoant. The State of Rhode Island and Providence Plantations has the island's namesake to thank for its state seal—the anchor. Dyer was the designer of the symbol that remains in use and appropriate today, more than 300 years later.

Although Dyer is presently inaccessible to cruising boats, we include it here to satisfy the curious, as it is a familiar yet unknown quantity to most boaters who bypass it each time they traverse this passage of the bay.

PORTSMOUTH
(MELVILLE AND
COGGESHALL POINT)

Charts: 13221, 13223

The presence of two excellent full-service marinas tucked behind Coggeshall Point, east of Dyer Island, in the northern reaches of East Passage, has made this stretch of Aquidneck Island's coastline more popular with cruising boats in recent years than ever before.

In past years, this land was owned by the Navy. Now, in addition to the two boatyards located here, the region has become a center for marine-related businesses. In addition to Little Harbor Marine, located at Melville, and East Passage Yachting Center (formerly Bend Boat Basin) just to the north, there are a host of marine enterprises including two ship's stores, Hood Yacht Systems, Hood Sailmakers, The Rigging Company, Newport Marine Electric, Liferaft and Survival Equipment, boatbuilders Tillotson-Pearson and Seahawk, and more.

Dockage/Facilities/Repairs. While there's little to do as far as entertainment for the cruising visitor here, these two yards may well be the most convenient on the bay for yachts needing repairs. Little Harbor has 50 transient slips, travel lifts with capacities to 160 tons, and easy access, with 15 feet at its docks mean low water and 20 feet in the entrance. Approaching Melville, look for the huge supply ship permanently berthed nearby, the *Cape Carthage*, which provides excellent shelter for boats docked in its lee.

Little Harbor can accommodate power and sailboats of up to 130 feet and is capable of performing any sort of repair job—but please note that they do not accept credit cards. You can reach them on VHF Channel 16 (see listing for further details).

East Passage Yachting Center, in a cove that is sheltered from virtually all directions, is also a full-service yard. Unlike Little Harbor, it has a head pump-out facility as well as CNG. Their lift has a capacity of up to 70 tons and the marina can accommodate boats of up to 115 feet in 10 feet MLW at their docks. The narrow entrance to the cove passes between unfriendly looking rocks, but is well marked. East Passage Yachting Center rents slips out as owners vacate, but have up to 30 open at any one time, and only require reservations if you are traveling with a large flotilla (see listing for further information). They can be contacted on VHF Channels 16 or 74.

At this writing, yet another large marina is being planned for this area of coastline, which would increase substantially berths for visiting yachts in the area.

Provisions. The complex sits in relative isolation on the west coast of Aquidneck overlooking Prudence Island, and there is little to do here in the way of shoreside entertainment, though Windsails Restaurant at East Passage Yachting Center provides a good meal ashore in a congenial atmosphere. In the way of provisioning, The Ship's Store, also at the yachting center, sells very basic grocery items. Gleeson's Package Store, about a mile uphill from both marinas, is the closest liquor store, and across busy West Main Road from Gleeson's there is a small convenience store. Major provisioning during a stop here will require a cab ride to Super Stop & Shop, the closest supermarket, a few miles south on West Main Road.

History. Coggeshall Point Cove functioned as a PT boat base during World War II, and all the acting PT boat skippers were trained here, including JFK. Nearby Melville was a storage tank form for military fuel.

Two British frigates were sunk off here in 1778, and divers say evidence of them can still be found on the bottom of the bay.

This north end of Aquidneck was the island's first settlement. Founders landed here in 1638 and established the town of Portsmouth, named after Portsmouth, England. A year later, a band of settlers broke from Portsmouth and headed as far south as land allowed. They named the new place Newport.

With its easy accessibility, its location just six miles north of Newport and not too far from Rhode Island Sound, plus its abundance of marine support services, this area may well become the place of choice for visiting yachts in the bay that find themselves in need of repairs.

For cruisers traversing north or south on the bay, it is well worth considering as an overnight stop.

The Upper Bay, Including Mount Hope Bay

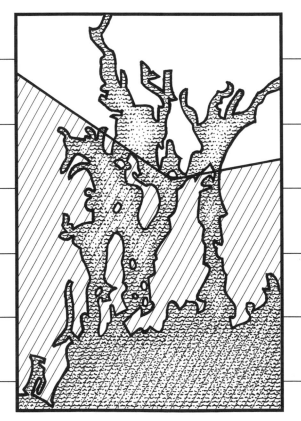

THE
UPPER
BAY,
INCLUDING
MOUNT
HOPE
BAY

94

The Upper Bay, Including Mount Hope Bay

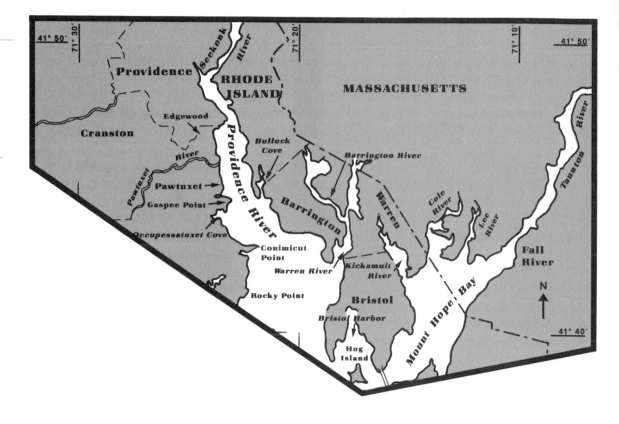

A
Glimpse
of
History

The shores of Providence River harbor a goodly number of local traditions, bits of history and romance. From Pawtucket down the whole stretch of shore there is not a bay or a little cape that has not been the scene of some exciting adventure in colonial days, either when the Indians were on the warpath or during the still more unsettled time when British revenue boats were poking into every nook and corner for contraband goods.

Mention a cruise of the Upper Bay to a habitual cruiser of the lower portion and you are likely to get an upturned nose. The truth is, the Upper Bay provides some of the most interesting cruising the bay has to offer. Although in places it is more urban than areas to the south, these waters harbor some of the bay's best hurricane holes and, because it is the oldest settled area on the bay, a cruise here provides some of the most fascinating glimpses of area history.

A few harbors in this region are filled to capacity with moorings and local boats, with no room to anchor. While this is not the case universally, it is something to be aware of when you head north. More often than not, mooring or docking will cost you, and it's wise to make a reservation in advance of your arrival for dock space or a mooring. While the harbors tend to be a bit crowded, there is surprisingly less pleasure boat traffic here than in the congested Lower Bay near Newport. Providence and Fall River, eschewed by cruisers in the past, are both undergoing waterfront restoration and revitalization, and now have much to offer the cruising visitor.

The Upper Bay in general has taken an undeserved bad rap over the years. While the flavor of cruising is different here than it is on other parts of the bay, it is no less interesting. We recommend giving it a try.

ROCKY POINT

(WARWICK)

Charts: 13221, **13224**

To the north of Warwick Point Light on Warwick Neck lies Rocky Point, a good stop for a day's outing at Rocky Point Park, particularly if you have kids aboard.

Approaches. Warwick Light is one of the bay's prettiest, and was built in the early 1800s to guide ships between Patience Island and Warwick Point on their way to Providence. The pass between Patience and Warwick is no longer the chosen route for shipping, but the light remains functional. Although it is automated, a Coast Guard keeper and family live in the neat white house next door. The light, which stands 51 feet tall, has a green signal that is charted visible for 12 miles, and is a helpful navigational aid for recreational and commercial fishing traffic.

Approaching from the south, landmarks to watch for near Rocky Point Park are a stone tower that calls Rapunzel to mind and a bulbous silver water tower. Both are clearly marked on NOAA Charts, and both are visible from a considerable distance.

Dockage. Rocky Point Park welcomes cruising visitors, although dock space is limited. There is a pier with room for six or seven small boats on a first-come, serve-yourself basis. Water depths at low tide are 3 to 4 feet at the inner docks, and 10 feet at the longer pier for larger boats on the outside. While water depths are adequate here, there is not much protection on windy days. Plan to put out plenty of fenders to save your topsides, as there is no padding on the pilings and it can get quite rolly. On summer days, slips fill up fast, so get an early start if you want a space.

Things to Do. Though not maintained by the park, visitors can swim (at their own risk), sun, and picnic in an area to the north of the docks. There is no beach, but swimming off the rocks along the shore doesn't seem to bother anyone here.

Rocky Point is among Rhode Island's oldest resorts, one of the few still remaining on the bay that hark back to the days when the Upper Bay was a resort area for the middle classes. During the Gilded Age it was Narragansett Bay's foremost amusement park, drawing revelers packed aboard excursion boats like the *Bay Queen*, a predecessor of the tour boat of the same name that plies the bay today. The park, established in 1849, was

For Merry Picnickers

A popular ditty "for merry-hearted picnickers" of the late 1800s was described by author Frederic Denison in a volume called *Narragansett Sea And Shore* (RIHS and R.A. Reid, 1879). The author instructs that it is "to be sung only at shore picnics and at 12 M." "The Shore Glee" was sung to the tune of "Yankee Doodle" and accompanied by mouth harp and kettle drum.

THE SHORE GLEE

Let gouty monarchs share their shams
   'Neath silken-wove pavillions;
But give us Narragansett clams—
   The banquet for the millions.
(Refrain) Yankee Doodle, etc.

Along the Narragansett Shore,
   Polite in their salams, sir,
Sat copper-colored kings of yore
   And feasted on their clams, sir.
(Refrain) Yankee Doodle, etc.

Successor to these doughty kings
   Sits now the Yankee nation,
And every jolly Yankee sings
   His *clam*-orous collation.
(Refrain) Yankee Doodle, etc.

But how each valiant Yankee crams
   We surely need not tell, sir,
If only you bring on the clams
   All smoking in the shell, sir.
(Refrain) Yankee Doodle, etc.

once heavily wooded, and the scenic promontory served as a site for hiking and picnicking before rides and other amusements were built.

Today, the park features rides with names like Corkscrew, Flume, and Cyclone as well as tamer entertainments, and also has one of the few shore dinner halls still accessible by boat on the bay. Admission to the park is reasonable, and kids under eight are admitted free with a paid adult. Don't leave without sampling some traditional Rhode Island seafood. The all-you-can-eat chowder/clamcake/watermelon special is a steal at $4.95, or if you want an entire clambake (including Indian pudding) it's available for less than $20 per person. The park is open daily from June 1 to Labor Day. Hours are 11 a.m. to 10:30 p.m., Sunday through Thursday; weekends the park stays open until midnight. Phone is 737-8000.

CONIMICUT

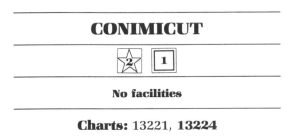

No facilities

Charts: 13221, **13224**

A classic sloop sails past Conimicut Point light in the Upper Bay. LYNDA CHILDRESS PHOTO.

Approaches. Between Warwick Point and Conimicut Point lies an extensive shoal. For the most part it is deep enough to be navigable—averaging 15 feet or so—but as you near Conimicut Point depths drop drastically to as little as 1 to 2 feet at low tide. Keep Conimicut Light to port when heading north; to starboard when sailing in the opposite direction. Since it is submerged, this tricky shoal is quite difficult to see. Don't be tempted to cut Conimicut Light or you will almost certainly run aground.

Not surprisingly, the shoal on the south side of the point is a favorite spot for quahoggers, and their skiffs—which often number in the hundreds—stretch across the water like stepping stones on any summer day. The landlike mirage this creates can be startling as you head north or south in these waters, especially on a hazy day. Despite their numbers, the shellfishermen leave plenty of room to the east of the shoal for recreational boats to go around them. Since these boats are anchored and engaged in scuba diving or raking for clams, avoiding the fleet is the seamanlike course of action.

Conimicut Light stands 58 feet tall, flashes white, and is charted as visible for 13 miles. Originally the light was placed here to warn ships off the dangerous Conimicut Shoal. Although it stands in the same spot, the structure there today is not the original light, which was built in the 1860s. Conimicut enjoys the distinction of being the last lighthouse in the United States to be electrified. Now it is both automated and unmanned.

Anchorages. Conimicut has a nice beach with a sprinkling of neat cottages lining the shore. Swimming is fine to the south of the point, but not recommended to the north of it. The north side of the point is classified by the Department of Environmental Management as "SC," which means OK only for recreational boating and other "secondary contact" water sports. Although it is a habitat for fish it is not clean enough for shellfishing or swimming. The north side is an acceptable place to drop the hook for lunch, but the low-lying point doesn't provide enough shelter from the prevailing southerlies to make it a good overnight anchorage, and it's exposed to

Rocky Point to Edgewood

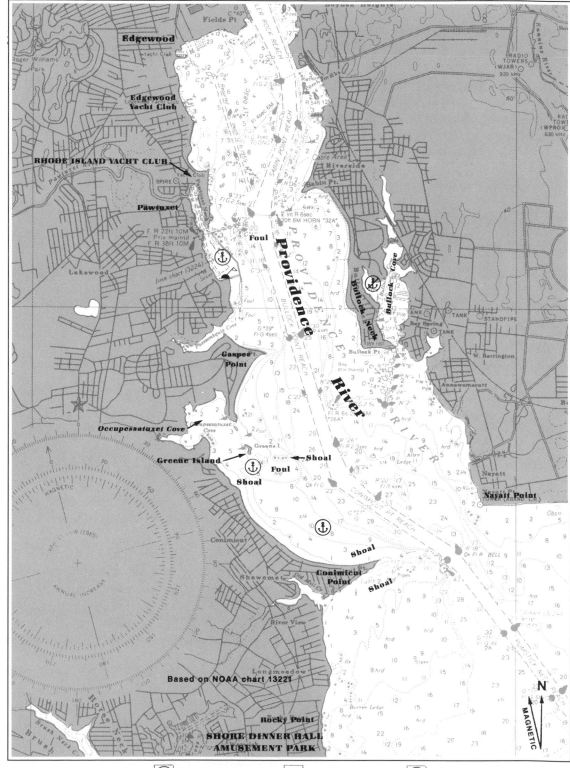

SCALE: 1"=.76 MILES   ⚓ **Do not anchor**   ⚓ **Mooring area**   ⚓ **Good anchoring**

the north and east. Holding ground is fair; the sandy bottom turns rocky as you near the shore. Anchor for an afternoon in 8 to 10 feet on the north side of Conimicut Point and walk across to picnic and swim in the cleaner waters on the south side, but find another spot to anchor for the night.

The point was named Conimicut for the granddaughter of Narragansett sachem Conanicus (after whom Conanicut Island was named), who was the daughter of an Indian princess named Quaiapen.

OCCUPESSATUXET

COVE

⭐4 4

No facilities

Charts: 13221, **13224**

A better anchorage lies just to the north of Conimicut Point: Occupessatuxet Cove. Pronouncing the name of this delightful place is probably the

most taxing thing you'll have to do while visiting here. Occupessatuxet is a wonderfully unpopulated and lovely anchorage for its proximity to Providence, the only drawback being that swimming and shellfishing are not recommended here. As is the case with Conimicut, residents seem to ignore the designation of the DEM, jumping in off private docks and waterskiing in the inner cove at high tide.

Approaches. This cove is one of the few in the Upper Bay that is unmarked, which is perhaps the reason the *Atlantic Coast Pilot* suggests entering only with local knowledge. Keep to the middle of the narrow entrance between Greene Island and the Conimicut shore. There are shoals along the shore as well as to the south and east of Greene Island; both are submerged. Proceed slowly with chart in hand and an eye on the depth sounder, being careful to avoid unmarked rocks south and east of the Greene Island shoal.

Anchorages. Occupessatuxet is not a big-boat anchorage, nor is there room for more than a handful of boats. The cove is shallow, offering 5-foot depths MLW at the eastern end and 2 feet or less in the inner cove to the west. Protection is good from every direction but due east. The

Deserted Greene Island is an oasis in the Upper Bay's Occupessatuxet Cove.

tongue-twisting Indian name means "small cove on tidewater"—an apt description of the anchorage, though the English version is much easier to pronounce!

To be on the safe side, anchor in the middle of the east end of the cove, going no further in than the western tip of Greene Island to starboard and the cluster of cottages ashore to port. Entering at dead low tide with 4½-foot draft, we bumped bottom gently a couple of times, but the bottom here is soft, forgiving mud that has the added bonus of providing excellent holding ground. When it came time to leave we were hard-pressed to extract the anchor. If you draw 3 feet or more it is probably a good idea to try to time your entry and exit at high tide.

Things to Do. The setting at Occupessatuxet is pastoral, surrounded by wildflowers, marshes and green meadows sprouting tall shade trees. The tiny, uninhabited islands Greene and No-Name poke their heads from the mud flats on the north side of the cove. An easy dinghy ride away, they provide excellent shelling, beachcombing, and birdwatching as well as protection from the north. Ironically, Greene Island is owned by a family named Brown, though it was named for a sea captain by the name of John Greene. At one time, it was a continuation of the mainland and the site of a large barn, which was washed away during the hurricanes of 1938 and 1954. No doubt it was also these storms that separated the island from the mainland, leaving only its tip in view, and creating the submerged shoal that surrounds it. At one time it was also called Turtle Cove.

A rooster crowed to greet the dawn each morning we awoke here, providing an alarm that preceded the rumble of early flights departing nearby Green Airport. The sound of an occasional jet must be taken for granted when cruising the west side of the Upper Bay, but here the intrusion is more obvious due to the tranquility of the setting. Because of its relative isolation, Occupessatuxet supports an abundance of bird life: chattering terns who may tamely land on your bowsprit, herons, egrets, sandpipers, and swans. During our stay an osprey took up residence on a large driftwood log on Greene Island; ordinarily, "fish hawks" are an uncommon sight west of the Sakonnet.

In addition to Greene Island, the inner cove is a delight to explore by dinghy. You may surprise a blue heron wading in the shallows or spot a rare cattle egret among his snowy counterparts on a deserted dock.

Occupessatuxet offers no facilities of any sort, but for bird–watching, spectacular sunsets, deserted isles, and as rural a setting as the Providence River has to offer, it can't be beat.

PAWTUXET COVE

Charts: 13221, **13224**

On the western shore of the Providence River lies the historic village of Pawtuxet, which perches on the line between Warwick and Cranston. The harbor is under the jurisdiction of both cities.

Approaches. Rocks on the approach to Pawtuxet are well marked, but this is known locally as a very tricky channel due to constant shoaling and no recent dredging.

The best tactic when negotiating this entrance is to stay exactly in the middle to stay out of trouble. The anchorage basin is to port as you enter, protected from the south and east by a stone breakwater and by land from the north and west. The harbormaster advises hugging Pettis's Boat Yard as you make the turn into the harbor.

Anchorages/Moorings. Like Occupessatuxet, Pawtuxet is a shallow-draft anchorage. Depth in the entrance channel is 6 feet at mean low water, with 4½ feet at low tide in the anchorage basin. We'd advise checking with the Warwick harbormaster before entering here for the latest local information on the condition of the channel and basin. He can be contacted on VHF Channels 8 or 16.

To the right at the end of the entrance channel is another channel, which leads north to a picturesque stone bridge and waterfall at the mouth of the Pawtuxet River and to Pawtuxet Cove Marina at the head of the channel to starboard. Depth at low tide here is a scant 2 feet; the passage has not been dredged in years. Although it may look passable because of the handful of large boats moored there, stay away unless you are a vessel of very shallow draft. According to the harbormaster, the big boats that call the channel home "don't move much." Only shoal draft boats can navigate the river to take advantage of the services of Pawtuxet Cove Marina.

In the anchorage basin the Warwick harbormaster has a 100-pound mooring marked "Harbormaster" that visiting boats are welcome to use, but he requests a call to ask permission first. There is definitely no swimming here and everyone pays heed, but fortunately there are other attractions to enjoy during your stay.

Salter's Grove State Park sits at the south end of the anchorage next to a waterfront condominium development, and the park is an attractive setting offering good paths for strolling and grassy expanses for a picnic by the water in the shade of tall trees. On the west side of the cove is a dinghy dock where visitors can leave the tender and take a short walk to explore town.

Provisions/Things to Do.

Pawtuxet is one of the oldest settlements on Narragansett Bay, and the village is a charming mix of affluent modern and historic homes, shady tree-lined streets, colonial streetlamps and a requisite white church. Gift and antique shops line the hilly streets of the village and there are good restaurants if you're in the mood for lunch or dinner ashore. Two of the best are the Bank Cafe, which serves regional American food at moderate prices, and the Driftwood, offering good Italian food in a more casual atmosphere. Lindsay's market in the

center of town carries all the provisions you'll need, and Cameron's liquor store, drugstore and bakery are nearby as well. A laundromat is just a short walk up the hill.

History.

Pawtuxet was settled by three farming families in 1638. In 1754 the land north of the Pawtuxet River became part of the town of Cranston, named for Samuel Cranston, governor of the colony from 1698 to 1727. The boundary today is the stone bridge crossing the river.

This now shallow cove was once a deep-water harbor, and as such was instrumental in the Triangle Trade between Narragansett Bay, the West Indies and Africa. The cove was once surrounded by thick woods, and was a favorite fishing ground for the Indians, who gave it the name Pawtuxet ("place by the waterfall"). A small, informative booklet on the history of the village is available at Cameron's.

Just to the south of the cove is historic Gaspee Point. Here, in 1772, Colonists burned the British schooner *Gaspee*, which had been patrolling Narragansett Bay in search of trading ships trying to elude Britain's hefty import tariff. The *Gaspee* chased the colonial packet *Hannah* up the bay to Warwick, where *Hannah*'s crafty skipper sailed into the shoal water near the point, hoping the *Gaspee*'s captain would pursue him. The ruse worked and the English ship ran aground while *Hannah*, armed with local knowledge, floated free and continued her journey to Providence. Word quickly spread of the incident, and a band of angry colonists ambushed the grounded *Gaspee* under cover of darkness, overpowered her captain and crew and torched the ship. This was one of the first acts of revolt against British policies that eventually sparked the Revolutionary War.

Every June in Pawtuxet Village, the uprising is reenacted as the crowning event in a two-week festival of arts, crafts and historical events called "Gaspee Days."

Pawtuxet has earned a rather bad reputation thanks to the polluted river of the same name in its midst. However, the water quality here is destined to improve with the cleanup of the river now mandated by the state. In the meantime,

this stop along the Providence River is still worth making to stroll through the village, picnic in the park, shop for antiques, or savor lunch or dinner in a picturesque setting.

STILLHOUSE COVE

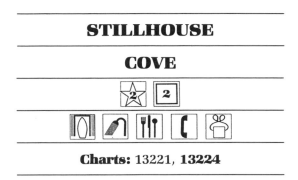

Charts: 13221, **13224**

This shallow cove north of Pawtuxet has a general depth of just 5 feet. Stillhouse Cove is home to the Rhode Island Yacht Club—and not much else. The area surrounding the club is residential, with no provisioning or entertainment within an easy walk, although there is a restaurant in the clubhouse.

The Cove is the site of an interesting moment in history. Colonists put the captain of the British ship *Gaspee* ashore here after they'd wounded him and burned his ship for attempting to enforce what they deemed were unfair trade tariffs. The incident occurred off Gaspee Point to the south of the cove. The name Stillhouse apparently was derived from a whiskey still that once graced the site.

We can see little reason for visiting boats to make a stop here unless a rendezvous with friends is planned.

EDGEWOOD (CRANSTON)

Charts: 13221, 13224, **13225**

The section of Cranston known as Edgewood has two facilities for yachts, neither of which is frequented often by transient boats.

Edgewood Yacht Club is a rustic, historic structure standing on pilings on the west shore of the Providence River north of Stillhouse Cove. The aging clubhouse has survived several major bay hurricanes and looks it—the pilings that support it show signs of rot, and in places the clubhouse deck is in need of repair. Despite this, the docks are clean and pleasant, thanks in large part to the friendly and cheerful dockside staff. The club is one of the most active on the bay and has produced some world-class sailors, among them Cranstonite Henry Childers, who sailed with Dennis Conner aboard *Stars & Stripes* in the 1987 America's Cup Races in Australia.

Dockage/Provisions/Fuel. If you take a slip at the yacht club, you'll find sodas and ice available at the docks, but you'll have to hike uphill a ways to a Cumberland Farms convenience store to find basic provisions. The area surrounding this club is mostly residential, and unless you've come to Edgewood with a purpose, we'd advise choosing another overnight stop. There is no anchorage in Edgewood.

Just to the north of the yacht club, also on the west side of the river, is Port Edgewood Marina. This primarily powerboat facility does not cater to transients, but it is one of the few places in the Upper Bay where gasoline is available, although the gas dock is sometimes closed on Sundays or holidays when you're most likely to run out. All the marina's slips are occupied by resident boats, but as with other ports in Cranston, there is not much to lure the visitor here anyway.

PROVIDENCE

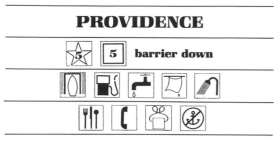

| ⍟ 5 | 5 | barrier down |

Charts: 13221, 13224, **13225**

It is worth the trip upriver to see Rhode Island's first settlement and capital city, founded nearly 400 years ago. From deck level the city looks imposing at the head of the Bay. Any city skyline can be impressive from a distance, but Providence seems more dramatic since it looms from comparatively rural surroundings.

Approaches. Heading upriver toward Providence, keep your chart at hand for ready reference. Stay well off Greene Island, which has a shoal extending eastward more than halfway be-tween it and the marked channel of Bullock Point Reach. Farther up, keep can "29" to port to avoid Gaspee Point Shoal.

As you head north you'll bypass 19th Century Ponham Rock, named for an Indian sachem, with its picture-postcard light on the Providence River's eastern shore. No longer active, the light is still home to a caretaker, who maintains the grounds. As a beacon it was replaced in 1974 by a 54-foot-high flashing red tower just to the west of the lighthouse.

The ship channel leading to the city of Providence is dredged to a depth of 40 feet. Outside the channel depths to either side are 10 to 18 feet, but tend to shoal to as little as 4 feet in places as you near the city, so don't put the chart away till you're safely at the dock. Shipping is likely to be heavy here, especially on weekdays, so stay alert, stay to the edges of the channel if possible, and stay out of the way of commercial ships.

Like San Francisco, Providence is a hilly city and, like Rome, it sports seven named slopes. It is the second largest city in New England and the third largest port. The city has about 25 wharves and docks to facilitate large ships. Roughly 10 miles of commercial waterfront borders either side of the river as you approach the city.

Dockage. To enter the anchorage basin in Providence, recreational craft must pass under a fixed hurricane barrier that was erected in 1966 to protect the city from severe flooding during hurricanes. The barrier is closed during severe storms, but generally remains open to water traffic. Each of the three gates has a horizontal clearance of 20 feet; unfortunately, the vertical clearance here is just 21 feet, making the inner harbor inaccessible to most sailboats. Waterfront developers are aware of the problem, however, and the city is now studying a way to open the top of the barrier during good weather to allow access to all types of craft. The basin offers good depth even at low water, ranging from 15 to 22 feet. The cove is sheltered from virtually every direction, making this an ideal hurricane hole—*as long as the hurricane barrier is closed.*

The Providence skyline looks imposing at the head of Narragansett Bay. LYNDA CHILDRESS PHOTO.

Providence Region

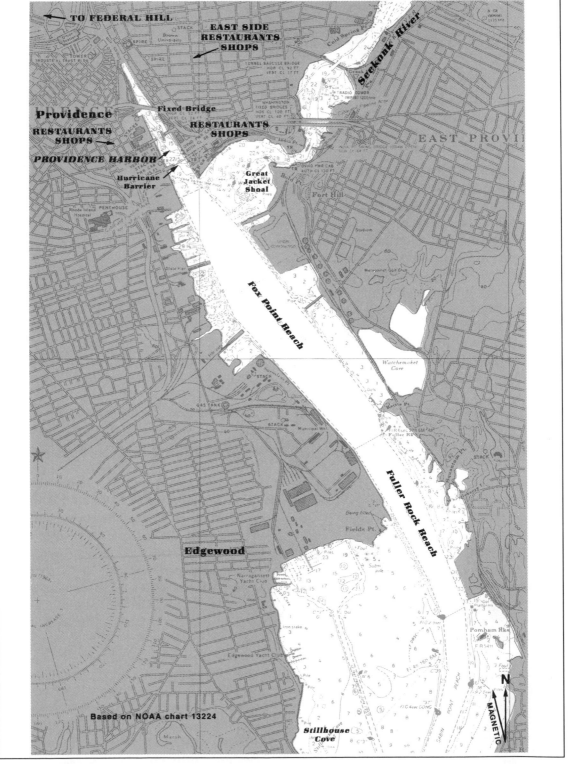

TO FEDERAL HILL

EAST SIDE
RESTAURANTS
SHOPS

Seekonk River

EAST PROVI

Providence

Fixed Bridge

RESTAURANTS
SHOPS

RESTAURANTS
SHOPS

PROVIDENCE HARBOR

Great
Jacket
Shoal

Hurricane
Barrier

Fort Hill

Fox Point Reach

Watchemoket
Cove

Fuller Rock Reach

Edgewood

Fields Pt.

Pomham Rks

Stillhouse
Cove

Based on NOAA chart 13224

N

MAGNETIC

SCALE: 1" = .46 NAUT. MI.

A boatload of revelers heads under the Fox Point hurricane barrier at Providence, bound for the popular Hot Club. LYNDA CHILDRESS PHOTO.

Things to Do.

Providence is undergoing a facelift similar to that of Baltimore and other waterfront cities. The rivers that run through the heart of the city, once covered by highways, are being uncovered. Buildings are being relocated and the maze of roadways rerouted to pass around, rather than through, the city center.

While the work is far from complete, the revitalized Providence is a delight to visit, offering all the entertainments that could be expected of a large city.

Within walking distance of the marina are scores of eateries, nightclubs and shops housed in attractively restored warehouses on cobbled streets. The Hot Club is a favorite with the local young business crowd, providing a lively environment on summer evenings when patrons can dine or sip cocktails on open-air decks along the river. Nearby Davol Square is a restored marketplace with indoor shops and restaurants.

A short taxi ride away is Providence's historic East Side, a mini-city within the city that is home to Brown University and Rhode Island School of

There is plenty of transient slip space at a brand-new marina, called Old Harbor as an indication of the developers' intent to restore the harbor to recreational use as it was in its early days. To date there are no moorings available, but additional marina space is planned for the future. There is no anchoring here.

Providence Harbor is now an attractive destination for recreational boaters. LYNDA CHILDRESS PHOTO.

Design. The East Side offers an abundance of interesting architecture and several good museums, among them the Rhode Island School of Design Art Museum, one of the best small museums of its type in the country. Roger Williams is buried on Prospect Hill, and the church he founded, the first Baptist church in America, is on North Main Street. Tours are available of most of the city's historic sites. For more information call the Greater Providence Chamber of Commerce at 521-5000 or the Rhode Island Tourism Division at 277-2601.

Where to Eat. Providence is renowned for its excellent ethnic restaurants, many of which can also be reached by short taxi ride. Three of our favorites are Thailand restaurant on Federal Hill, an excellent choice for spicy and delicious oriental food; Angelo's on Atwells Avenue for superb Italian food, and Taj Mahal on the East Side for equally satisfying Indian cuisine. Thailand and Taj Mahal are BYOB establishments; atmosphere at all three is casual, with prices that give the word "reasonable" new meaning. If you're in the mood for something more elegant, Hemenway's on the river is a good choice for any type of seafood imaginable, local or flown in from ports around the world and Al Forno is a nationally acclaimed Italian grill. For a different sort of night out, take a taxi over to Providence's premier comedy club, Periwinkles, for dinner and a show. The club is housed in the Arcade building, a restored indoor marketplace similar to Boston's Faneuil Hall.

Provisions. If you need to provision while you're here, we highly recommend a visit to the neighborhood Italian markets on Federal Hill. The short taxi ride is worth the savings you'll find on Atwells Avenue, where cheese, pasta, pastry and bread are made fresh daily, and espresso is served in the bakeries.

A few of the cab companies in the area are Checker Cab (273-2222); East Side Taxi or Laurel Cab (521-4200); and Walsh Cab (861-5450).

History. Providence was founded in 1636 by religious dissident Roger Williams, who was banished from the Pilgrim settlement at Plymouth for his beliefs. After an arduous journey south on foot in the middle of winter, Williams was welcomed to the land west of the Seekonk River by the Indians, with whom he began a mutual friendship. Justifiably feeling quite lucky to have arrived in one piece, he thanked "divine Providence" for delivering him safely, and christened the city Providence.

When Providence was attacked and burned in 1675 by the Indians during King Philip's War, the angry throngs spared Roger Williams, telling him he was the only good and honest man in the confines of that city. Most of the city's buildings were burned, however, and residents fled south, many to Aquidneck Island, to avoid the conflagration.

Present-day Providence, while somewhat tamer by comparison, is an exciting and worthwhile place to visit by water, and only promises to become more so in the future.

SEEKONK RIVER

Charts: 13224, **13225**

Since Roger Williams crossed the Seekonk River by canoe to found Rhode Island in 1636, it has suffered a fate familiar to many big-city rivers: devastating pollution. The river is about 5 miles long and stretches inland from Providence to the Blackstone River in Pawtucket. It was named by the Indians to mean "at the outlet." The Seekonk is the northernmost point of Narragansett Bay tidewater, and separates the cities of Providence and East Providence.

East Providence, on the east bank of the river, was the original stopping place for Roger Williams when he fled Plymouth Colony. Williams attempted to settle here first, but ultimately crossed the river to found Providence on the west bank when he was ordered off the land by angry leaders of Plymouth Colony, who claimed the east bank belonged to them. Originally part of Seekonk, Massachusetts, the land on the east bank was annexed to Rhode Island in 1862.

Once a pleasant waterway between woodlands, the southern end of the Seekonk is now framed by highways and heavy industry. Farther up, the surroundings grow more pleasant, though pollution is still highly visible.

Approaches. The channel entrance is well marked to starboard with red nuns, but buoys grow fewer and farther apart as you head north. Depths are 18 to 20 feet, but beware of Green Jacket Shoal off Bold Point, with only 1 to 2 feet at low tide. Stick to the middle of the channel to be on the safe side. There is plenty of water for a considerable distance upriver. A short distance upriver is the Washington Street Bridge, which has a horizontal clearance of 100 feet and a vertical clearance of 40 feet. At this writing, plans are afoot to upgrade Bold Point Park at the entrance to the river. A floating pier for fishing and small boat tie-up are to be installed and a decrepit pier removed. A launching ramp for small boats already exists at the park.

Dockage. Boats cruising Narragansett Bay may wish to end their Seekonk River sojourn at the Oyster House Marina and restaurant just south of the bridge. The marina has three slips for transients who wish to visit the restaurant and offers a good meal, though staying here overnight will be noisy due to nearby highway traffic.

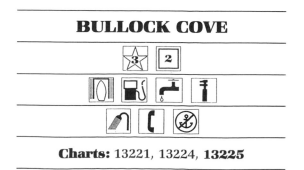

BULLOCK COVE

Charts: 13221, 13224, **13225**

Bullock Cove is formed by one of two peninsulas in the town of Barrington, southeast of Providence on the east shore of the Providence River. The cove is an attractive place but hasn't been dredged in almost 30 years and has silted up quite badly in places.

Approaches. The entrance is extremely narrow and shoal, though well-marked, and passes startlingly close to land on either side in places. Depth at low water is only 4½ feet, and some of the moored boats rest on the bottom at low tide in the cove, where depths are only 1 to 3 feet except for dredged areas around marinas.

If your vessel draws more than 4½ feet you should most definitely plan to enter and exit this cove at high tide, and even then it's possible you'll bump bottom. The bottom is soft mud, so no harm is done, and large boats enter here quite frequently. Even boats with up to 12 feet of draft get in and out of this cove successfully, but usually do so on an extra-high moon tide.

The cove is an attractive place, surrounded by marshes and trees. Its shoal nature has prevented excessive overcrowding, though boats are tightly packed into dredged areas near marinas.

Dockage. There is no room to anchor here, so don't be tempted by the inviting, empty cove to port as you head up the channel—it's less than a foot deep at low tide. Neither are there transient moorings, but two marinas provide slips. Cove Haven, on the eastern shore of the cove and Stanley's, to the north of Cove Haven, both welcome transients. Bullock Cove Marina at the southwest end of the cove has no facilities for transients, and hardly room for local boats moored and docked there. Lavin's Boatyard, across the way, does not offer transient slips either, but does have a fuel dock.

If you intend to visit Bullock Cove you must call well in advance to reserve a slip. (See marina listings, page 194.) Both Cove Haven and Stanley's rent slips to transients on a variable basis, as yard owners come and go. Depths at Cove Haven are 9 to 12 feet at most docks. As you enter the area north of A-Dock, hug the pier and steer clear of the area between pilings to port—it's shallow. The marina has a swimming pool that guests can enjoy, a plus if you have kids aboard, since Bullock Cove is classified "SC"—no swimming—by the Department of Environmental Management.

Repairs/Fuel. Cove Haven's 150-ton travel lift is one of the largest on the bay. For this reason it is popular with large commercial boats, visiting charter yachts and large racing and pleasure yachts needing repairs or service. This was the yard of choice for many America's Cup yachts in years past. Cove Haven does not provide fuel, but nearby Stanley's does, with depths of 5 feet at the dock at low water, and so does Lavin's.

Things to Do. Haines State Park is just next door, with picnic tables and stone fireplaces set on a carpet of pine needles and plenty of shady acreage on the waterfront. There are 10 miles of trails for jogging and biking here, making this a good place for a morning or evening workout, even if you are on vacation.

Provisions. Aside from the park, the area surrounding the cove is residential, with no restaurants or provisions within an easy walk. However, there is a small marine supply store at Cove Haven and a larger, better stocked one, the Boat Barn, right across the street. This place has all the boating supplies and gear you're likely to need. Visiting Almac's grocery store, a drugstore or laundromat requires a cab or a ride if you need to provision or do laundry during your stay here.

History. This quiet cove once was a hunting and fishing ground for the Wampanoag Indians. At one time it was also part of Plymouth Colony, and the town's English name comes from a Viscount Barrington, a British lawyer who believed in religious freedom and was one of the early settlers here. The area remained a part of Massachusetts until 1746, when it was transferred to the Colony of Rhode Island. Originally, the land was part of Warren, but split to become Barrington in 1770.

Bullock's Cove is a pleasant stop on the bay, but transient space is very limited, so if you plan a visit, make a reservation well in advance. If you find yourself here with no reservation, and there's no free slip, give Occupessatuxet Cove a try, just across the river. (See page 99.) For repairs while on the bay, Cove Haven is well worth considering.

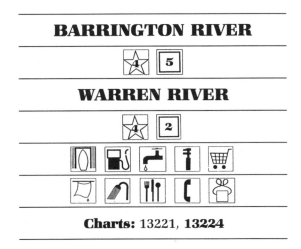

BARRINGTON RIVER

WARREN RIVER

Charts: 13221, **13224**

These two rivers are grouped together for the simple reason that the Warren River turns into the Barrington River when you head north between the towns of Warren and Barrington. The rivers are a pleasant area in the Upper Bay.

Approaches. The mouth of the river is fairly wide open and exposed, but becomes progressively narrower and more protected as you head north. On approach, beware of unmarked but visible Rumstick Rock, which sits at the northwest end of Rumstick Shoal. Can "1" marks the southern edge of the shoal. Nun "2" across from it marks a pair of rocks to be avoided called The Brothers. These two buoys mark the beginning of the narrow channel; follow it carefully when entering and exiting. Don't deviate, because the channel takes quite a dogleg west around Lower Middle Ground shoal and then snakes east around yet another shallow area called Upper Middle Ground. As you approach, a church spire and town are visible dead ahead. Blount Marine and Dyer (home of Dyer dinghys and boats) are prominent on the east bank. Depths in the channel are more than adequate for most vessels. There is 20 to 26 feet at the mouth of the river and 9 to 10 feet as you head north. The large tourist ferry *Bay Queen* docks on the river at Blount Marine, so be prepared to meet it in the narrow channel when entering or exiting.

Warren, named for British navy admiral Sir Peter Warren, is a delightful, rambling 18th Century town situated on the east bank of the river. To the west is Barrington, an affluent suburb of Providence. Stately homes with well manicured lawns and pruned trees line the west bank overlooking Warren, which in contrast is disarmingly ramshackle in places. Locals joke that Barrington residents pay exorbitant taxes for a view of Warren, while Warren residents pay half the amount and are treated to Barrington's neatly trimmed green lawns on the other shore.

Anchorages/Moorings. The current in both rivers is quite strong, 3 to 4 knots, so don't attempt to anchor in the river itself. Smith Cove, with 7 feet of water at low tide in its basin, provides protection from the current but not much from the prevailing southerlies. The cove is known locally as a good place to swim, but because it is open to the south, you may want to head upriver to spend the night. Barrington Yacht Club welcomes transients and is glad to provide a mooring if one is available for $5 a day—one of the best deals on the bay. Call ahead on VHF Channel 68 to be sure there is space; you need not be a member of an affiliated club to get a mooring as long as there is space available.

To reach the club, follow the channel to the mooring basin south of the stone highway bridge across the river. You'll see the club off to starboard. When approaching the fuel dock, keep north and west of the floating red barrel that marks a bothersome rock, which club officials say no amount of dredging has been able to dislodge.

The mooring area is a pleasant, protected place to spend the night. There is a small sandy beach beside the yacht club with a float to swim out to. Hundred Acre Cove to the north of the bridge is a scenic area to explore by dinghy, but you'll need

an outboard to buck the current. Horizontal clearance under the stone bridge is 56 feet, with a vertical clearance of 9 feet. Farther up is a 32-foot-wide trestle bridge with only a 6-foot vertical clearance.

Where to Eat. There are no restaurants or provisioning stops near the club, but if you're fortunate enough to have a motorized tender, try motoring downriver to one of several good eateries along the waterfront on Water Street, most of which have small-boat docks for patrons. The Wharf Tavern serves good food, but is a bit pricey. Be prepared for a long climb up the ladder to the outdoor patio at low tide. Another good bet is TavVino's. When we visited, the restaurant had no sign facing the water so finding it was an adventure in itself. The restaurant's dock is located just south of the Wharf Tavern beyond a wall of high pilings. TavVino's serves steaks, seafood, chicken and light entrees but is apt to be both noisy and crowded. A short and scenic walk uphill from Water Street is Chezwick's, on Market Street, for everything from enchiladas to pasta at reasonable prices. It's good if you can get past the rather startling purple and black decor. Warren is a seafaring town, and the atmosphere and dress are casual in all these places.

Provisions. Main Street in Warren runs parallel to Water Street, a block up the hill. Along this pleasant thoroughfare you'll find a liquor store, drugstore and all the conveniences except a market.

History. The land surrounding the rivers was once owned and occupied by the Wampanoag Indians, who hunted and fished along the river banks. The town of Warren stands on the site of Sowams, royal residence of Indian sachem Massasoit, who died here in 1661. A trading post was established on the river by Plymouth Colony in 1632, when relations between colonists and Indians were good. Some years later, the town was leveled by Indians in the conflict between colonists and Indians that became known as King Philip's War. The war was spearheaded by Wam-

panoag chief Massasoit's son, King Philip, who had requested and was granted an English name when the Indians were on better terms with the settlers. The town's first name, bestowed in 1667, was Swanzey.

Eventually, the town was rebuilt and prospered as a center for trade, shipbuilding and whaling. Many of the wharves that line the river today date to the 1700s, and the waterfront is still lined with Colonial-era homes. Warren was the original site of Brown University, which was moved to Providence in 1770 after five years in the town.

Awakening early in the morning on the river, you may feel the boat gently (or not so gently!) rocking as the quahog fleet moored north of the yacht club heads out at dawn. Resident ducks quietly quack as the sun comes up and the hum of commuter traffic on the bridge is audible, but not intrusive. Every evening we were here, an unusual looking goose patrolled the area, honking insistently with cohorts in tow. The yacht club is active, and you'll see similar processions of boats in the evening, particularly on Tuesday—race night. While the water is clean enough to swim here, there is a lot of boat traffic to contend with along with the strong current. If you choose to swim, stay near the stern of your boat and don't wander. Don't be surprised to find your boat laying to the current rather than the wind in this mooring area.

The Barrington Yacht Club staff does a superb job of making visitors feel welcome and does everything it can to assure that guests enjoy their stay. Despite the shortage of transient space, the Warren and Barrington Rivers are worth exploring.

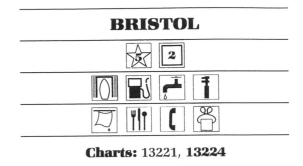

BRISTOL

Charts: 13221, **13224**

Bristol Point thrusts out into the bay like the chin of a stubborn Yankee. The shape of its two peninsulas has been compared to an open lobster claw, with Bristol Point and Popasquash Neck forming the "jaws" of the claw that surround Bristol Harbor.

Approaches. The harbor is roomy and has plenty of water for recreational craft. Depths in the channels and mooring basin range from 10 to 20 feet, with shallower areas as you near shore. Hog Island guards the entrance, dividing the approach in two. Approaching in the West Passage, avoid tiny Castle Island, well marked by a 25-foot-high, flashing red tower, and the rock-dotted shoal that extends north of Hog Island to a red and green buoy marking the northern end of the shoal. Keep can "3" to port and the red and green buoy to starboard. Approaching from the other direction, follow the buoys and don't stray in too close to shore, particularly in the area near Walker Island, which is studded with unmarked rocks.

A Coast Guard Aids To Navigation station is located in Bristol, serving Narragansett Bay and vicinity. The guardsmen and women keep the buoys in the harbor in tiptop condition, so don't be surprised if you find one missing for servicing on approach, as we have several times. Keep the chart handy just in case.

Anchorages/Moorings. While Bristol is a port of call on the bay that shouldn't be missed, it affords disappointing protection at best in strong southerly winds, particularly in the designated anchorage area to the south of the moored boats in the harbor. On our most recent visit we sailed

Bristol Harbor and Hog Island Anchorages

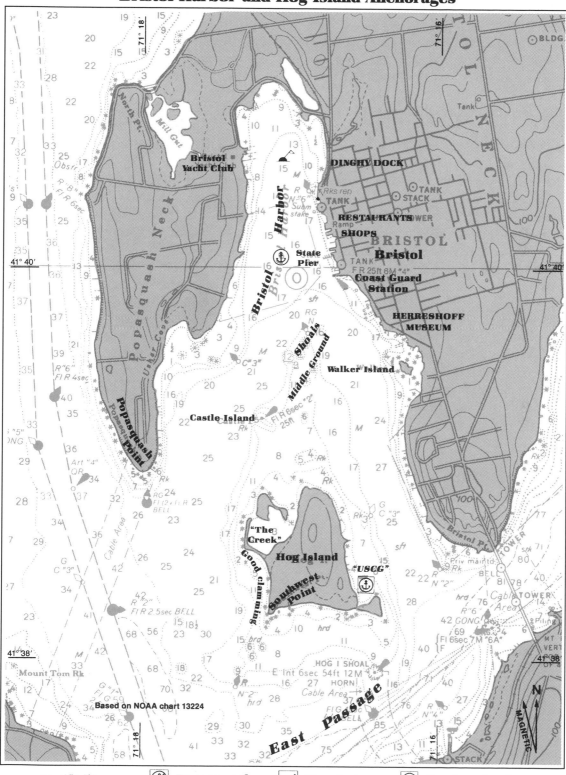

Based on NOAA chart 13224

SCALE: **1″=.50** NAUT. MI.   🚫 **Do not anchor**   ⚓ **Mooring area**   ⚓ **Good anchoring**

in on the wings of a smokey sou'wester and found it most uncomfortable in the anchorage area, so we moved in to find a place among the moored boats, where it is more protected and marginally more comfortable in a blow. Holding ground is good here once the anchor is set, but on a windy day in Bristol Harbor you're bound to have difficulty accomplishing this feat. To be on the safe side here, if it's really blowing, we use the dinghy to set a second anchor at a 30°- to 45°-angle to the primary anchor.

By far the most picturesque and comfortable place to drop the hook in Bristol is the extreme northern end of the harbor. Unfortunately, there's not much room to anchor here as the space is filled with moored boats. Two State of Rhode Island Guest Moorings are located here—disappointingly, these are no longer available for use by visitors to Bristol. The moorings are under the jurisdiction of the harbormaster, and Bristol's has chosen not to make his moorings available to visitors. He will attempt to find you a private mooring if he knows of a vacancy—for a $10-per-night fee. The state pier outside his office in the armory at the entrance to the harbor has one transient slip, which costs $25 per night regardless of boat size. There is ample water dockside for most midsize boats. Joe and his crew work nights, from 7 p.m. to 2 a.m., and can be contacted on VHF Channels 16 or 17, or by telephone at 253-1700. If you dock at the state pier, don't be surprised by the hourly appearance of the tiny Prudence Island ferry, which docks nearby.

Things to Do. Independence Park, just north of a prominent factory building that manufactures thread and is lit up like Manhattan at night, has both a dinghy dock and a rock/sand beach where dinghies can be tied or pulled up. This is as good a place as any to leave the tender while you explore town, as it's centrally located.

Bristol is one of the bay's most attractive harbors. The anchorage area is bordered to the west and north by grassy lawns and sprawling homes; to the east the quaint town brims with colonial charm. Bristol has a nice, homespun feel to it. Like Newport, it has much to offer the visitor in the way of history and shoreside entertainment, but unlike that city, it isn't overrun with tourists—except on the Fourth of July.

In Bristol, the Fourth is almost bigger than Christmas, and as that holiday approaches the town rolls out the red (white and blue) carpet and gets ready to celebrate. Stately, pillared homes and businesses lining the town's streets hang flags and bunting. Virtually every building is swaddled in red, white and blue, to match the stripe painted down the center of the town's main street. The tradition dates back to 1785 and is one of the country's oldest and grandest celebrations. The parade includes thousands of marchers (and spectators), colorful floats, marching bands, military units, politicians, and even a procession of the area's antique fire engines. It wends its way for hours along Hope Street, a block up from the waterfront and an easy walk uphill. Fireworks are generally held a day or two later and are visible from the harbor. If you can time your visit to coincide with this celebration, by all means do so. Arriving by boat is far easier than battling the traffic by car, and the patriotic spirit the town displays is guaranteed to touch the heart of even the sternest cynic.

If you have access to a car, try a visit to Colt State Park's Coggeshall Farm, an 18th-century homestead with live animals such as a working team of oxen. Historical farm activities include 18th century crafts, and an historical herb and vegetable garden. The farm is open Tuesday through Sunday from 10 a.m. till dusk. On the waterfront but not accessible by dinghy is Blithewold Gardens and Arboretum, a turn-of-the-century 45-room mansion on 33 acres of beautifully landscaped grounds overlooking the bay and harbor. There is a water garden, bamboo forest, and a giant sequoia tree. During the cruising season, Blithewold is open Tuesday through Sunday from 10 a.m. to 4 p.m., and is closed holidays.

Where to Eat. There are a number of excellent restaurants along Bristol's waterfront. Maison Robert serves good food in an attractive bistro atmosphere. S.S. Dion on Thames Street on the waterfront offers excellent and imaginative fare and diners have the choice of eating inside in the dining room or outdoors on a pleasant canopied terrace overlooking the waterfront. Peaberry's, on Hope Street a block uphill from the water, is a good choice for gourmet coffee in the morning or for a hearty, homemade lunch.

There are no full-fledged grocery stores within walking distance, but a shopping plaza two miles from the harbor has an Almac's grocery store and can be reached by taxi. There are two Cumberland Farms convenience stores in town, one on Hope Street and one at the north end of town. Both sell basic grocery items as well as ice. There is a liquor store on Hope Street as well as one on Thames Street closer to Independence Park; both also sell ice. Hope Street is a stately street to stroll along, with antique shops and other window shopping opportunities as well as plenty of interesting colonial architecture. The street is lined with homes that call to mind the Old South, framed by draping centuries-old trees, and also provides such modern conveniences as a drugstore and various other shops as well as a library and post office. Pay phones are available at various locations in town.

History. Like most places on the bay, Bristol is rife with history. The land was once the home of the Wampanoag Indians, led by chief Massasoit, who occupied the territory until it was claimed by Plymouth Colony, and named for Bristol, England. The land was desirable to the colony because Narragansett Bay provided a safer harbor than did Plymouth. Eventually, it became an important trade arm for Plymouth as well as for the colonists who had fled the colony to settle here. While it's a long way around by water from Bristol to Plymouth, the residents of Massachusetts soon discovered it was easy to move cargo by small boat from Bristol to Tiverton or Fall River, then transport it overland from there.

As with other places on the bay, Bristol retains a lasting Indian influence, with several streets, businesses and other sites carrying long Indian names. Popasquash Point, which forms one of the "jaws" of the Bristol lobster claw, may well

have been named by the Indians. The point was the most remote—and therefore safe—place for the tribe to sequester its children and women (papooses and squaws) during conflicts with white settlers. Some believe Popasquash is an anglicized version of the point the Indians called "Papoosesquaw." Other subscribe to the theory that the land was named by one of the town's first settlers, who lived on the point and planted the first flowers and vegetables—you guessed it— poppies and squash.

Like other towns on the bay, Bristol was a booming port both before and after the revolution, trading with the West Indies, Europe and the Orient. Shipbuilding was a major industry here, and you shouldn't leave without a visit to the Herreshoff Museum. The Herreshoff family, including famous Captain Nat, designed and built not only five America's Cup winners, but, beginning in 1863, also produced steam and sailing yachts, engines, fittings, and eventually even torpedo vessels for the U.S. Navy. The museum was founded in 1971 to collect, preserve, and display Herreshoff creations; the fascinating exhibits and old photographs provide an excellent overview of Bristol's nautical heritage. The museum is located south of the Coast Guard station, and visitors are welcome at its docks. From the water the museum is flagged by the cluster of Herreshoff designs nearby, both in the water and on the hard behind the docks. The museum is directly across the street. Exhibits are open from 1 p.m. to 4 p.m. Tuesday through Sunday, May through October. The museum is closed Mondays. For more information call 253-5000.

Today, boatbuilding is still booming in Bristol. The town is home to several boatbuilders: Albin, Bristol Yachts, Shannon, Goetz Custom Sailboats (builders of the Cup challenger *Heart of America*), C.E. Ryder, Carroll Marine (builders of Frers custom racer/cruisers), and such notable marine equipment manufacturers as Hall Spars, Lewmar and Brookes & Gatehouse U.S.A.

Whether you visit to help celebrate Fourth of July in truly grand old fashion or arrive at any other time during the summer, Bristol has much to offer.

HOG ISLAND

★ 4	2

No facilities

Charts: 13221, **13224**

Hog Island guards the entrance to Bristol Harbor, separating its entrance into parallel passages. The island lies between the tips of the "lobster claw" of Popasquash Neck and Bristol Neck, and, perched just west of the Mount Hope Bridge, is close to the dividing line between East Passage and Mount Hope Bay. The terrain is wooded, with a few houses. Roughly three-quarters of Hog's small coastline consists of pebbly beach strewn with clamshells bleached white by sun and salt. The island is 200 acres in size and rises to 40 feet above the bay at its highest point.

Approaches. The isle is surrounded by shoals of varying depths. The most notorious is Hog Island Shoal, which extends from the south end of the island eastward and is marked by Hog Island Light and, to the west, red nun "2." In places, depths on the shoal are a comfortable 11 feet, and there is 9 feet at mean low water just inside the light, but the bottom rises rapidly as you near shore, particularly near Southwest Point. Pleasure boats in a hurry or sailboats on a favorable tack sometimes cut the light and buoy; if you elect to follow suit, keep an eye on your depth sounder and don't stray in too close to shore, where depths drop sharply. Also beware of a cluster of unmarked rocks between nun "2" and Southwest Point, which are submerged at a depth of 6 feet at low tide.

Hog Island Shoal was the scene of many a shipwreck in early days on the bay until a lightship and, eventually, Hog Island Light were placed at the outer edge of the shoal to warn of the danger. The present light was built in 1901, and its familiar sparkplug shape is a comfortable presence in the Upper Bay. The light has been au-tomated since 1964, and its white flash is visible for 12 miles at a height of 54 feet above the water. Like most lighthouses on the bay, this one was once the home of a lighthouse keeper, and its interior has several different levels for eating, sleeping, working, and storage, in addition to the lantern room at its peak. There is also a foghorn on the light.

Anchorages. Hog Island has one small anchorage that is popular with pleasure boats drawing 5 feet or less—the unnamed cove formed by a sandpit at the island's southeast corner. The island is a delightful place to visit for lunch and a hike along the shore, and you'll find more shells in one place here than just about anyplace else on the bay. Anchor in the bight in 5 to 8 feet at low water and dinghy ashore for a walk or a swim, or simply sit back in the cockpit and enjoy the sunshine.

Holding ground and shelter at Hog are fair to good. Set your anchor in the mud/sand bottom but pay out plenty of rode. When the prevailing southwesterly wind pipes up in the afternoon and funnels over the low sandspit, boats with too little anchor rode out invariably begin to drag—which can be a bother, particularly if you've gone ashore and are watching someone drag down on your boat from that vantage point. Some boats do anchor here overnight, but since the anchorage is exposed from the north and a bit from the east, we prefer to lunch here and head elsewhere—such as nearby Potter Cove on Prudence Island, or the Kickamuit River just north of Mount Hope Bridge—to spend the night. For Upper Bay boaters out for the day, Hog is an ideal, uncrowded spot.

Things to Do. The water is fine for swimming anywhere near Hog, but shellfishing in the anchorage is prohibited due to industrial runoff from nearby Bristol. Off the west coast of the island, shellfishing is fine, and nowhere else will you so easily unearth delicious littleneck clams to enjoy with cocktails at sunset. In this area, snorkeling or scuba gear is a help, as good shellfish beds are submerged just offshore. If you have neither, try wading out and "digging" with your feet, or bending down to feel for telltale shells hidden in the sand. (See "Bay Fish And How To Catch Them," page 167, for more information.) The good shellfishing grounds are just a short walk west along the shore from the anchorage area, and, while it's often too windy on this exposed side of the island for swimming, the hike is worth it for the shellfish you'll find here.

On the northwest part of the island is a perfectly sheltered, albeit very shallow cove that is ideal for exploration by dinghy or small boat at high tide. Depth is only 2 to 3 feet at low water, but birdwatching here is excellent. Neither of Hog's coves has been named, but this one may at one time have been known as "The Creek," a name that has surfaced on old land deeds.

History. Perhaps because of its diminutive size, Hog Island holds a special fascination. Although it is just a stone's throw from Bristol, the island belongs to the town of Portsmouth on nearby Aquidneck Island. In colonial times, it was the subject of a heated dispute over ownership between Massachusetts' Plymouth Colony and Portsmouth, which never relinquished its claim to the island despite pressure from the Pilgrims to the north.

The island gets its American name from the simple fact that during colonial times, swine were kept corralled here. On Hog, the water surrounding the isle effectively kept the livestock in one place and the natural predators, such as foxes, wildcats, and wolves, at bay.

The Indian name for the island is "Chesawanoke" or "Chisawannock," interpreted as "island of many shells," which makes perfect sense when you encounter the piles of shells that line the island's beaches today. Hog was once a lucrative oystering ground as well as a bountiful site for clams.

At one time the island reportedly had its share of deer, but because of its small size, the herd dwindled as Hog's human population grew. At one time, it was the site of a summer camp for children; at another, much of it was owned by a wealthy family named Knight, whose Spanish-style mansion stood on the hill near the eastern shore and was the site of gala parties and dances in the early 1900s.

There isn't much to do on Hog besides stroll the beaches, swim, gather shellfish, and relax, but there's a pervading sense of restfulness here that may be the basis for the other interpretation of Hog's Indian name: "Island of peace and quiet." If you can use a dose of that—and who can't?—Hog Island is the spot.

Mount

Hope

Bay

☐

At the very entrance to the bay . . . the most prominent object in the landscape is an attractive hill, that in a flat country takes upon itself all the dignity and importance of a mountain. All values are relative, and the lofty crest of Mount Hope would be hardly more than a respectable mound in the Hudson Highlands, and might sink to the level of a depression in a more mountainous region. To tell the truth, it is only 200 feet above sea level, but that is pre-eminence in its neighborhood.

Nestled between the shores of Rhode Island and Massachusetts, and named for the noble hill that presides over its western shore, Mount Hope Bay is one of the most pleasant places on Narragansett Bay for a day on the water. The bay is about 7 miles long and 2 to 3 miles wide, and is bordered by several navigable rivers, including the Kickamuit, Lee, Cole and Taunton.

Spanning the entrance to the bay is the Mount Hope Bridge, which, in addition to joining the mainland and Aquidneck Island, forms a gateway for mariners to Mount Hope Bay. At the time it was built in 1929, Mount Hope Bridge was one of the largest suspension bridges in the world, and was awarded a prize for beauty in its class. From 1698 until 1929, a ferry provided transportation between Bristol to the west and Portsmouth on Aquidneck Island to the east, and the ferry landing site in Portsmouth just north of the bridge is known, not surprisingly, as Bristol Ferry.

The Mount Hope's span across the water is an unmistakable landmark that can be seen from as far away as Newport on a clear day. The width of its center span is a healthy 400 feet, and charted vertical clearance is 135 feet.

Still visible under the western end of the span on Bristol Point, but made obsolete when the well-lit bridge was completed, is the old Bristol Ferry light and keeper's house, one of the prettiest on the bay. The pristine little light, active since 1855, has been replaced by the navigational lights on the bridge, a red nun buoy off Bristol Point, and a flashing white tower and gong on the east shore opposite the old light.

On the west shore of the bay just north of the bridge, the modern campus of Roger Williams College lies partially hidden among the trees overlooking the water; along the east shore just under the bridge, a sprinkling of boats tethered to moorings buck with the wind and swell.

Pilotage. Average depth of the bay is 15 to 20 feet, and a dredged ship's channel leading to Fall River is marked by buoys to port and starboard. Depths in the channel range from 24 to 35 feet. Be on the lookout for shipping traffic in these waters, and note that breezes can be flukey

Mount Hope Bay and Kickamuit River Anchorages

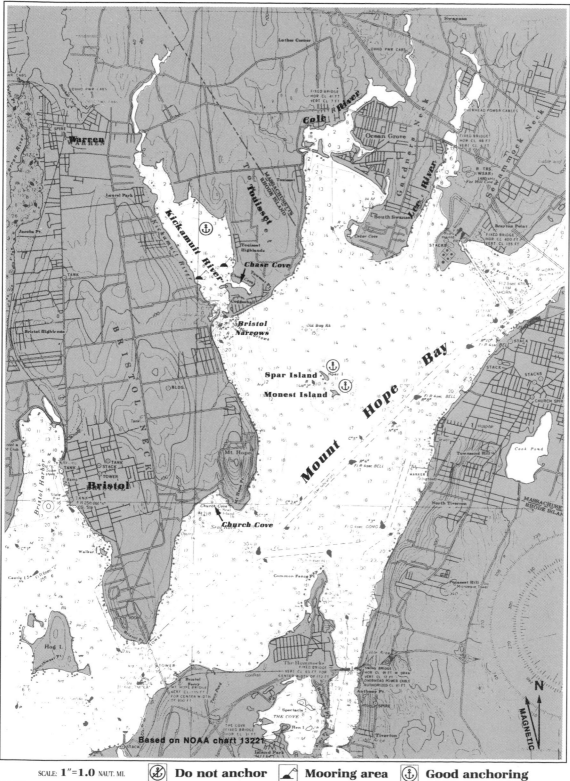

Based on NOAA chart 13221

SCALE: 1″=1.0 NAUT. MI. ⚓ **Do not anchor** ⚓ **Mooring area** ⚓ **Good anchoring**

as they deflect off Mount Hope and off the base of the bridge pylons.

At this writing, no major marinas exist on Mount Hope Bay with facilities for transients; however, just south of Battleship Cove the brand-new Borden Light Marina is under construction. (See marina listings for more specific information.)

History. While it may not lay claim to much distinction as a mountain, Hope and environs are the site of some of the bay's most fascinating history. "Hope" is said to be the "Hop" of Norse legend, and some believe Leif Erikson and his fellow Vikings made camp here while they explored the bay almost 1,000 years ago. Some claim that "Hop" (or "Haup") means "fjord fed by a river and open to the sea" in the ancient Viking tongue, and that they left their mark upon a large gray boulder that rests at the eastern base of the hill. A crude boat and a series of undeciphered angular symbols were said to be inscribed on the rock, which is approachable from seaward in a small boat. The inscription, if indeed it ever existed, has been long since worn away with time and tide, but on a moonlit night it is not hard to imagine a fleet of Viking ships bobbing at anchor in the lee of the mountain, their crews clustered around campfires ashore.

Later inhabitants of the area were the Wampanoag Indians, who some say garbled the Viking name "Hop" to "Montaup," giving rise to the present day name of the hillock. The mount has achieved notoriety as the domain of King Philip, or Metacomet, son of Wampanoag chief Massasoit who was given an English name at his own request by colonists. The Indians also called his abode "Pocanoket."

Legend has it there is a stone formation on top of Mount Hope that was the "chair" of King Philip when he preached to his tribe. Atop the tiny mountain, the leader made what he thought was an impenetrable stronghold against white settlers during a war that history later named for him. But during a December snowstorm, an Indian traitor led a band of settlers to attack the area, forcing Philip to retreat. Eventually, he made

his way back, only to find his wife and children slain and his village almost deserted. The English were camped on the bay's opposite shore, and the angry young Indian determined to strike one last blow against his enemies. His remaining constituents did not agree, and eventually Philip was driven into a swamp on the west side of Mount Hope, where he was slain by a vengeful member of his own race.

According to local lore, Philip's ghost still roams the mountain on moonless nights, stepping from stone to stone in the marsh. Strange wailings, whisperings and lights are said to haunt the area to this day.

On sunny summer days, there is no better sailing ground than the wide expanse of bay that is guarded by and named for the mysterious Mount Hope.

CHURCH COVE

No facilities

Chart: 13221

Lying at the base of Mount Hope is Church Cove, an attractive place surrounded by cottages and wooded hills that is unfortunately an untenable anchorage. In addition to being mined with unmarked rocks, the cove is exposed to the north, south and east—and since westerlies are rare on the bay during the boating season, it can be all but ruled out as a viable place to drop the hook. A web of rocks and a tiny island called Seal make tucking up near shore a tricky business, and anchoring for any length of time here is not recommended.

SPAR ISLAND

No facilities

Chart: 13221

Tiny Spar Island, in the middle of Mount Hope Bay, erupts from the sea bottom like a treeless tropical motu, and is almost more of a navigational hazard than a true island. The spot is marked on its west side by a red nun buoy. However, at twilight or in poor visibility, it is almost impossible to see; be sure you steer clear of the area if visibility is bad.

Marked on nautical charts as simply "Spar," the island is actually a pair of islands—Spar, the northernmost, is 1,500 square feet of low, pebbly sand beach. Just to the south is a larger, 10,000-square-foot island, unnamed on the charts but known locally as Monest Island, named after a former owner.

Not long ago, the islands were acquired by the nearby town of Tiverton after taxes went unpaid. Locals recall that the island was once the site of a pair of buildings that the owners tried to operate as a mid-bay refreshment stand. But locals would have none of it, and the buildings were removed after the attempt to peddle fast food in the distinctly non-fast lane of Mount Hope Bay failed to catch on with potential boating patrons.

Now both are town property, and boaters are free to anchor nearby and go ashore to explore or merely stay afloat and observe the wide variety of birdlife that inhabits the sandspit.

Anchorages. Indeed, the islets are surrounded almost entirely by deep water, making the spot an ideal place for an afternoon or early evening outing by boat. Except at the very northern end, which has a depth of 4 feet near shore, and the passage between the two isles, which has shoaled over and breaks at low tide, depths average 10 to 12 feet on all sides almost clear up to the shoreline. The sole hazard is a trio of rocks

just off the west shore of Spar, marked by a red nun buoy. In prevailing southwesterlies, anchor in the islands' lee on the northeast side.

The only inhabitants of Spar Island today are the birds, and visitors are advised to be careful not to disturb their unique environment. Because of its isolation and inaccessibility to humans, the island attracts "shy" species that are rarely seen in the more populated areas of the bay. On our most recent visit we spotted a pair of timid—and rarely seen in this area—American oystercatchers. These large, exotic looking birds have black and white plumage and long, bright orange beaks, which they use to crack open and extract tasty morsels from oyster and clam shells. The fact that so many birds gather here may be how the island got its name. Originally called Sparrow Island, the last three letters may have been dropped from the name at some point in its history, perhaps by a careless cartographer.

Swimming here is not recommended, and shellfishing is off-limits due to the area's proximity to the polluted waters of Somerset and Fall River—though quahogs are so plentiful that, should the area ever reopen, shellfishermen will have a field day gathering them like pebbles from the muddy bottom.

Spar Island is not a place to stop on any but a calm day, and even then only briefly. But as one of the few islands in the bay that belongs entirely to nature, it's worth a visit. Spar is an excellent place for patient ornithologists to await a photo opportunity or two, particularly in the evening, when the small landscape is silhouetted by the sun setting over the western reaches of Mount Hope Bay.

KICKAMUIT RIVER

No facilities

Chart: 13221

Known locally as the best hurricane hole on Narragansett Bay, the Kickamuit River actually seems more like a pond than a saltwater arm of the ocean. Situated just north of Mount Hope, the river is about as close to landlocked as you can get and still be in the "ocean."

Approaches. The narrow entrance to the Kickamuit is nearly hidden, nestled close along the western shore of Mount Hope Bay and shielded to the southwest by the loom of Mount Hope. The entrance must be negotiated carefully, as it is not very wide and has fairly drastic shoals to either side. Hug the red nuns to starboard when entering the channel, which is shallowest at the southern end and deepens as you proceed north, offering depths of from 6 to 10 feet. Passing into the river brings you uncomfortably close to shore on either side, and the slogan "reach out and touch someone" suddenly takes on new meaning as fishermen and swimmers sidle by almost at arm's length along the pebbly beach. Once through the narrow entrance, the river is well worth the minor anxiety of entering. Holding ground is soft mud and is excellent, and depths range from 7 to 16 feet in most of the river basin.

Once past can "1," the river opens up and you feel as though you have sailed through the looking glass from bay to inland lake. A few residences dot the shoreline and there are pockets of moored boats here and there, but the overall impression is one of a sweeping, sheltered expanse of flat water surrounded by pines, shade trees, and marshes. Despite its rather considerable size and fetch, the river provides excellent protection from all directions, and the shoreline surrounding it is forgiving mud and eelgrass, with a few rocks to damage a wanton keel or bottom.

Anchorages. Anchoring is good almost anywhere there is adequate depth and swinging room. Our favorite place to drop the hook is in the north end of the river basin just west of another small cluster of moored boats. Here the setting is pastoral, there is plenty of swinging room, and protection is still good, even in a blow. Hidden behind the nearby trees, cows and horses graze in peaceful pastures and a colonial farmhouse or two can be glimpsed through the brush.

Even on a summer weekend, there are few visiting boats here, which offers you a sense of privacy that sometimes is hard to find on the bay at the height of the season. Swimming, windsurfing and waterskiing are excellent, and shellfishing is legal in most areas of the river except after a heavy rainfall, when certain areas may be off-limits. Signs are posted marking safe and restricted areas, but check with local authorities after a rain. The Kickamuit is one of the few spots on the bay where edible oysters can still be picked, though they are considerably harder to find than quahogs. Forage the rocks surrounded by grass around the pond's perimeter in safe areas and you may be surprised to find these now-rare Narragansett shellfish. (See "Bay Fish And How To Catch Them," page 168, for more information on catching oysters.)

In addition to peace, soothing scenery, and a host of recreational activities, the Kickamuit is excellent for exploration by dinghy or small boat. Several small coves await the adventurous, uninhabited save for stalking great blue herons, perching red tailed hawks, paddling ducks, cormorants, and egrets.

The Kickamuit, pronounced "Kick-a-MYU-it," was once the site of an Indian village of the same name. Translated, it means "at or around the spring" or "source of water."

The only sounds to disturb the peace here are the occasional whine of a ski boat or, in the early morning, the muted hum of a quahog skiff or two. The Kickamuit offers shelter in a storm, but it's also a wonderful spot to spend an afternoon, evening or weekend when the weather is fine. Luckily for those who have discovered its fair-weather attributes, this is a revelation that seems to have escaped the attention of those who flock here only when the hurricane flags are flying.

COLE RIVER AND LEE RIVER

No transient facilities

Chart: 13221

Cole and Lee, the two rivers to the east of the Kickamuit, in our opinion have little appeal for the visitor. Used mostly by local mariners who moor or dock their boats here, neither offers much in the way of attractive setting, recreation or facilities for transients.

Gasoline is available at Swansea Marina, tucked into the northeast corner of the Cole River, but unless you're in the vicinity and find yourself short on fuel, we can see little reason to venture in here.

To the east, the Lee River lies in the shadow of a power plant whose stacks are visible on its southeast banks. Thanks to this structure, the river and environs have earned the distinction of one of the most polluted areas on the bay.

FALL RIVER (BATTLESHIP COVE)

Charts: 13221, 13227

Eighteen miles southeast of Providence, in Massachusetts at the head of Mount Hope Bay, lies the Upper Bay's other big-city port of call. As a place for potential exploration, Fall River's reputation once was at the bottom of the barrel. At the turn of the century, Edgar Mayhew Bacon's book advised: "To really appreciate Fall River, one should never approach nearer than the opposite side of Mount Hope Bay." Now all this is changed, and present-day Fall River is undergoing a revitalization that makes it a worthwhile overnight stop when cruising the Upper Bay.

Approaches. To reach the mooring and anchorage area in Battleship Cove, follow the dredged shipping channel north under the Braga Bridge, which offers a horizontal clearance of 400 feet and a vertical clearance of 135 feet, as well as a privately maintained fog signal. Ahead looms the battleship *Massachusetts*, after which the cove is named, an unmistakable landmark when approaching this area.

Anchorages/Moorings. Turn east into the cove, keeping the red nun off the battleship's bow to starboard. Ahead and to starboard is the mooring area, which offers depths of 8 to 27 feet; to port is an empty basin where transients can anchor in 10 to 23 feet, albeit with a little less shelter from the southwest.

Fall River

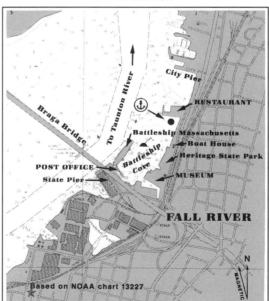

Based on NOAA chart 13227

SCALE: **1"=.34 NAUT. MI.**   **Do not anchor**

 Mooring area   **Good anchoring**

Moorings in the cove are available at no charge—call the Heritage State Park Boathouse on VHF Channel 14 to see if one is available. The boathouse is open from 12 noon to 8 p.m. daily during summer. All the moorings here are private, but owners leave word with the boathouse staff if they will be away, so be sure to check before you pick one up as all assignments are handled through the park. There are usually several available at any given time.

Sheltered by the battleship, which forms an unusual sort of breakwater, this cove is protected from almost any direction but due west—and prevailing westerlies are almost unheard of here during summer months. Should the battleship ever be moved, the cove will be far less sheltered and somewhat exposed to the southwest. Although you'll sleep undisturbed by swell in the lee of the ship, bring a set of earplugs for an overnight stay. The traffic from the nearby bridge and highway can be a deterrent to a good night's sleep.

Things to Do. Fall River's harbor is polluted, and swimming here is out of the question. Even retrieving the anchor rode or mooring pennant can leave an unhealthy looking residue on your hands. Fortunately, there are plenty of so-called "secondary contact" watersports to be enjoyed here as well as a host of shoreside amusements.

Heritage State Park is a clean and pleasant waterfront area with shade trees, flower gardens, neat paths, and a boardwalk bordering a grassy lawn on the waterfront. A visitor's center boasts a museum chockablock full of exhibits and programs on area history and heritage—thus the park's name. If you dinghy ashore, leave the tender on the east side of the boathouse dock; the west side is reserved for the park's sailboats and paddleboats. These are available, free of charge, to persons of appropriate age and ability, for a spin around the bay. Visitors can also take a narrated mini-cruise aboard the park's excursion boat, the *River Queen*.

At Fall River, yachts can moor in the lee of the Battleship *Massachusetts*. LYNDA CHILDRESS PHOTO.

From the boathouse, it is an easy stroll along the boardwalk to the museum and the cove's other attractions. The battleship and other ships are open for tours, including the USS *Joseph Kennedy, Jr.* and the submarine SS *Lionfish*. A marine museum housing several PT boats and other marine exhibits is also included in the modest admission fee. Visitors can take guided tours or wander about at will, and this is an interesting and educational way to spend an afternoon, particularly if you are cruising with kids. For further information contact the Battleship Museum at (508) 678-1100.

At the battleship complex, there is a gift shop, small post office, and telephone. Another pay phone is located in the boathouse itself.

Admission to the Heritage State Park museum is free. In the evening, the park sometimes sponsors special events, such as outdoor concerts on the lawn by the water, that can be enjoyed from a shoreside vantage point or from the shelter of your own cockpit. For more information on programs at Heritage State Park, call (508) 675-5758; for information on the battleship and related attractions, call (508) 678-1100.

Fall River has earned notoriety for its plethora of factory outlet stores. The outlet district is not far away from the cove by cab, and tremendous bargains can be found here on almost any type of merchandise from leather to designer clothing. Most of the old mills have been refurbished into mini-malls where vendors peddle their wares in pleasant specialty shops. Although some of the bargains to be had here are too unwieldy to transport by boat, a shopping expedition to the mill store outlets is a worthwhile project if you find yourself here on a rainy summer day.

Where to Eat. If you're in the mood for eating out, Leone's Restaurant (formerly the Gangplank) just north of Battleship Cove is a short walk north along the waterfront, or a short hop by tender or shoal-draft cruiser. The restaurant has docks for patrons and is a busy place on a summer evening. If you're feeling adventurous, we highly recommend taking a cab to sample some of Fall River's distinctive Portuguese cui-

sine. There are several worthy establishments, including Sagres' and others, but our favorite is Lusitano. Here the atmosphere is casual, the food is spicy and superb, the meals are reasonably priced, and the folk music and festive atmosphere are guaranteed to make you feel as though you've crossed the Atlantic and made landfall in Portugal.

History. Most people are familiar with the grisly rhyme, "Lizzie Borden took an axe, and gave her mother forty whacks . . ." Fall River has earned infamy as the city where the alleged murders and trial took place in 1892. Although Borden was acquitted, the legend of Lizzie Borden remains.

The name "Fall River" is a derivation of the Indian name "Quequechan" ("falling water"). The name comes from the river that runs through the center of town and spills out into Mount Hope Bay. The site was purchased from the Indians in 1659 by Plymouth Colony and widely settled more than 20 years later. Originally part of Freetown, it was incorporated as the town of "Fallriver" in the early 1800s, and was renamed "Troy" for a time before resuming its original name.

Once a farming community of only a handful of families, the town's abundance of water power, prime harbor and moist climate led to an influx of manufacturing, particularly textiles, and by the late 1800s the city had become a leading cotton textile center. Employment opportunities drew workers from Britain, Ireland, French Canada, Poland and Portugal, and because of this influx, the city had one of the highest concentrations of immigrants of any major U.S. city for roughly 40 years. This cultural diversity is still preserved today.

Fall River today is much different than the city Bacon recommended avoiding back in 1904. Like Providence, its flavor is distinctly urban, but a visit by boat is both worthwhile and entertaining.

TAUNTON RIVER

Charts: 13221, 13227

The Taunton River meanders north from the city of Fall River past the Massachusetts towns of Somerset, Assonet, Freetown and Dighton. The city of Taunton, named for Taunton, England, lies at its head.

Approaches. Mildly industrialized at its mouth, the river becomes progressively rural as you head north. Depths in the marked, dredged channel vary from 24 to 36 feet until just past Somerset Marina, when the marked channel becomes drastically shallower, offering 7 feet to Peters Point. Four-foot depths in the channel have been reported past Peters Point. Don't stray out of the channel (depths are shoal). Boats drawing more than 2 feet will be hard pressed to find a spot to anchor this far upriver.

On a voyage up the Taunton, mariners should beware of several bridges and overhead power cables. The first set of cables stretches across the river just south of the Brightman Street bridge, and at a height of 145 feet above water, presents no problems for recreational craft. About 1 mile past the Braga Bridge at Fall River is the Brightman Street bascule bridge. This span offers horizontal clearance of 98 feet and vertical clearance of 27 feet, but a bridge tender will open the bridge for boat traffic if necessary. Contact him on VHF Channel 16 or Channel 13.

Farther upriver is another set of overhead cables, also at a height (150 feet) that presents no problem for pleasure boats. About 5 miles up, a swing span crosses the river at Berkely. Here the clearance is just 7 feet, and as such marks the end of the road for sailboats and larger powerboats. Sailboats venturing this far upriver should negotiate the channel under power, since it is too narrow to provide room to maneuver under

sail. Beyond the bridge at Berkely is a highway bridge with 10-foot clearance, and a final railroad bridge with 9-foot clearance lies 2/10 mile past the highway bridge.

Anchorages. The Taunton River is noteworthy as a viable hurricane hole. Anchoring is permitted anywhere you can find a spot, though most of the many sheltered coves are shallow, with depths of just 3 to 5 feet. Outside the channel, the river is not particularly well charted, so proceed with caution.

The Assonet River, which forks off the Taunton to starboard just past Somerset, offers depths of 10 to 15 feet at its mouth and protection here is excellent. However, it is not charted at all beyond this point, so if you explore here, take it slowly and let the lead line precede you.

History. The town of Taunton was purchased from the Indians by a woman, Elizabeth Poole, in 1638, and the river theoretically is the end of Portuguese explorer Miguel Corte Real's journey of exploration on Narragansett Bay. Some historians believe the adventurer preceded Verrazano to the bay by as many as 20 years. His ill-fated flotilla departed Lisbon in 1502 to explore the New World and was never heard from again. Some historians theorize he came to grief somewhere along the New England coast, and later made his way to Narragansett Bay and headed north to Mount Hope Bay, where he may have lived among the Wampanoag Indians for his remaining years.

In the northern reaches of the Taunton River near Assonet Neck once stood a famous pictured rock, on which Corte Real allegedly inscribed his name, the Portuguese coat of arms and the date: 1511. Dighton Rock, as it is called, has since been removed from the river and is now preserved in the Dighton Rock Museum and State Park at Berkely, just opposite the Taunton Yacht Club on the river's eastern shore. Although there is a small dinghy dock at the park as well as shady trees and picnic tables, park management curiously does not welcome waterborne guests, and when we attempted to disembark we were asked to leave by an apologetic young ranger, who agreed it is a shame the park is closed to visitors in boats.

Some observers have compared the Taunton to an English river as it wends its way through the countryside. As you proceed upriver, you'll be surprised by an increasing sense of isolation among wildlife. Near Peter's Point we glimpsed a great blue heron sunning on a rock, a falcon on the wing, and numerous species of ducks and geese paddling among the grasses near the riverbanks.

If you have the time to proceed this far north, the green riverbanks, shade trees, and marshy shallows make an exploration of Narragansett Bay's Massachusetts corner a worthwhile pastime.

TAUNTON
RIVER

125

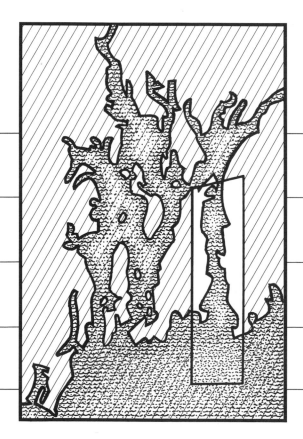

The
Sakonnet
River

The Sakonnet River

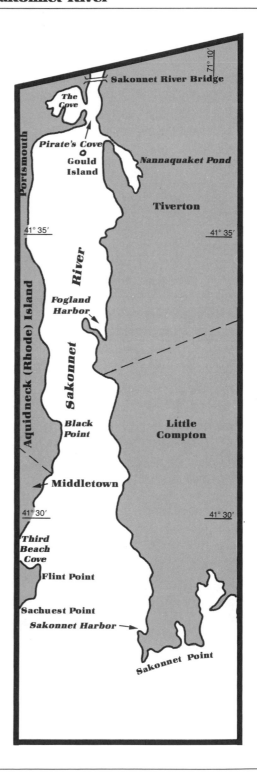

The Cove

Sakonnet River Bridge

71° 10'

Pirate's Cove

Gould Island

Nannaquaket Pond

Portsmouth

Tiverton

41° 35'   41° 35'

Aquidneck (Rhode) Island

Fogland Harbor

River

Sakonnet

Black Point

Little Compton

Middletown

41° 30'   41° 30'

Third Beach Cove

Flint Point

Sachuest Point

Sakonnet Harbor

Sakonnet Point

SCALE: **1"=2.1** MILES

An

Overlooked

Secret

The arm of the bay that flows between Aquidneck and the eastern shore is called Saconnet [sic] or Seaconnet [sic] River, though it is properly not a river, but a strait, and so it used to be called on old maps . . . Along the length of the Saconnet, the eye travels past points and bays to where a distant sail looms upon the rim of the Atlantic . . .

The Sakonnet River, which should more properly be named Sakonnet Passage, is in actuality the third north-to-south salt waterway of Narragansett Bay. It is also the most beautiful, the least crowded, and the most overlooked by cruising yachtsmen.

Pilotage. From Rhode Island Sound, the abandoned Sakonnet River light is a prominent daytime landmark, perched on rocks just west of Sakonnet Point. Give the point a wide berth, as the area around it is full of rocks and two small craggy islands named East and West. Keep nuns "2" and "2A" to starboard when approaching from the south and steer clear of Cormorant Reef to port. The reef is partially visible, and is marked by breaking surf as well as can "1."

Since not all the buoys marking the approach to the Sakonnet River are lit, we don't recommend entering the river at night without local knowledge. In poor visibility, use extreme caution.

Conditions in the river are excellent for both the powerboater and the sailor. In prevailing southwesterlies, winds are fresh and fair but surrounding hillsides keep the water surface flat, producing almost lakelike conditions. If winds are from the north or due south a chop can develop, but in the season's prevailing southwesterlies, there's no better place to sail than the wide expanse of the Sakonnet.

The river's 10-mile length and 1.5-mile width is bordered by some of the most rural scenery on Narragansett Bay. On the west side, the emerald shores of Aquidneck slope gently to the sea. To the east, a patchwork quilt of Little Compton farmlands rolls away into the distance as far as the eye can see, dotted with grazing cattle, groves of stately old trees and isolated colonial farmhouses.

The Sakonnet's name is a derivative of the Indian word "Seekonk," ("place of the black goose"). Indeed, the fields on either side of the river are favorite gathering spots for endless flocks of Canada geese, who throng to the river's wide open spaces. Ospreys find the Sakonnet a lucrative hunting ground, and you are more likely to spot these soaring fish hawks here than in any other spot on the bay.

The Sakonnet is well marked and easy to navigate in daylight. Although it is shallower as a whole than either the East or West Passage, you will find comfortable depths of more than 20 feet in most areas within the marked channel. Outside the buoys, there are good depths until you near shore except in the river's northwestern end, near Island Park and west of Gould Island, where there are pockets of 5- to 7-foot depths and some uncharted shoaling in spots. Currents are less than 1 knot in the lower river, but stronger in two notable areas at the north end of the Sakonnet: in the narrow channel between the remains of an old stone bridge that once crossed the river, and just beyond it in the narrow passage under a highway bridge that threads through an open railroad bridge. At the stone bridge, the current runs to 2½ knots, and the white water kicked up between the buoys and to either side can convince you that you are sailing onto a shoal—which may indeed occur if you stray outside the channel here. Keep inside the buoys, and be prepared for unsettled water. Small boats without auxiliary power should time their passage through here on a favorable tide.

Spanning the Sakonnet, and visible from its upper reaches, is a highway bridge connecting the town of Tiverton on the mainland with Ports-mouth on Aquidneck Island. The bridge is more than one-half mile long, and travels on a downgrade from the hills of Tiverton to the considerably lower marshlands of Portsmouth. The charted vertical clearance at the center span is 65 feet. When passing beneath this bridge, traffic must also pass through a permanently open railroad swing bridge, which has a charted horizontal clearance of 99 feet. However, only the westernmost opening is navigable due to obstructions on the other side. The charted distance refers to the entire horizontal span, and you'll find considerably less room than this in the one open channel. Keep well to port or starboard when passing through here to allow oncoming traffic to pass, and be mindful of the dangling lures of line fishermen who favor the old railroad bridge as a fishing spot.

Through the railroad bridge, currents and back-eddies swirl at up to 1½ knots, and you can expect to feel the effect on the helm as you steer slowly through the narrow pass. Take note that the 5 m.p.h. speed limit is strictly enforced here, as well as in the waters well north of the bridge. There are mooring areas to either side of the channel until well past the bridge, and skippers who are tempted to increase their speed in this area should keep in mind that they are responsible for damage or injury caused by their wakes.

Sailing on the Sakonnet, rarely will you have

The strong current at the Old Stone Bridge on the Sakonnet River is notorious, and is clearly visible in this photograph. LYNDA CHILDRESS PHOTO.

to share the sapphire valley of water with more than a handful of other pleasure boats. Almost never will you encounter commercial traffic here, except for an occasional fishing boat plying the waters north or south, or trolling lazily to and fro in the river.

The waters beneath the shelter of the hilly shores provide some of the best anchorages in the area, with good mud and sand holding ground and few rocks to foul anchors. Anchorage is permitted along the river's shores anywhere skippers deem suitable. Boats are often seen snugged up near the banks on either side of the river as well as in its coves, enjoying solitude in beautiful surroundings. Thankfully, these shores have not yet succumbed to large-scale development, and one can only hope they remain as rural and beautiful as they are today.

The Sakonnet is our favorite Narragansett Bay cruising ground—and we almost hate to let this cat out of the bag. Perhaps we're biased, but we think this expanse of clear blue water provides cruising at its best.

EASTON'S BAY

No rating/No protection

No facilities

Charts: 13221, 13223

As you approach the Sakonnet from the southwest, you will first pass Easton's Bay. On Aquidneck Island's south shore to the east of Brenton Reef and the cliffs of Ocean Drive, it is probably one of the area's most beautiful spots. Easton's Bay is bordered by mansions and cliffs to the west, a white sand beach to the north, and Easton's Point to the east. Unfortunately, the bay is an open roadstead, and under no circumstances would we recommend that cruising boats venture in here. In boisterous summer southwesterlies, breaking waves kick up a surf that makes the

beach a favorite spot for surfers and wave-jumping boardsailors.

Many times over the years we have observed boats, lured in by the bay's scenery in the calm of early evening, heading toward the beach and dropping the hook, only to awake in the morning bobbing merrily in the surf. Wide and deep, Easton's Bay tempts a few adventurous souls each year, and a few have ended up on the beach, so sacrifice the scenery for safety and head elsewhere.

History. While not a good destination for cruisers, the bay still has its share of history to offer. The bay, the point to the east, and the beach (also called "First Beach") were all named for Nicholas Easton, one of Newport's founders. It has always been a popular bathing beach for locals. Until the 1938 hurricane the beach was a major resort that boasted a boardwalk, Ferris wheel, and other amusements. Today it remains one of the island's best bathing beaches, though it is plagued with seaweed in warm weather. A merry-go-round, bathhouses, and kiddie rides are all that remain in the way of amusements.

The cliffs along the western shore of the bay allegedly house tunnels that were used to smuggle slaves north on the Underground Railroad, and, later, the bay is said to have been a popular spot for smuggling of another sort during Prohibition.

Easton's Bay is also the setting for one of the area's better "unsolved mystery" stories. In 1750, so the tale goes, a brig owned by a Newport merchant, on a passage from Honduras bearing a valuable cargo, was long overdue. When another incoming ship finally reported seeing the overdue brigantine, the owner and some of his friends set themselves up at the harbor mouth to wait. At long last, they spied the ship, sailing toward them from the east. She appeared over the horizon under full sail, but as she drew closer it appeared she had set a course not for East Passage, but for Easton's Bay. As she approached the outlying reefs off Easton's Point she altered course to avoid them, then resumed her previous heading, sail-

Third Beach Cove and Sachuest Anchorages

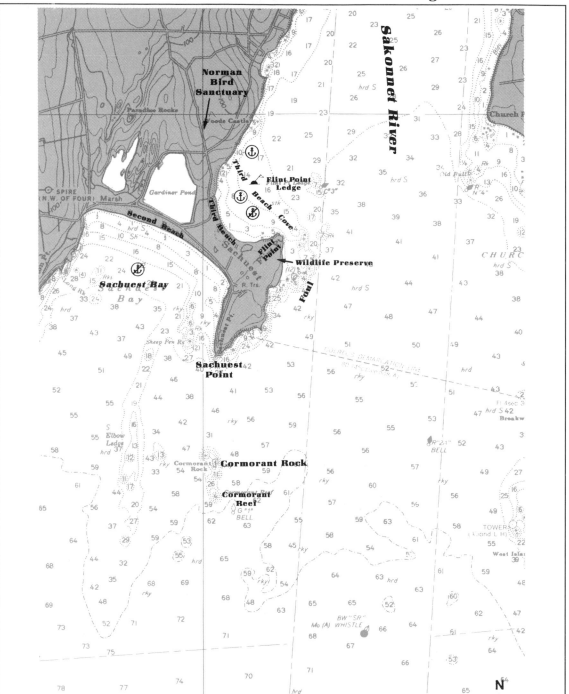

SCALE: **1"=.67** NAUT. MI.   **Do not anchor** **Mooring area** **Good anchoring**

ing quietly into the bay until she gently came to rest on the sand at the northeast end.

Reaching her and going aboard, the mystified owner and friends found no one but a dog and cat. Oddly enough, the saloon table was set for breakfast and a fire blazed merrily in the stove, a full kettle of tea boiling away on top. No trace of captain or crew was ever found on the ship that sailed herself home.

If ghosts don't keep you out of this bay, its orientation should. It's scenic, it's deep, and it's home to one of the island's best beaches, but the risk involved in anchoring here isn't worth it.

SACHUEST BAY

No rating/No protection

Chart: 13221

Sachuest Bay is one of the most spacious and scenic on Aquidneck Island, and is also home to Sachuest, or "Second" Beach. However, like adjacent Easton's Bay, it is completely exposed to the prevailing southerlies and the surf here can be monstrous by island standards.

Although you're apt to see small runabouts and ski boats in here, this is not a good port for cruising boats, and should be bypassed in favor of a more secure spot.

Towering above the bay and very visible from well off the coast is a quadruple church spire perched on a hill. The tower and church are part of the campus of St. George's School, and the hill on which they sit may have given the cove its name. Bestowed by the Indians and still lingering today, "Sachuest" has been translated to mean "near the great hill."

The name "Sachuest Cove" has occasionally been inaccurately applied to the excellent anchorage north of Flint Point in the Sakonnet River, locally called "Third Beach Cove." Newcomers to the area should not confuse the two. Complete information on the cove at Third Beach follows.

THIRD BEACH COVE

Snack bar/No other facilities

Chart: 13221

Nestled behind Sachuest and Flint Points almost immediately to port as you enter the shelter of the Sakonnet is a cove marked by rocky cliffs to the north, a boulder-strewn shore to the south, and a scythe of white sand beach sandwiched between. The natives call it Third Beach Cove, but it has also been dubbed Sachuest Cove by others. Since we think the latter is apt to be confused with Sachuest Bay just around the corner, we prefer the former name for this cove.

Third Beach Cove is in the town of Middletown, which was named for its position between the island's two older towns. The lands of the town were the site of a fair bit of action during the Revolutionary War, when the British landed and headed toward Newport. The town was incorporated as a separate entity in 1743.

Approaches. Approaching from the south, beware of foul ground off Flint Point. To be on the safe side, leave can "3" to port before you turn west to head into this pleasant and increasingly popular anchorage.

Anchorages. Third Beach Cove offers depths of 8 to 11 feet well in toward shore. The mud bottom provides excellent holding ground, but with eelgrass increasing as you head toward the southern end of the anchorage. Anchor anywhere in the cove except in the channel or approaches leading to the launch ramp ashore, which is clearly marked by brightly colored rows of mooring floats.

Until recently, there were no moorings in this cove and only rarely did yachts poke in here. Now, both private moorings and weekend visitors have made this cove quite crowded on weekends, even though it is somewhat exposed to the north and east.

SACHUEST
BAY

THIRD
BEACH
COVE

133

The popularity of the cove is partially due to the fact that it borders one of Aquidneck Island's best swimming beaches. With no surf to speak of, the sugary sand beach is an island favorite, particularly with boardsailors, who find here that elusive combination of good wind and flat water. On Saturday and Sunday afternoons, with wind-surfers, water-skiers, and swimmers all vying for space in the waters of the cove, it calls to mind the beach scene from the film "Jaws."

On weekends, the Middletown harbormaster presides over the scene in an attempt to preserve order. He is a member of the Middletown police department, and the boat is so marked. He can be contacted on VHF Channel 16.

Despite the activity, Third Beach is a fun spot to drop anchor for an afternoon or overnight, and is even better during the week when work responsibilities keep crowds away.

You'll find calm anchorage here in prevailing southwesterlies except when the wind pipes up to 20 knots or more. Then, though the low-lying beach keeps the water flat, it can be uncomfortably cool and windy even in mid-summer.

Swimming here, both off the boat and off the beach, is excellent, though if you take a dip off the stern beware of the water traffic around you. Anchoring in the cove's south end—the crowded part—leaves you vulnerable to runaway board-sailors, Hobies and runabouts on busy weekends. To preserve your topsides and your peace of mind, we suggest dropping anchor in the north end of the cove, in the company of quiet (and stationary) cliffs, and a rock formation resembling a sleeping lion. See if you can pick him out off the north end of the cove.

Things to Do. On the north end of the beach you'll find a snack bar ashore, where soft drinks and fast food are available. The middle of the beach is owned by the Navy, and its large beach club (beside the row of tiny beach houses) sometimes is rented for parties and other gatherings. Anchored off the beach one Friday night, we were treated to the sounds of an excellent live band and, after cocktails and a barbecue dinner aboard, cruising friends joined us for an impromptu "sock hop" on our foredeck, which nearly buried our boat's bow.

Generally, the frenetic daytime activity in this harbor evaporates after the sun goes down, and the cove is left to the enjoyment of the cruising boats anchored there. Since there are no city lights anywhere near this anchorage, it is an excellent spot for stargazing, and Orion is a quiet companion after the moon has risen over Little Compton and marched away across the night sky.

Third Beach Cove provides other shoreside at-

Third Beach Cove, viewed from the wildlife refuge on the cove's southern shore. LYNDA CHILDRESS PHOTO.

tractions. The entire area to the west and south of the cove is a national wildlife refuge, which welcomes visitors provided they stick to marked trails. Reaching the sanctuary entails a healthy but pleasant hike along the sand-turned-rocky shore at the cove's south end. Just around the bend of Flint Point, you'll find a path leading into the sanctuary, and a wood observation platform nearby provides excellent views of the Sakonnet and the cove, as well as providing a good spot to observe or photograph wildlife. A small museum, trail maps, and naturalist's headquarters are located southwest of the platform. Trails are all well worn, so you won't have trouble picking them out. Hike at your leisure through the rambling terrain, or bask in the sun on the warm rocks near shore. Please, do not enter the sanctuary by bushwacking through the brambles elsewhere along the shore, since you may disturb the habitats of small animals and birds that live there.

If you're really in the mood for a hike, about one-half mile down Third Beach Road, which runs parallel to the beach, you'll find the Norman Bird Sanctuary, a 400-acre expanse of deep woods, cliffs, ravines, small lakes and streams, and excellent hiking trails, as well as a small natural history museum.

If you've been on the boat awhile and are craving earthy terrain, the bird sanctuary is an excellent remedy. It will certainly allow you to stretch your legs, do some birdwatching and enjoy some spectacular views. There is a $2 admission fee for hiking the trails for non-member adults. Children are admitted free.

As long as you don't mind some excitement by day, Third Beach Cove is an excellent stop along the shores of the Sakonnet.

Sakonnet Harbor

Based on NOAA chart 13221

SCALE: 1″=.59 NAUT. MI.

 Do not anchor

 Good anchoring

Mooring area

SAKONNET HARBOR

Chart: 13221

Sakonnet Harbor's a gem reminiscent of a Maine fishing village, but there's a catch. The approach is mined with lobster pots and fish traps. Approach from due south and hug Breakwater Point. KENNETH S. GROSS PHOTO.

Sakonnet Harbor, which lies to starboard as you enter the Sakonnet from points south, is as close as Rhode Island comes to a Down East Maine fishing village.

Approaches. Sheltered from the south and east by land and from the southwest by a large breakwater, this harbor is protected in all but northwest winds. A skeleton tower on the north end of the breakwater stands 30 feet high, flashes white, and bears the number "2." The harbor has prevailing depths of 7 feet, but shoals and rocks line the northeast shore, so stick close to the breakwater when entering.

Anyone attempting to enter Sakonnet Harbor, even on a clear, sunny day, should exercise extreme caution to avoid lobster pots and fish traps strung across the harbor entrance, virtually blockading safe entry from the west. The traps stretch in an arc from north to south outside the harbor entrance. Strung together and marked by barrel floats, they are almost impossible to see in any conditions other than flat calm. These traps are an annoying navigational nuisance and one wonders why they are allowed to remain in this particularly inconvenient spot—unless the fishermen in question are attempting to send a not-so-subtle message to visitors to the harbor.

The only way to safely negotiate this harbor entrance is from due south, hugging Breakwater

Point as closely as possible while staying in deep water. Though this approach is clear of the strings of fish traps, it is mined with individual lobster pots, so watch your prop. Sailboats should plan to negotiate this entrance under power to increase maneuverability.

Moorings/Dockage. Depths in the basin have been dredged to 7 feet, and once you go through the trouble of getting in here, your stay in Sakonnet Harbor will be worth it. There is room for only a few transients at any one time in this harbor, where the primary focus is on commercial fishing. Prior to 1988, there were no facilities here for visitors. The harbor is full of moorings, all of which are privately owned, but the harbormaster, who is also a fisherman, may be able to steer you to one he knows is vacant. Call him on VHF Channel 6. There is one—and only one—spot large enough to accommodate an anchored boat in the harbor, between two moorings near the mouth of the cove. If you can't locate it, ask anyone on the docks to point it out.

Currently, the Sakonnet Point Marina offers some transient dockage, as well as fuel and showers. (See listings in the Appendix for more information.) While this pleasant, spanking-new marina is a welcome addition to the harbor from the point of view of visitors to Little Compton, it has caused some concern and controversy locally. The marina displaced some of the harbor's fishing fleet, who were forced to relocate their boats to moorings in the harbor or find dockage elsewhere.

At this writing, dredging is in progress on the southeast side of the harbor next to the marina for installation of a town dock. Ask locally for progress on this project.

The marina also monitors VHF Channel 6 (even though FCC regulations stipulate the channel should be used only for ship-to-ship) and, due to limited space, reservations are suggested. A free dinghy dock is located at the marina near the Foc'sle Restaurant inside the finger pier.

Provisions. Ashore here, you'll find the Foc'sle a lively place to enjoy a steak or seafood dinner, and the restaurant is crowded on summer evenings. A small grocery store, phone, ice cream parlor, and gift shop are located behind the Foc'sle, facing the open Atlantic. The view of open ocean from the point is unsurpassed, obstructed only by the rocks and small islands off the point and the loom of the lighthouse near West Island. The light itself stands on a clump of rock called Little Cormorant Island, and was deactivated in 1954 after being damaged in a hurricane. However, it has been completely restored and maintained by a private group in Little Compton.

The long jetty forming Breakwater Point is a favorite summer evening strolling spot for locals, and there's hardly a more scenic spot to enjoy the sunset over the Sakonnet, or, in the morning, to catch the sunrise over the harbor.

Things to Do. Little Compton is primarily a rural farming community and unlike many neighboring towns that have succumbed to the temptations of development, Little Compton has staunchly resisted. The result is a community that remains very similar in character to the one that was settled in 1675. Without question, it is one of the state's prettiest areas, rivaling anywhere in rural New England for scenic beauty and country charm.

Originally, Little Compton was part of Plymouth Colony, but was annexed to Rhode Island in 1746. The daughter of Pilgrims John and Priscilla Alden lived and died in the town, and her headstone is in the old cemetery on the common.

Locals and visitors alike know that Rhode Island's state bird is the Rhode Island Red chicken; few know the bird was first bred in this small and unassuming farming community.

About five miles from the harbor is one of the town's best kept secrets. Sakonnet Vineyards, owned by Earl and Susan Samson, welcomes visitors and produces award-winning and delicious wines with names like "Rhode Island Red," "America's Cup White," and "Eye of the Storm"—a memento of Hurricane Gloria, which struck the region in 1985.

The vineyard and its tasting room are well worth a visit. Tours are available during summer months and there are picnic tables so visitors can bring lunch to enjoy with their wine. A retail shop assures that you'll be able to stock your liquor locker with your favorite selections.

Earl and Susan provide transportation for visiting yachtspeople who are genuinely interested in a visit to the vineyard. If they are particularly busy, they may not be able to take the time, but they will do everything they can to oblige. If you're interested, give the vineyard a call at 635-8486 to arrange a time that is convenient for all. If you can get there, you won't regret it—and the drive through the rolling countryside is worth the expedition in itself.

Since this harbor is small, with limited room for visitors, we suggest making slip reservations well in advance. If you arrive without notice, it's best to get there early in the day.

Whether you stop for an overnight stay before jumping off for the nearby Elizabeth Islands of Massachusetts or make this harbor your ultimate destination, Sakonnet Point is one of the bay's best places to spend some quiet time afloat.

BLACK POINT

 ⭐5 | 3

No facilities

Chart: 13221

The full sails of a visiting tall ship are visible behind some unsuspecting waterskiers at Black Point on the Sakonnet River. LYNDA CHILDRESS PHOTO.

In the lee of Black Point in prevailing summer southwesterlies is a fine anchorage that is a quiet alternative to Third Beach Cove to the south, offering far more privacy as well as better shelter from the southwest. As you round the point and head in to anchor, you'll notice a distinct rise in temperature as the prevailing southwesterly passes over warmed land to the anchorage, and the distinct smell of earth and mown grass assaults the senses.

Anchorages. Like Third Beach Cove, Black Point is unprotected from the north and east, so if you overnight here be sure of the forecast and set an adequate amount of ground tackle.

Depths here are good as long as you don't stray in too close to shore. Anchor in the southern portion of the cove, but keep away from the point because swells from boat traffic in the river wash around it and quickly prove annoying. Drop the hook slightly west of the point in 8 to 9 feet and set it well, for the bottom here is harder and rockier than in most other parts of the river, particularly near shore. In fact, it is so rocky in the shallow water near shore here it is impossible to safely beach a dinghy—swimming the short distance is a better alternative.

Things to Do. Snorkeling is fine in this secluded spot. Whelks—which some consider a delicacy—are plentiful and can be freely picked from the bottom like southern conch, though the taste is considerably different. (See "Bay Fish And How To Catch Them," page 170.) It's probably a good idea to wear a pair of old sneakers ashore to save your feet here. Once past the submerged rocks, you'll find a secluded sand beach with privacy ensured by a border of trees. Since this beach is not easily accessible by car, you're almost sure to find it deserted. Seashells of all types are plentiful, and are mostly undamaged due to lack of surf action in the river. Sift through the sand here and you'll find hundreds of perfectly formed miniature shells.

The land surrounding the shoreline is privately owned, so don't stray away from the beach. However, on a fine sunny Sakonnet River day, you'll have little reason to want to leave this balmy stretch of sand.

FOGLAND HARBOR

⭐5 | 3

No facilities

Chart: 13221

While Fogland Harbor is a popular destination for Sakonnet River sailors, it has managed to avoid excessive weekend overcrowding encountered at places like Third Beach Cove.

Approaches. Like Third, Fogland has a fine sand swimming beach ashore, with another south-facing beach on the windward side of Fogland

Fogland Harbor and Black Point Anchorages

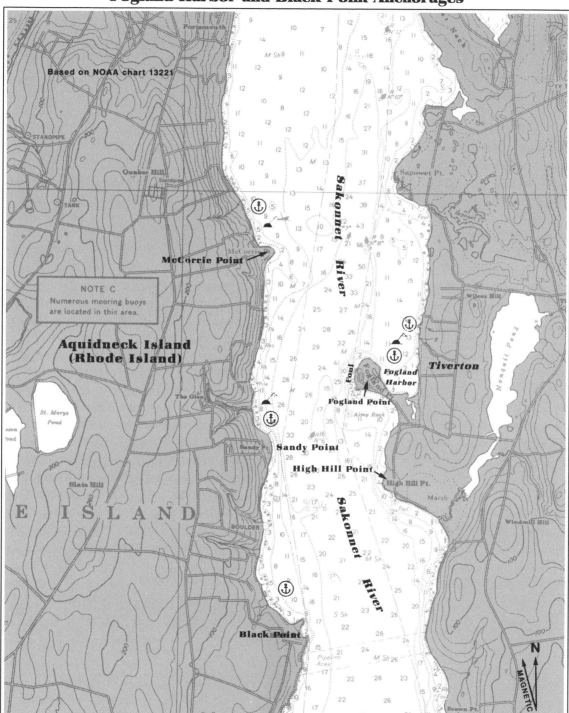

Based on NOAA chart 13221

Portsmouth

STANDPIPE

Quaker Hill
Standpipe

TANK

McCorrie Point

NOTE C
Numerous mooring buoys
are located in this area.

**Aquidneck Island
(Rhode Island)**

St. Marys
Pond

The Glen

Slate Hill

E I S L A N D

BOULDER

Sandy Point

Black Point

Sakonnet River

Sapowet Pt.

Wilcox Hill

Nonquit Pond

Tiverton

Fogland Harbor

Fogland Point

High Hill Point

High Hill Pt.

Marsh

Windmill Hill

Pipeline
Area

M Sh

Brown Pt.

Sakonnet River

N

MAGNETIC

SCALE: **1″=.72** NAUT. MI.   🚫⚓ **Do not anchor**   ⛴ **Mooring area**   ⚓ **Good anchoring**

FOGLAND
HARBOR

139

Point within an easy walk. It is also a popular scuba diving spot, so keep an eye out for divers' flags as you enter.

Approaching Fogland from the south, give the point a wide berth to avoid rocks near shore. From the north, if you draw 5 feet or more, keep nun "8" to *port* to avoid a 5-foot shoal midway between it and shore.

Anchorages. The harbor, in the lee of Fogland Point, is protected from all directions but north-northwest, and is a fine overnight anchorage during the summer months. There are a handful of privately owned moorings in the harbor, but the majority of boats to be seen here during the summer are visitors swinging on anchors. Holding ground is good in soft sand farther out, but depths of 11 to 12 feet in the center of the harbor suddenly jump to 1 and 2 feet as you close on the shore, so keep an eye on your depth sounder when readying the anchor. There are scattered rocks as you near shore, but the bottom here is primarily smooth sand.

Our favorite spot to drop the hook here is opposite the end of the point tucked up close to the eastern shore. Here the shelter from prevailing winds is best—and the scenery is nothing to complain about, either.

Things to Do. Fogland is a popular spot for digging littlenecks, but because it is accessible by automobile from shore, the shellfish crop tends to be a bit overpicked in the summer. Strolling the beach ashore you're bound to see—or stumble upon—clamdiggers' "potholes" left in the sand at low tide.

If you come to Fogland, arrive well-provisioned because there are no supplies of any kind anywhere near here. We've heard there is a farmhouse to which one can walk and arrange a taxi to town. On our many visits, we have seen no evidence of such a place, and the caliber of the few homes that line the harbor suggests that none would welcome sandy, salty strangers at their doors asking to use the telephone.

Fogland Point was at one time the site of a fortification that was hastily built by the British during their occupation of the area in 1778. The point is also the former landing spot for a ferry that provided service between Tiverton and the opposite shore near McCorrie and Sandy Points.

At both McCorrie and Sandy Points, you may notice clusters of moored boats, and visiting sailors occasionally tuck in to anchor among the moored fleets and enjoy the beaches on the river's western shore. These spots both tend to be crowded, however, and our vote stays with Fogland as the best beach/anchorage in the upper Sakonnet, particularly if you plan to stay the night.

Just to the south of Fogland, near High Hill Point, you'll find a silver barrel mooring belonging to the Country Harvest Restaurant, which sits uphill overlooking the river. Dinner guests are welcome to pick up the mooring and hike up to sample the restaurant's excellent continental fare or enjoy the sweeping view of the river from the outside patio bar. The mooring spot is a trifle exposed, so we'd suggest heading north to Fogland to anchor for the night after you've enjoyed your meal.

Only one word can be used to describe Fogland Harbor, particularly when you awaken here in the glassy calm of a sunny summer morning: pastoral. Rising before the wind picks up, you are likely to be treated to the delightful vision of an armada of hot air balloons drifting silently over the treetops and fields. The Sakonnet is a popular ballooning spot, with a launch site fairly near Fogland, and the colorful balloons hovering over the anchorage add to the magic of the place.

Forget about material pastimes when visiting this lovely spot. In fact, forget about everything, including your troubles, as you sit back and enjoy one of the Sakonnet's most peaceful anchorages.

GOULD ISLAND

No rating/No protection

No facilities

Chart: 13221

Tiny Gould Island, the second island by that name in Narragansett Bay, lies in the center of the Sakonnet River just off Nannaquaket Neck. The island is a familiar landmark to Sakonnet River sailors, and though there is no anchorage here, we include it for curiosity's sake if nothing else.

Although the island has one small south-facing cove, the remainder of it is sheer cliff and very steep-to. Depths around the island range from 34 to 81 feet, except off the south end, where there is 10 feet of water at low tide. Unfortunately, the cove is wide open to prevailing southwest winds, and the area is littered with unmarked rocks. The bottom here is rocky close to shore, with soft mud farther out, but holding ground is notoriously poor.

The waters surrounding the island are popular with area fishermen, who hover off the island on all sides in small skiffs fishing for blackfish, flounder, scup, and bluefish.

Locals call this "Snake Island" and it is rumored that the island is infested with rattlesnakes. There may well be snakes on the island, but its main population these days consists of flocks of shore birds who find the craggy island a delightfully isolated nesting spot. The island belongs to the Rhode Island Audubon Society, and is open to visitors brave enough to land here from October 4 through March 31, but is strictly off-limits during nesting season from April 1 to October 3. Birds including snowy egrets, cattle egrets, great egrets, blue, green and black-crowned night herons, gulls, and owls have been sighted on the island. For the preservation of this important nesting ground, perhaps it is just as well that the island's terrain is inhospitable to human visitors.

History. Until it was donated to the Audubon Society, Gould was private, and gets its name from Thomas Gould, the original English owner, who purchased it from the Indians in 1657. During the time when nearby Island Park housed a huge amusement park, Gould was the site of a dance hall to which park patrons were ferried to party the night away, then shuttled back to shore in the wee hours of the morning.

During the Revolutionary War, the thickly wooded Gould was the site of a fort called "The Owl's Nest" for its lofty spot high in the trees overlooking the Sakonnet. From here, colonists were provided with a perfect spot to sight British warships advancing up the Sakonnet.

For the foreseeable future, it looks as if Gould will be left to the auspices of nature—but now, when you pass this rocky speck in the middle of the Sakonnet, you'll know a little more about the mysterious "Snake Island."

"PIRATE'S COVE"

(TIVERTON AND

PORTSMOUTH)

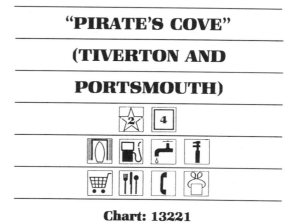

Chart: 13221

Sandwiched between the towns of Tiverton to the east and Portsmouth to the west is a sheltered anchorage which, over the years, has absorbed the name of the marina on its western shore. The name "Pirate's Cove" was applied by a man with the appropriate name of Donald Kidd to his own establishment, but it has been adopted by locals to refer to the entire cove, which has no charted name.

Moorings/Dockage. There are several excellent marinas in the vicinity. In addition to Pirate's Cove Marina, facilities include Standish Boat Yard, on the Tiverton shore, and Brewer's Sakonnet Marina just north of the cove past the Sakonnet River Bridge. All of these facilities offer transient slips and/or moorings and are full-service yards.

Tiverton Yacht Club offers reciprocal privi-

"PIRATE'S
COVE"
(TIVERTON
AND
PORTSMOUTH)

142

A sloop sails into so-called Pirate's Cove, with the shores of Tiverton visible in the background. LYNDA CHILDRESS PHOTO.

leges to members of other clubs, and may have dock space open for transients. Anchoring is not suggested in the cove; as mentioned, the current runs fast through here thanks to the cove's constricted entrance and exit.

Fuel/Provisions. Standish, Pirate's Cove and Brewer's marinas all have gas and diesel available. Brewer's has a clean, New England atmosphere and offers the added bonuses of a swimming pool and Jacuzzi, but a small ship's store and a variety store down the road to the west are all you'll find nearby in the way of supplies.

On the Portsmouth shore at the west side of the cove, you won't find groceries nearby, but just south of Pirate's Cove Marina is an excellent waterfront restaurant named for its address: 15 Point Road. Here you can sit behind lace curtains in a comfortable and easygoing bistro atmosphere and enjoy the view of activity on the Sakonnet. Farther down the road in Island Park (the name lingers, although the amusement park that once stood here is long gone) is Moriarty's Liquor Locker as well as another restaurant, The Sportsman, popular for its family atmosphere and excellent seafood. Moriarty's will deliver to marinas

at no charge; you can contact them by phone at 683-4441. If you can arrange a ride, you'll find the area's best fried seafood at a beachfront shack called Flo's, at the west end of Island Park. Patrons here are given small, festive beach rocks bearing hand-painted order numbers. When your number is called, turn in your rock at the window for steaming hot food served in paper bags and cartons. If you haven't yet sampled stuffies (stuffed quahogs) and clam cakes (fried fritters), try some of Flo's with hot sauce. The fried clams here are as close as you'll come to fried-food heaven. Small, shoal-draft boats can tie up temporarily at Flo's moorings off the beach across from the restaurant. Next to Flo's is a small variety store with a basic supply of grocery items.

Ashore on the Tiverton side, you'll find a liquor store, small Cumberland Farms variety store, and a bank all within walking distance of the waterfront, as well as several small cafes. The whitewashed buildings of Tiverton perch above the cove on a steep hillside, where neatly kept homes nestle among tall trees punctuated with an old New England church spire or two.

History. A short walk uphill from Main Road is historic Fort Barton, named for Colonel William Barton of Tiverton, who was the perpetrator of one of the Revolutionary War's most daring coups. Follow the sign from Main Road to reach the fort.

Apparently, Colonel Barton had a notorious sense of humor, and one day decided it would be great fun to penetrate a British camp in Warwick on the mainland and kidnap the troops' commanding officer, General Prescott. No one tells this tale better than Edgar Mayhew Bacon:

> "The story of Barton's raid should have been put into heroic verse or found a place in ballad literature, for no legend can outmatch the stealing of General Prescott by a Yankee Colonel from Tiverton.
>
> "Colonel Barton started out with 5 whaleboats and 40 volunteers to cross Narragansett Bay, the lower part of which was held by the British. The enemy were in possession of Conanicut, Prudence, and Hope, and had numerous gunboats pa-

Pirate's Cove and The Cove

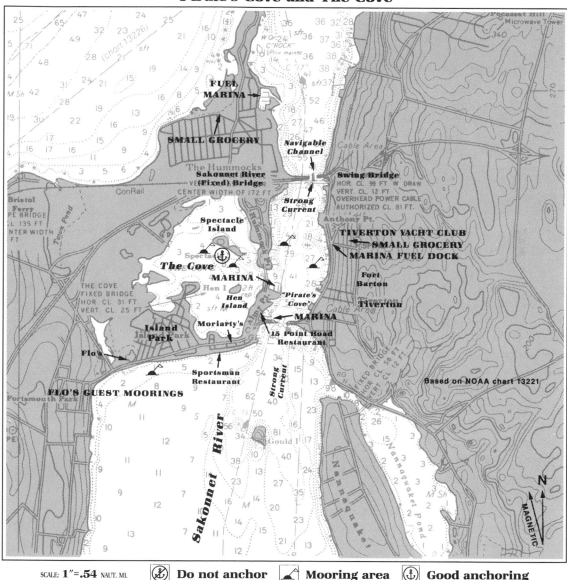

SCALE: **1"=.54** NAUT. MI. ⚓ **Do not anchor** ⚓ **Mooring area** ⚓ **Good anchoring**

"PIRATE'S
COVE"
(TIVERTON
AND
PORTSMOUTH)

143

trolling the waters in between, besides several war vessels and miscellaneous shipping.

"... The little flotilla of Americans dodged between Patience and Prudence, and then, continuing down the west shore of the latter, rounded its lower end and reached the west shore of Rhode Island without mishap ... concealed their boats, and made a landing.

"... A servant in the household of the

British General is said to have acted as guide; it is certain that someone well acquainted with the position of headquarters was with Barton's party, for they went at once to the farmhouse where Prescott was living.

"They do not seem to have made any effort to avoid the sentinel, who challenged them as a matter of course. Instead of answering the challenge, Barton cried, 'We are looking for deserters. Have you seen any?' For a moment the soldier was thrown off guard, and as the American impatiently repeated his question he allowed the party to gather around him.

"In a moment he was overpowered and threatened with death if he cried out. When the coast was finally clear and guards disposed of, the servant led the way to General Prescott's room, and finding it locked butt it open.

"Prescott was sitting up in bed when his captors entered . . . The plan had worked without a hitch from beginning to end."

This fine prank has an interesting historical epilogue: Prescott was only handed back to the British when they in turn relinquished the colonies' own General Lee, who had been held captive by the British army for quite some time.

Fort Barton today is the site of an observation tower from which you can see miles down the Sakonnet and out to sea beyond, making it easy to see why the spot was ideal for monitoring the activities of British troops during the war. There are several acres of hiking trails behind the fort, and it is certainly worth the walk if only for the perspective it provides on the river.

Both Portsmouth and Tiverton are among the area's oldest, and Aquidneck Island's founders landed on this north end when they founded Portsmouth, the second Rhode Island settlement, in 1638. Tiverton originally was part of Massachusetts Bay Colony, and like Portsmouth was named for a town in its founders' homeland of England. The town was annexed to Rhode Island in 1747. The land to either side of the cove was called "Pocasset" by the Indians, which is said to mean "where it widens"—no doubt referring to the waters north of the cove.

If you have an auxiliary powered tender or shoal-draft powerboat, don't miss a visit to "The Cove"—a shallow area west of the highway bridge on Pirate's Cove's west side. Two uninhabited islands, one of which is a public right-of-way, make it easy to while away an afternoon sunning and swimming here (further description follows).

This area of the Sakonnet, while less peaceful than areas to the south in the river, offers less shoreside entertainment than some of the bay's other more populated areas. Nonetheless, it is worth a stop for a healthy dose of picturesque New England.

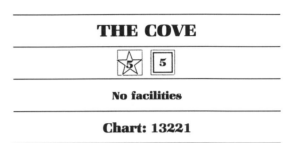

THE COVE

☆5   5

No facilities

Chart: 13221

The almost entirely landlocked area known simply as "The Cove" is a popular spot for shoal-draft boats to gather on summer weekends, and the two uninhabited islands lure squadrons of boats that raft up here for a good time.

Approaches. The Cove is not accessible to deep-draft boats or sailboats, since in order to enter you must pass beneath a highway bridge with only a meager amount of uncharted vertical clearance. At low tide, prevailing depths in the cove are just 3 to 4 feet, though there is a pocket just inside the bridge where depths of 8 to 15 feet can be found.

Use caution when navigating through the waters of the cove, as shoal spots abound. Proceed with an eye on the bottom here at all times.

Anchorages. The soft mud, shallow water and nearly perfect protection here provide a snug spot for shoal draft boats to anchor. If you draw less than 3 feet and can maneuver under the bridge, this is definitely a spot to spend some time exploring.

The most popular spot to anchor here is on the south side of Spectacle Island, an unpopulated oasis owned by the Central Baptist Church of Tiverton. The island was willed to the church in 1897, by a farsighted man named Isaac Church of Tiverton. Church added as a codicil to his last will and testament that the island must "forever remain in the natural state." Thanks to the vision of this turn-of-the-century fellow, The Cove's three acre site remains wild for visitors to explore and enjoy. No buildings are permitted on the island per its benefactor's will, nor is cutting of trees or shrubs allowed. If you visit here, do so with respect for the island's natural state.

The other island in the cove, Hen Island, is privately owned, and boaters are asked not to go ashore. If you really have a hankering for an island to yourself, however, the house on the island can be rented. For information, call Newport attorney John Sheehan at 847-8220.

History. For years, Hen Island was the private home of the Haffenreffer family, who owned the local brewery that once produced Narragansett Beer. The brewery closed several years ago, and the beer bearing the name of the bay was relegated to the history books.

The Cove is thought by some to have been the landing place of Portsmouth's founders, though others claim it was on the northwest side of the island at a place called Founder's Brook, which appears on early maps near the west side of Common Fence Point.

NANNAQUAKET
POND

| ☆5 | 5 |

| 🛈 | 🛒 | 🍽 |

Chart: 13221

Nannaquaket Pond, a small, almost completely landlocked cove, is snugged in behind Nannaquaket Neck on the northeastern shore of the Sakonnet.

Approaches. The entrance is northeast of Gould Island, and unless you know it's there, it is very difficult to pick out thanks to its narrow girth.

Like The Cove, Nannaquaket is inaccessible to deep draft sailboats due to limited depths and a highway bridge that spans its entrance with a charted vertical clearance of just 12 feet. Horizontal clearance here is 56 feet, and depths in the approach are 8 to 10 feet. Beneath the bridge, there are shoals of just 2 feet that sit cheek-by-jowl with a small, circular 15- to 26-foot deep pool. Shoals are to either side of this deep area, as well as beyond it to the south—in fact, outside this area the entire pond is just 1 to 3 feet deep at low tide. Although there is a red and green buoy marking the entrance to the cove well west of the bridge, the remainder of it is devoid of navigational aids. For this reason, those entering here without local knowledge should use caution, keep the chart in hand and monitor depth continually.

Things to Do. Nevertheless, the spot is popular with local small to mid-size powerboats and a favorite place for water-skiers. At the cove's south end is the new location of Don's Marine, a small boat-and-motor dealership where engine repairs can be obtained if necessary. Also in this end of the cove is Evelyn's, a favorite summertime eating spot for locals, which serves fried clams and other seafood in a pleasant spot outdoors overlooking the pond.

While sailboats and larger vessels cannot pass beneath the bridge, there are two excellent retail seafood shops near the mouth of the cove, west of the bridge, where boats can temporarily tie up to purchase fresh seafood. Both Manchester's and the market just to the west sell top-grade fresh local fish and shellfish.

Small boats can proceed to the inner pond, which is surrounded by woods and meadows, and is calm in virtually any wind direction. The land surrounding the pond apparently was at one time prime Indian terrain; the name "Nannaquaket" means "hunting ground."

Although Nannaquaket is not the place for large boats, it is an excellent, sheltered harbor for smaller boats seeking a quiet cove in the upper Sakonnet. Remember, however, that the water here is shoal, and proceed cautiously.

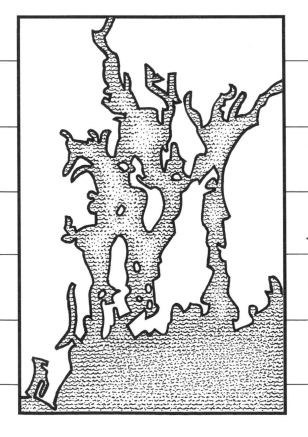

More About The Bay

Hurricanes and the Bay

The possibility of hurricanes exists on Narragansett Bay and elsewhere in the North Atlantic between June and November, but increases during August and September, when the formation of storms in the tropics is more likely. However, hurricanes in this region are by no means frequent. In the past 90 years, only six hurricanes have scored direct hits; a seventh was downgraded before reaching the area. Still, anyone cruising the bay during hurricane season should be aware of the possible occurrence of these storms. At the first indication that a tropical storm or hurricane is approaching, monitor National Weather Service and local weather broadcasts continually and make preparations to head for shelter. (See page 153.)

Formation

Hurricanes and tropical storms that affect the Narragansett Bay area breed over the waters of the open ocean, typically either in the western Caribbean, or in the Atlantic Ocean east of the Cape Verde Islands. Formation occurs over the warm ocean waters of the Intertropical Convergence Zone, between 8° and 20° North latitude. In this region, thunderstorms that maintain their identity for more than 24 hours are called tropical disturbances; these can organize into tropical depressions. Tropical depressions are characterized by surface rotary circulation and wind speeds of up to 38 miles per hour, or 33 knots. These organize still further into tropical storms, which display distinct rotary circulation with constant wind speeds of 39 to 73 miles per hour (34 to 63 knots). At this stage of development, storms are issued a name by the National Weather Service and are watched very carefully. Once development begins, it progresses fairly rapidly, marked by a sharp drop in barometric pressure across the area. A hurricane is born when winds in a tropical storm reach a sustained speed of 74 miles per hour, or 64 knots, and rotary circulation around a center, or eye, becomes pronounced.

Hurricanes and tropical storms that form in the lower latitudes generally move slowly west–northwest for a time before turning north toward the U.S. East Coast. Skirting the Bermuda High, which sits over the ocean to the east of the U.S. mainland, such storms generally hug the coastline as they head north. Many times such storms veer east near Cape Hatteras, North Carolina, where their path out to sea is no longer blocked by the Bermuda High. However, if weather patterns indicate that a high pressure area is stationed north of the Bermuda High, this may force the storm to continue traveling north instead of heading out to sea. Such a scenario historically has spelled trouble for Narragansett Bay, as storms blocked by high pressure to the east traditionally skirt the Mid-Atlantic states and zero in on the southern New England coastline. The most severe hurricanes to strike this area generally begin their northward curve over the Atlantic east of Florida and come ashore from the south-southwest.

How Dangerous Will

a Storm Be?

How much damage a hurricane can be expected to cause depends on four things: the track of the storm's center in relation to Narragansett Bay; the degree of the tide at the onset of the storm; the storm's size and internal wind strength, and the speed of its advance.

Winds in a North Atlantic hurricane revolve around the eye in a counterclockwise direction, and this, combined with the storm's forward motion, causes one side of the storm to be more powerful than the other. If a hurricane's spiraling clouds are bisected by an imaginary line, the semicircle to the right of the line is considered the most dangerous area of the storm. In this area, the forward movement of the hurricane combines with wind speed and direction within the storm to increase overall velocity. The op-

posite side, or left semicircle, is considered safer, since wind direction in the storm as it continues its counterclockwise spin opposes the storm's forward path, and velocity is decreased. If, for instance, winds within a storm are 80 miles per hour, and it is moving toward the coast at a speed of 20 m.p.h., combined wind speed in the dangerous semicircle would be 100 miles per hour. In the so-called "navigable" semicircle, the storm's 80-m.p.h. internal winds are blowing in the opposite direction from its 20-m.p.h. forward speed, decreasing overall velocity.

In relation to Narragansett Bay, if the eye passes to the west, the bay lies in the dangerous semicircle. Flood danger is also increased, particularly if the storm strikes at high tide. Conversely, if the eye of a storm passes to the east of the bay, the bay is in the safer semicircle, and both flood danger and wind speeds are likely to be lower. Five of the seven hurricanes that have hit southern New England in this century have passed west of the bay. Only two, Edna in 1954 and Diane in 1955, left the bay in the less dangerous semicircle, and Diane had been downgraded to tropical storm status by the time she passed well to the east of the bay.

Hurricanes that hit at low or ebb tide are likely to cause far less damage from storm surge than storms that arrive at high tide. Storm surges build over the open ocean, caused by a combination of hurricane winds, the storm's forward speed, and low barometric pressure. A surge is caused as this water reaches gradually shoaling coastlines. Usually surges are gradual, but sometimes onset is fast, causing what is called a "tidal wave" to occur. Normally, storm surge is less severe along ocean-facing coastlines, ranging from six to eight feet above normal high tide. On bays and inlets such as Narragansett Bay, which are particularly vulnerable to surge travelling up the coast, the surge is more significant, ranging from 12 to 15 feet above normal high tide. During the hurricane of 1938, a sudden storm surge inundated the Lower Bay with a tidal wave of 30 feet, and Providence was flooded with water that rose more than 13 feet above the normal high tide mark.

The extensive damage caused by storm surge in the 1938 hurricane as well as others that followed it prompted the Army Corps of Engineers to propose construction of a series of hurricane barriers at sites around the bay. Designated barrier locations included the stretches of water between Conanicut Island and the mainland; between Fort Wetherill and the south tip of Aquidneck; and at the Old Stone Bridge on the Sakonnet River. The Army also proposed a series of dikes at Island Park beach, as well as a barrier spanning the Providence River just below the city.

The only barrier ever actually built, however, was the one that today protects downtown Providence from repeat episodes of flooding during hurricanes. The Fox Point hurricane barrier was built after a 1954 hurricane, and extends half a mile across the head of the Providence River just below the harbor. With its gates closed, it provides a 25-foot-high barrier that protects the harbor and downtown area. Dikes are pulled across to seal off street access, then 53-ton gates are lowered by electric motors. In addition to providing a dike effect, the structure is capable of pumping more than 3 million gallons of water per minute through the barrier and out of potentially flooded areas inside its walls.

Construction of Lower Bay barriers was never carried out due to public outcry at the high cost and concern about effects on the environment if the bay's normal flushing action were tampered with, and the hindrance to recreational and commercial traffic entering and leaving the bay.

Hurricanes That Have Hit the Bay

Records show that Narragansett Bay experienced hurricanes as early as 1635, when, on August 15, a violent storm struck the area at high tide. Ac-

Providence during the Great Gale of 1815. Copy by John Russell Bartlett of an original painting by J. Kidder, 1835–1840. COURTESY OF THE RHODE ISLAND HISTORICAL SOCIETY.

This photograph, snapped during Hurricane Carol on August 31, 1954, shows the shorewide devastation hurricanes can cause. COURTESY OF THE NAVAL HISTORICAL COLLECTION, NAVAL WAR COLLEGE, NEWPORT.

cording to written records, the tide "rose at Narragansett 14 feet higher than ordinary and drowned eight Indians flying from their wigwams." Less than 200 years later, history noted another fierce storm. The so-called "Great Gale of 1815" swept over the bay on September 15, with high winds, rains and floods that inundated Providence, causing widespread devastation.

It was more than 100 years, however, before the granddaddy of hurricanes bore down on Narragansett Bay. Like its predecessors, it came as a complete surprise to bay residents, who awoke on the morning of September 21, 1938, to a cloudy forecast of intermittent rain. Later, residents uniformly recalled a strange cast to the sky that day, an odd glow that seemed to permeate the overcast. That afternoon, southern New England was walloped by one of this century's most powerful hurricanes. The storm, traveling upwards of 30 m.p.h., arrived at high tide, packing sustained winds of 95 m.p.h. with gusts reported as high as 120 m.p.h., and left a swath of destruction in its wake. The "Great New England Hurricane" passed to the west of Narragansett Bay, placing the bay in the dangerous semicircle, and the resulting storm surge caused tidal waves along the south coast and submerged downtown Providence. Two hundred sixty-two persons died in the hurricane, and damage was in excess of $8

million—an enormous sum by the standards of those days.

Six years later, another hurricane paid a visit. On September 14, 1944, the "Great Atlantic Hurricane" punched its way through the bay and south coastal areas with winds of 82 m.p.h. and gusts to 100 m.p.h. Fortunately, this storm struck at ebb tide, and damage was far less widespread.

During the 10 years before Narragansett Bay was again the target of a high caliber hurricane, meteorologists began assigning each storm a woman's name, using the names of their wives, mothers and girlfriends. On August 31, 1954, again with virtually no warning by weather forecasters, Hurricane Carol blew virtually straight up the coast after forming north of the Bahamas, packing sustained winds of 90 m.p.h. Like the 1938 hurricane, it arrived at high tide and downtown Providence again was flooded by the accompanying tidal surge. Carol departed leaving damage estimated at $90 million.

Following on the whirling skirts of Carol came Edna, which careened through southern New England 12 days later, and also struck at high tide, but with far less vengeance: sustained winds were 40 to 50 m.p.h., but gusted to 90 m.p.h.

Although the bay was the recipient of the rainy backlash from a hurricane dubbed Diane that lost strength after detouring inland in August, 1955, all remained calm until September 12, 1960, when Hurricane Donna began a deadly dance northward from the Caribbean after a segue over the Florida mainland. Unlike her forebears, Donna was well forecast; residents were prepared for her arrival with wind speeds of up to 81 m.p.h., and as a result no lives were lost and property damage was far less than in previous hurricanes.

In the ensuing 25 years, Narragansett Bay residents were allowed to become a bit complacent about hurricanes; none headed this way until 1985. On the morning of September 27, Hurricane Gloria aimed toward the coast, and her power more than made up for the hurricane-free interval. Classified by the National Weather Service as one of the most powerful hurricanes of the century, Gloria fortunately lost some strength by the time she reached Narragansett Bay, but still packed winds of 81 m.p.h. with gusts to 91 m.p.h. The hurricane passed to the west of the bay at a forward speed of 40 m.p.h., again placing the area in the dangerous semicircle. However, thanks to up-to-the-minute weather forecasting that allowed those in and around the bay to prepare for the storm well in advance, Gloria did far less damage than storms of her size and strength that hit in the early part of the century.

Preparing for

a Hurricane

Fortunately, today's tropical cyclones are monitored from the moment of their birth in the lower latitudes, and those living in the potential path of a hurricane have ample time to prepare for its arrival. The National Weather Service updates forecasts continually when a hurricane or tropical storm threatens land, and local television and radio meteorological coverage is excellent.

The National Oceanic and Atmospheric Administration (NOAA) publishes a hurricane tracking chart, which allows you to track a storm's progress by its coordinates, which are given in all forecasts and advisories issued by the National Weather Service as a storm approaches. Tracking charts can be obtained from the National Weather Service, Public Affairs Office, Washington, D.C. 20402. There is no charge.

At the approach of a hurricane, forecasts should be monitored continuously and boat owners should prepare to secure their vessels hauled and on land, moorings, or at anchor in a good hurricane hole.

Choosing a

Hurricane Hole

While the safest course of action for boat owners is to secure their boats as well as possible and proceed to shoreside shelter for the duration of a hurricane, liveaboards or visiting cruising yachts caught in the bay during the onslaught of a storm may wish to remain aboard. While this is not the generally recommended course of action, if you choose this alternative the next best step is to proceed to an appropriate hurricane hole well in advance of the approaching storm. Look for the following characteristics when choosing a Narragansett Bay anchorage in which to hole up and weather a storm:

- Search out a deep, narrow anchorage, surrounded by land high enough to reduce the effects of the wind and to provide shelter from storm surge. It should be protected from the wind in all directions.

- The farther away you can get from Rhode Island Sound and the open sea near the mouth of the bay, the better.

- Holding ground should be excellent, preferably heavy mud.

- The shoreline surrounding the anchorage should be marshy, with few rocks or other obstructions; if your boat does drag ashore, less damage will result.

- Water depth should be three to four times your boat's draft; shallow enough to allow for up to 15 feet of storm surge, but deep enough to prevent your keel from hitting bottom in the troughs of any waves produced by the storm's winds.

The best known hurricane hole on Narragansett Bay is the Kickamuit River, but it is a popular spot and fills up fast at first word of an impending hurricane. You may also hole up in the northern reaches of the Taunton River or the southern portion of Greenwich Cove in Greenwich Bay. The northern reaches of both Potter Cove on Prudence Island and Allen Harbor meet most of the criteria for good hurricane holes; however, both are sheltered from the east only by low-lying sandspits, which would be inundated in any significant storm surge, and which would not provide much protection from winds from the east. In choosing a spot to weather a storm, keep in mind the criteria of a good hurricane hole and exercise prudent seamanship.

Once you have chosen a hurricane hole, everything possible should be done to prepare for the arrival of the storm. Although hurricanes often take unexpected twists and turns, by monitoring forecasts you should be able to determine the storm's likely track and probable wind direction, thus determining which semicircle you will be in. Set storm anchors, using sufficient rode to provide holding power in a storm surge, but leaving plenty of swinging room to allow for likely wind shifts. Standard fair weather scope is between 5:1 and 7:1; in a hurricane, use at least 10:1. Use storm anchors well above the weight you would use under normal conditions; the more chain rode, the better. You may wish to set multiple anchors or to augment holding power by tying off to a secure tree or other object ashore. Use plenty of chafing gear to protect the anchor rode from parting under stress of heavy loads, and lead lines around winches so as to avoid excess stress. Avoid leading multiple lines to one cleat, and avoid leading lines at right angles to the base of the cleat to reduce potential of failure.

Clear decks of all removable items. Sailboat

Where to Turn for the Latest Storm Information

National Weather Service broadcasts on VHF/FM radio are aired continuously over a 24-hour period. Forecasts are updated every six hours, more often if a hurricane or other weather disturbance threatens the area, as frequently as once per hour. In addition to NOAA weather radio, local Coast Guard stations broadcast weather advisories as they are received from the National Weather Service. Coast Guard advisories are announced on VHF Channel 16, then subsequently broadcast on VHF Channel 22.

Area VHF Weather Channels	Frequency
WX 1 = Hyannis, Massachusetts	162.55 MHz
WX 2 = Providence, Rhode Island	162.40 MHz
WX 3 = Boston, Massachusetts	162.475 MHz

In addition to NOAA and Coast Guard broadcasts, you may find local television weather satellite maps and forecasts helpful if you carry a 12-volt television set aboard. Local TV stations air constant live updates from the National Hurricane Center in Miami as a storm nears the New England Coast, as well as continually updated local forecasts.

decks should be stripped of sails and sail covers to decrease windage. Also remove dodgers, bimini tops and other deck gear and stow it below. All running rigging should be secured, as well as all ports and hatches—downpours are apt to be heavy. Finally, top off fuel and water tanks and make sure batteries are fully charged. Above all, remember: While you should do everything possible to save your boat in a hurricane, ultimately it is replaceable. Human lives are not. If at all possible, go ashore for shelter after doing everything possible to secure your boat. If you choose to stay aboard, be fully prepared to cope with the worst in seamanlike fashion.

Hurricanes are not a frequent occurrence on Narragansett Bay, and with modern satellite and computer-assisted weather forecasting, it would be rare indeed for cruisers to be caught unaware in the bay during a hurricane. Nonetheless, it pays to study the characteristics of past hurricanes to be better prepared for those that may pass through in the future, and to arm yourself with a list of options should one occur during your stay on the bay.

Local Color: Narragansett Bay People and Food

Narragansett is the home of the quahog and the quahogger, otherwise clamdigger. The Indians, who appreciated the large and luscious bivalve at its proper value, would have refused to affront it with a plebeian name of only four letters. They looked at the goodly shell, tipped with purple, and saw possibilities of wampum in it; they tasted the salty morsel of marine manna with which Providence provided them each day, and they rolled their pious eyes to heaven and reverently called the treasure poquauhock. The Rhode Islander, catching the reverent spirit of the Indian, if not his exact pronunciation, adheres to quahog. In Connecticut men go clamming, which is a much more prosaic occupation.

The People

Three hundred and fifty years ago, Narragansett Bay belonged to the Indians. Today, fewer than one percent of the area's people are descended from Indians. The immigration that began when Roger Williams stepped ashore at Providence and formed the first official settlement here has continued over the centuries, and today Rhode Island and Narragansett Bay are home to a wide range of ethnic groups.

Early English immigrants were soon followed by the Irish. Large numbers of French Canadians arrived here after 1860, followed by groups from Italy, the Azores, and Cape Verde Islands, and from Poland and Germany. Most recently, Rhode Island has attracted immigrants from South America and Southeast Asia.

Virtually all of these newcomers brought with them maritime skills passed down through generations of seafaring ancestors in their native countries. Perhaps it is the many ethnic enclaves still strong in the area, or maybe it is the nautical heritage. Whatever the reason, the result is a group of people who cling stubbornly to tradition in the face of modern life.

Visitors will notice an accent that is unique to this area. Bloodlines no doubt have something to do with this; linguists say accent is inherited, and "Rhode Islandese" sounds like a mix of twisted cockney, Irish brogue, Italian slang, and Boston Brahmin. The regional accent may also be due in part to immigrants who arrived here through Boston and New York, having picked up distinctive local twangs along the way. Some speculate that the accent stems from the first New World colonists, who came from an area near London known for its distinctive manner of speech and who settled in Massachusetts Bay Colony before making their way south to the bay area.

Accents vary, even in a region as small as Narragansett Bay, being less pronounced in southern areas and on the islands than in the Upper Bay near Providence. Near the city, visitors often react with bewilderment bordering on awe when first confronted with Rhode Island-speak.

Like other New Englanders, Rhode Islanders are prone to dropping r's where r's should be and inserting the letter where it doesn't belong. But don't ask a native to say "park the car,"—everyone is wise to that ruse and will purposely exaggerate the vowels every time. Catch the phrase when it is uttered unselfconsciously, however, and you are likely to overhear something like "pok the coh," a guttural and nasal pronunciation that contrasts noticeably with the Kennedyesque and distinctly more close-mouthed "paahk the caah" heard in Boston. Rhode Islanders are apt to tell you they "sore" the sights, use "umbrellers" when it rains, and eat plenty of fruit like "bannaners" and "payahs." "Hot fun" here isn't what one has in the summertime, it is the organization promoting cardiovascular fitness to which one donates annually at the office.

Lazy-tongued natives shorten words and phrases into pithy little packages. The state's name often is pronounced "Rodilan" and the area north of Greenwich Bay is known as "Wawik" to many Upper Bay inhabitants.

What the rest of the world knows as a milkshake, Rhode Islanders call a "cabinet"—or, for the more erudite, a "frappe" (pronounced "frap"). The origin of the word cabinet as it applies to an ice cream drink is enough to mystify the most dedicated linguist. This travesty is topped by the native term for the large sandwich most Americans call a "hoagie" or a "sub." Here, this is unconditionally known as a "grinder," and while locals may tolerate the use of the term "sub" when you're ordering lunch, forget about being understood if you order up a steak and cheese hoagie.

Requesting a cup of coffee in a bay area cafe can be an adventure in semantics as well. In Connecticut, they sip coffee with cream and sugar; in Rhode Island, they drink it "regular."

Colloquial expressions and accents lend to the charm of any area, and Narragansett Bay is no exception, though Rhode Islandese is hardly lilting. No doubt about it, a thick Rhode Island accent is unmistakable, and once you hear one, you aren't likely to forget it.

The Food

Fortunately, the ethnic mix of Narragansett Bay has produced more than the unusual accent, and along with rich cultural diversity, visitors here will experience an array of interesting ethnic and native cuisines. For a small state, Rhode Island has a surprising number of delicacies that can't be had anywhere else, and no one should cruise the bay without sampling at least some of them. Recipes follow on page 158.

COFFEE SYRUP. Rhode Island children are brought up on this elixir; mixed with milk, it beats chocolate syrup any day. The sweet syrup

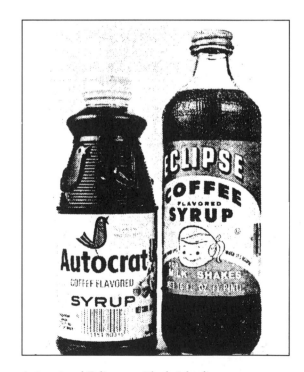

Autocrat and Eclipse are Rhode Island's biggest sources of coffee syrup, an unusual concoction that many people feel is the best thing to happen to milk since the cow.

is made in Rhode Island and is rarely seen elsewhere, as bay residents who move away (and unfailingly mail order it by the case) soon discover. No one seems to know why the tall bottles of syrup are so popular here. Give some coffee syrup a try while you're here—but be warned—it's addicting. Better buy several bottles to bring home.

DEL'S FROZEN LEMONADE. On a hot day, a slushy sip of this tart concoction is enough to make you weep with pleasure. Rhode Island's own frozen lemonade is made in the Upper Bay port of Cranston using a family recipe that has been passed down for generations. It's said to have originated in Italy, where its inventor allegedly made the first batch with freshly fallen snow. It is widely available at shops and stands around the bay, especially near the shore. It is made with fresh lemon juice and most of the lemon itself, studded with pulp and peel nestled among the slushy ice. The company has revealed it squeezes more than two million lemons annually to satisfy consumer demand, but won't divulge the secret ingredient that sets the lemonade apart from the rest. Trust us. This is the best frozen lemonade you will ever taste.

CHOURICO/LINGUICA. Chourico (pronounced shur-eece) and linguica are spicy, Portuguese pork sausages made locally and found only in Rhode Island and eastern Massachusetts. Chourico is generally spicier than linguica, and both can be found prepackaged among the other sausages in the supermarket. The reddish tinted links keep well on a boat with refrigeration or an icebox. Try them instead in any recipe in which you'd use Italian sausage, as well as in omelets, or fried with green peppers and onions and served on a *grinder* roll. They're delicious. These should not be confused with the Spanish sausage similarly named *chorizo*—the two are quite different. Aboard our boat, we have introduced many of our guests to this sausage. All become hooked instantly.

PORTUGUESE SWEETBREAD. Also made locally, particularly in and around Fall River, oversized loaves of this delectably sweet bread can be found in the bread or bakery section of local markets. Toasted and buttered, it's as close as toast comes to perfection, and it's delicious served with soups and stews. A cousin of sweetbread are "bolos," sweet muffins shaped like oversized English muffins.

RHODE ISLAND JOHNNYCAKE MEAL. In colonial Rhode Island, water-powered grist mills ground an Indian strain of corn called whitecap flint, native to Rhode Island. The corn is known for its delicious nutty flavor, and on the shelves of Rhode Island markets in the baking section you'll find packages of stone-ground whitecap flint

LOCAL
COLOR:
NARRAGANSETT
BAY
PEOPLE
AND
FOOD

157

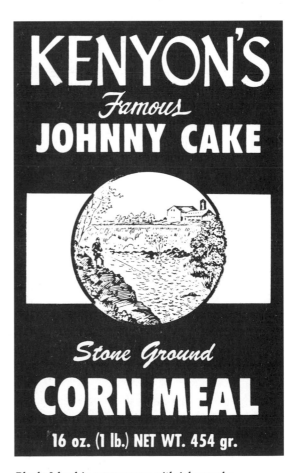

Rhode Island is synonymous with johnnycake, stone-ground whitecap flint cornmeal. Two mills, Kenyon's and Gray's, have produced the nutty mix for more than a century.

cornmeal produced by two mills that have been in operation for more than a century, Kenyon's and Gray's. Rhode Island is synonymous with johnnycakes and natives use only Kenyon's and Gray's Meal.

CLAM CAKE MIX. Next to the johnnycake mix in the markets you'll find red, white, and blue boxes of Kenyon's Clamcake Mix, a combination of Rhode Island corn meal, flour and other ingredients. The recipe for clam cakes is on the box. Give them a try!

HOPE LAGER BEER. Rhode Island's state motto is "Hope," a suitably Puritan virtue that was adopted by a local brewing company as the name for the only malt beverage now brewed in the state. The beer has an excellent strong flavor for those who like full-bodied beer, and is worth a taste during a visit here. Certainly it is leagues above the state's previous home-brewed beer, which carried the name of the bay and was known locally as "Nasty Narry."

SAKONNET VINEYARDS WINES. Several years ago a vineyard in Little Compton on the Sakonnet River began producing wines that have gone on to receive national acclaim. Don't leave the area without enjoying some of the wines produced by this local vineyard. Vintages have names like "Rhode Island Red," "America's Cup White," and "Eye of The Storm," a pleasant blush wine originally produced with grapes picked early to beat the arrival of Hurricane Gloria in 1985.

Seafood Recipes

Whether you provision in the supermarkets and neighborhood markets, or harvest seafood from the waters of Narragansett Bay, we'd like to share some ways of preparing foods indigenous to the area. Here are some of our favorite recipes using locally available ingredients and native seafood.

For information on catching and cleaning fish and shellfish in the bay, see "Bay Fish And How to Catch Them," page 162.

"Stuffies"

This is Rhode Islandese for "stuffed quahogs," and no one should visit Narragansett Bay without trying one of these large shells stuffed with bread, spices, quahog meat, and, sometimes, ground chourico. There are probably as many recipes for stuffies as there are quahogs in the bay, but here's our own way of preparing them.

> Meat of 6 quahogs
> ¼ cup butter
> 1 onion, finely chopped
> 1 red pepper, finely chopped
> 1 green pepper, finely chopped
> 2 cups seasoned stuffing mix
> ½ tablespoon lemon juice
> 2 to 3 tablespoons white wine
> Water, as needed
> 1 tablespoon paprika
> 1 tablespoon grated parmesan cheese

After cleaning and shucking the quahogs, remove meat (see page 170 for method) and clean and reserve 6 half-shells. Tenderize the quahog meat by pounding with a meat mallet. Mince the meat finely, preferably using a meat grinder or food processor. In your largest frying pan, melt butter and add quahogs, onions, peppers. Saute until quahog meat turns white and firm and onions turn translucent. Add stuffing mix, lemon juice, and wine, and stir until moist, adding more wine or water to moisten if necessary. Spoon into quahog shells. Top with paprika and grated cheese and bake at 350° for 30 minutes, or until stuffing is browned and bubbly. Makes 6 stuffies; allow at least 2 per person for an appetizer.

Rhode Island Clam Chowder

Rhode Island clam chowder is made with quahogs, which is how the shellfish earned the nickname "chowder clams." In Rhode Island the broth is clear, with no cream or milk added. Do not even consider polluting this elixir with tomatoes. Here, this practice is regarded as sinful and transforms true chowder into the soup they eat in Manhattan.

Meat of 1 dozen quahogs
2 large onions, diced
4 potatoes, peeled and diced
¼ cup chopped parsley
2 bay leaves
1 tablespoon oregano
1 tablespoon thyme
2 cloves garlic, crushed
1 or 2 small chunks chourico sausage

Steam open clams in enough water to cover. Remove shells and extract meat, reserving broth. Grind clams and return to broth. Add remaining ingredients and simmer for at least 2 hours over low heat. Stuffies are a perfect accompaniment.

Rhode Island Clam Cakes

In Rhode Island, when it comes to clam cakes, there is no such thing as a fritter. The delicious breaded and fried morsels studded with bits of minced quahog are clam cakes, nothing else. Making your own batter is possible, but for the cakes to be truly authentic, you must use Rhode Island stone ground corn meal along with flour, so it's just as easy to buy the pre-packaged mix. To the mix, we add:

    1 to 2 cups chopped quahogs, with juice
    1½ cups water
    1 teaspoon curry powder (non authentic, but good!)
    ¼ teaspoon cayenne pepper (ditto)

Mix and drop by spoonfuls into hot oil to fry. One box of mix makes 3 to 4 dozen clamcakes, so you may wish to halve the recipe. Serve with hot sauce or cocktail sauce, lemon wedges and a bottle of Hope Lager beer.

Steamed Clams

If your appetite isn't up for a whole clambake, steamers by themselves make a delicious light meal or appetizer. In a large pot, place:

2 quarts steamers
½ cup white wine
½ cup water
2 cloves garlic
1 tablespoon butter
1 tablespoon chopped parsley

LOCAL
COLOR:
NARRAGANSETT
BAY
PEOPLE
AND
FOOD

159

Cover and steam until shells uniformly open. Discard unopened shells. Serve with broth and/or drawn butter and lemon wedges.

To prepare clams for eating: Freshly dug steamer clams are quite sandy and must be thoroughly cleaned before eating. To clean, place clams in a bucket or sink full of cold water. Jostle gently with your hands. The water will become sandy. Drain it and repeat the process until the water remains relatively clear. If you soak the clams for any length of time, the water must be changed frequently to keep the clams alive. Never eat a clam that is dead before you cook it, or one that floats to the surface as you are cleaning. Clams with broken shells should be discarded.

Littlenecks On The Half-Shell

Littlenecks, as the name implies, are a tiny hard-shelled clam found in mud flats around the bay. Although these can be prepared in the same manner as steamer clams, they are best eaten on the half shell (yes, raw!). Oysters are eaten this way as well.

    1 dozen littlenecks (or oysters)
    Crushed ice
    1 cup catsup
    ¼ cup horseradish
    2 fresh lemons

Shuck littlenecks and arrange on a platter over crushed ice. Mix catsup and horseradish with a dash of lemon juice and place in dollops atop each clam. Top with additional lemon juice and slide deftly into your mouth by lifting the shell to your lips with your hand. Forks are not an acceptable means of propelling these morsels to your mouth.

Spicy Steamed Mussels

Once relegated mainly for use as bait, blue mussels now have gourmet status. Mussels can be picked from rocky beds at various sites around the bay (see "Bay Fish and How to Catch Them," page 168). To clean, rinse with water and scrub shells thoroughly to remove the "beard," or stringy residue, on the outside of the shell where the mussel was attached to the rock. The meat of mussels is sweet and succulent, and many prefer the firmer consistency to that of the softer steamer clam. Eat only blue mussels; leave the ribbed ones to the seagulls.

> 2 quarts mussels
> ½ cup water
> ½ cup sweet vermouth
> 2 cloves garlic, crushed
> 1 tablespoon (or more) sweet basil
> 1 tablespoon oregano

Clean mussels and place in a large pot. Add remaining ingredients. Cover and bring to a boil; reduce heat and steam until shells are open and meat is orange colored and firm to the touch. Discard unopened shells. Serve with broth for dipping, crusty bread and a cold bottle of Sakonnet Vineyards wine.

Lemony Baked Fish

Blackfish and summer flounder are both prevalent on the bay in summer and quite often are the catch of the day. This recipe works well for either, but is especially nice for blackfish, or tautog, as the Indians called it. The ingredients tenderize the sometimes chewy flesh of the blackfish.

> 2 blackfish fillets
> ¼ cup dry white wine
> ¼ cup butter, melted
> ¼ cup lemon juice
> 2 cloves garlic, crushed
> 2 tablespoons grated lemon peel
> 2 tablespoons seasoned bread crumbs

Place fillets in lightly greased baking pan. Combine wine, butter, lemon juice and garlic and pour over fish. Top with lemon peel and bread crumbs. Bake at 350° for 20 minutes, until fish flakes easily with a fork. Do not overcook.

OTHER RHODE ISLAND FARE

Rhode Island Johnnycakes

Johnnycakes have been part of life on Narragansett Bay since colonial times, when they were also called "journey cakes" by those who toted them around for sustenance while traveling. The proper way to make a johnnycake depends on whom you talk to: West Bay residents prefer theirs smaller and cakier, while those on the eastern shore want them larger, thin, and crepelike. This debate has been raging for years, and at one point it prompted a local paper to comment that cows would probably learn to fly before the issue was resolved. One thing is certain; whichever way you make them, true Rhode Island johnnycakes must be made with whitecap flint corn meal, a locally grown strain developed by the Indians, who taught colonists how to use the meal in the first place.

East Bay Johnnycakes

> 2 cups johnnycake meal
> ¾ cup cold water
> ½ teaspoon salt
> 1½ cups milk

Combine first 3 ingredients and slowly stir in milk. Drop batter in spoonfuls onto a hot greased skillet and fry until the edges are golden brown.

West Bay Johnnycakes

> 2 cups johnnycake meal
> 1 teaspoon salt
> 2 cups boiling water
> ¼ cup milk

Combine cornmeal and salt. Add boiling water. Let stand for 5 to 10 minutes. Add milk, mix thoroughly. Fry spoonfuls on oiled skillet over medium high heat. Cakes should be 2 to 3 inches in diameter.

In olden days, johnnycakes were eaten more like cornbread is today; now, they are most often eaten like pancakes; topped with maple syrup. We'll leave it up to you to decide which recipe wins your vote!

Portuguese Soup

Also called "kale soup" locally, there is nothing better than this thick and hearty potage after a cool early summer or fall day out on Narragansett Bay. Serve with plenty of Portuguese sweetbread and a bottle of Rhode Island Red wine. This version is simple, and truly delicious. Don't substitute the beans; Campbell's beans come in tomato sauce, which is the key to this broth.

    1 package chourico, sliced
    1 bunch fresh kale (or ½ package spinach),
        washed and chopped
    1 small head cabbage, shredded
    2 1-pound cans Campbell's baked beans in
        tomato sauce
    Water to cover

Into a large soup kettle, place all ingredients. Add water and stir. Bring to a boil; lower heat and simmer for 1 to 2 hours, until broth absorbs the spicy taste of the chourico and thickens slightly. Serves a crowd.

Eggs Portuguese

    4 eggs
    2 Portuguese sweet muffins (bolos)
    1 can artichoke hearts, sliced
    1 package hollandaise sauce mix
    1 package chourice or linguica sausage

Poach eggs; split sweet muffins in half and lightly toast. Heat artichoke hearts and prepare sauce according to directions on packet. (On the boat, we prefer the mix; it's much easier. At home, we make our own hollandaise.) Place half a roll on each plate; on each half place a poached egg and a few artichoke hearts. Top with Hollandaise. Serve with a side of pan-fried chourico or linguica. Your guests aboard will never suspect this breakfast, lunch or light dinner feast was so easy.

LOCAL
COLOR:
NARRAGANSETT
BAY
PEOPLE
AND
FOOD

161

Bay

Fish

and

How

to

Catch

Them

Some of the densest shellfish beds and best in-shore angling along the U.S. East Coast are found in the cool, plankton-rich waters of Narragansett Bay.

Fishing in Narragansett Bay is dictated by seasonal changes in water temperature. Cooler autumn temperatures send marine life to more stable climates in deep offshore waters, or signal a migration to warmer waters to the south. Warming temperatures in the spring bring marine life back to Narragansett Bay for the summer spawning season. The seasons mentioned in the angling section refer to the migratory seasons when these fish are easiest to catch. There is no license required for recreational angling; however, there are size restrictions and bag limits.

Shellfishing is pursued year-round in Narragansett Bay for most species. There are size and harvest limits to be observed and, most importantly, there are areas of the bay which are closed to all shellfishing due to the possibility of contaminated stocks. Also, heavy rainfall affects sewage treatment plants that empty into the bay, resulting in temporary closing of some shellfishing areas. For the latest information on areas closed to shellfishing, call the state Division of Water Resources, 277-2900. Nonresidents of Rhode Island are required to obtain a license before taking shellfish. All licenses are issued by the state Division of Boating Safety, 22 Hayes St., Providence, RI, phone 277-3576.

Each spring, anglers and shellfishermen should pick up a copy of the latest fishing regulations, which are available at local tackle shops, or by contacting the state Division of Fish and Wildlife, Wakefield, RI, phone 789-3094.

The Bait

Nearly anything that swims or crawls in the ocean can be used for bait and it seems the more unsightly the animal is, the better the bait it will be. Turning mossy rocks or digging mud holes at low tide exposes crawlsters and other marine life that the weekend angler can parlay into a seafood feast by the end of the day. If angling time is more important than digging your own bait, numerous tackle shops carry a variety of live, frozen, and artificial baits.

You can find *blood worms* at low tide in mud and under rocks. Blood worms have large black pincers at the mouth, and will attempt to bite your hands, but the bite is weak and harmless. When stuck with a hook, the blood worm oozes red fluids that help attract predator fish. Force the hook down the mouth as deeply as it will go, then out the side. This is excellent bait for flounder.

A fat, fuzzy, cousin of the blood worm, the *sea worm* is found at low tide in mud and under rocks and logs. Black pincers emerge from the mouth, but they are more psychologically annoying than physically harmful. Force the point of the hook down the mouth as far as the hook will go, then out the side. When hooked, the sea worm will ooze fluids that attract predator fish. Scuba divers gathering quahogs in the depths of Narragansett Bay often have flounder swarm around their hands slurping up sea worms they have exposed. It can be productive to fish down-current from a quahog boat to take advantage of the quahog fisherman's natural chumming action.

Many small *crabs* inhabit the Narragansett Bay shoreline. *Fiddler* and *green crabs* can be found hiding in eelgrass and in rocky areas. They can also be caught by tossing a fresh fish head to the bottom of a tidepool. In five to ten minutes, crabs will suddenly come forth to eat the bait and can be added to your bait bucket. Hook these crabs by penetrating the seam of the upper and lower shell from the rear center into the main body. *Hermit crabs* are found inhabiting abandoned shells of other bay dwellers. Crack the shell open to expose the crab. Remove the large claw, then set the hook from mid-underbody up through the top. Crabs are excellent bait for tautog (blackfish).

Clams are turned out of the sand and mud along the shore using pitchforks or shovels at low water. Setting a hook in clam flesh is little more certain than setting a hook in Jell-O, though

BAY
FISH
AND
HOW
TO
CATCH
THEM

163

A shovel or pitchfork is a big help when digging for clams at low tide. STEVEN KROUS PHOTO.

the neck is somewhat more durable. If the bait stays on long enough, there is a good chance a flounder or striped bass will take the clam's place on your hook.

Bait stores around Narragansett Bay supply fishermen with *American eels* for bait. These eels are greenish-brown in color. The best size eel for bait is an inch in diameter and 12 inches in length, although these eels can grow more than three feet in length. They live in muddy areas of brackish water. Eels can be captured in baited minnow traps or by using fresh cut bait on tiny hooks. A Little Compton fisherman says, "If you don't catch anything on a live eel, then there is nothing around

American eel, not dangerous, just slippery. COURTESY OF THE RHODE ISLAND DEPARTMENT OF ENVIRONMENTAL MANAGEMENT.

to catch." Handling eels is not dangerous. They have tiny jaws and sandpaper for teeth; however, they are slippery. Use a rag or cotton glove to grip an eel while forcing the hook up from the bottom and out through the top jaw forward of the eyes. Do not let the eel swim to the bottom, as he will wind himself and your line into the rocks. At the first sign of a strike, let the catch run for a distance before setting the hook. Rarely will a bass or bluefish swallow the eel and hook on the first pass.

The *pogy* is a small fish that is most commonly known in other regions as Atlantic menhaden. Pogy are silvery with brassy sides. Adults have dark spots on the sides. They average nine inches in length and can grow to 14 inches, and are often seen in schools just breaking the surface near shore and in anchorages while feeding on tiny zooplankton and fry. At times, schools of pogy froth the surface in an attempt to escape the jaws of swarming bluefish. The flesh is dark and oily, making it excellent for cut bait or for grinding into chum. A live pogy hooked through the back from the right side to the left side, avoiding the backbone, will prove effective for catching bluefish, bass and mackerel. An angler can catch his own pogy by fishing specks of cut bait on tiny #11 hooks floated near the surface. A more common method is to cast a 7/0 weighted treble hook into a school of pogy. Snap the rod back sharply through as great an arc as possible, then quickly reel in the slack in preparation for another snap. Using this technique, you will almost certainly snag a pogy. Such a blind fishing method is surprisingly effective.

Shrimp and *squid* are excellent bait for all types of fishing in Narragansett Bay. An angler can catch his own shrimp and squid using special nets and jigs during seasonal runs. Most often these baits are bought fresh or frozen at nominal expense at tackle stores. Shrimp and squid spoil easily. As with any bait, use only when fresh and take great care to keep it that way. Rancid bait that has been fermenting in the sun is as unattractive to a fish as it is to a fisherman.

Chum is ground-up bits of fish that is gradually released in the water, creating a trail for fish to follow to your baited hook. A fisherman can cut or grind up leftover parts of fish after fillets have been removed or grind up whole pogies or other inedible fish with a hand-operated grinder. The chum can be discharged directly overboard or frozen in plastic buckets and hung overboard in an onion sack to thaw gradually. Holes poked in cans of oily cat food and hung overboard can form an effective chum line. It is important to keep an uninterrupted slick of chum flowing to lead fish to your hook.

Catch in the Bay

Bluefish. This sometimes fierce fish can make sharks and barracudas appear as tame as bowl fish. The jaws of bluefish are dangerous to fishermen and have been known to nip permanent chunks from legs and hands. Immobilize a bluefish with a gaff as the fish is hauled aboard then be sure to club the fish or contain the fish in an icebox before releasing the gaff. Larger blues should be returned to the ocean unharmed as they are not suitable for human consumption. For this reason, barbless hooks should be used when schools of blues are hitting hard. With the fish alongside and slack in the line, it is easy for the barbless hook to back out of the fish's jaw. For any fishing, common steel hooks should be used. If for any reason the fish escapes with the hook still in its jaw, a steel hook will eventually rust away, a stainless steel hook will not.

Season: To fuel their long migrations and spawning, bluefish feed furiously when Narragansett Bay water temperatures edge upward into the low 60s, around early June. To prepare for their southerly migration, another heavy feeding spell begins when water temperatures dip into the mid 60s in September.

Size: Average size is five pounds, but 10-pound catches are common. The record catch is 24 pounds.

Edibility: Fair. With their oily, dark flesh, fish over five pounds are too oily and strong tasting.

BAY
FISH
AND
HOW
TO
CATCH
THEM

165

Bluefish, when small, a tasty catch. COURTESY OF THE RHODE ISLAND DEPARTMENT OF ENVIRONMENTAL MANAGEMENT.

The dark strip should be removed from the fillet before eating.

Fishing methods: Will strike on any live or cut bait and any type of lure when they are actively feeding.

Atlantic Mackerel. These are small but strong fighting migratory fish related to tuna and skipjack.

Season: May through November.

Size: One to two pounds, but can reach four pounds.

Edibility: Excellent. Mackerel have a slightly oily but rich flavor with medium texture. Mackerel are high in Omega-3 acids which are reported to reduce the risk of heart attack. As with tuna, mackerel must be gutted and iced immediately to avoid scombroid poisoning, which is the result of humans ingesting histamine and other compounds that rapidly develop in tuna that has not been handled properly.

Fishing methods: Drift-fishing with live shrimp or cut bait, jigging just off the bottom with mackerel jigs or trolling with silver spoons or feathers.

Tautog. These are known locally as blackfish. Tautog are territorial bottom fish that can be found in rocky areas feeding on mussels.

Season: April through November, then they migrate to deeper water.

Size: Average size is three pounds. The record catch is 21 pounds.

Edibility: Fair. Tautog has lean, firm, white flesh that is bland if not cooked with seasonings.

Tautog, known locally as blackfish. COURTESY OF THE RHODE ISLAND DEPARTMENT OF ENVIRONMENTAL MANAGEMENT.

Fishing methods: Legal minimum size was 12 inches in 1989. Bottom fishing with crabs, seaworms, clams or cut bait works well.

Striped Bass. Bass are an important coastal game fish whose numbers have been declining.

Season: June through November.

Size: Average is five to 35 pounds. The record catch is 73 pounds, but the fish can reach 100 pounds.

Edibility: Excellent, with soft white flakey flesh similar to South Florida grouper.

Fishing methods: Legal minimum size was 36 inches in 1989. Anglers should check frequently for latest state regulations. Caught near shore with live and cut bait or by casting into wave washed rock using "popper" type lures.

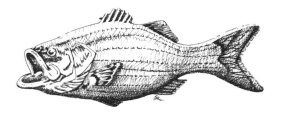

Striped bass, popular game fish with declining numbers. LAURA HOLT. COURTESY OF THE RHODE ISLAND DEPARTMENT OF ENVIRONMENTAL MANAGEMENT.

Scup. Also called porgy. These are small, bottom-feeding fish.

Season: April through October.

Size: 12 to 14 inches in length and one to two pounds in weight, but can grow to 18 inches and three to four pounds.

Edibility: Excellent pan fish, but boney.

Fishing methods: Bottom fishing with small hooks, such as #5 hooks, and small shrimp, worms, crabs or cut bait.

Weakfish. Known locally as squeteague, these fish are strong fighters named for the ease with which a hook will tear from their mouth.

Season: May through mid-October. Catches are better in spring months.

Size: Average two to four pounds, up to 10 pounds. Legal size limit in 1989 was 12 inches.

Edibility: Excellent.

Fishing methods: They feed extensively at night. Use most cut and live baits, silver lures, bucktail jigs.

Summer Flounder. These fish are also called fluke, and are a flat, bottom dwelling fish, with both eyes on the top side. They are easily distinguishable from winter flounder since they possess a large, heavily fanged mouth and the gill slit extends from the left side of the fish towards the center.

Season: Late April through September but late June or early July is the peak.

Size: Most often two to five pounds but 10 pounders are often taken.

Edibility: Excellent. Firm white meat with a delicate, rich flavor.

Fishing method: Minimum legal size was 14 inches in 1989. Bottom fishing with cut or live bait or deep trolling with artifical lures. Chumming is very effective.

Winter Flounder. Also known as flatfish, these are distinguished from summer flounder

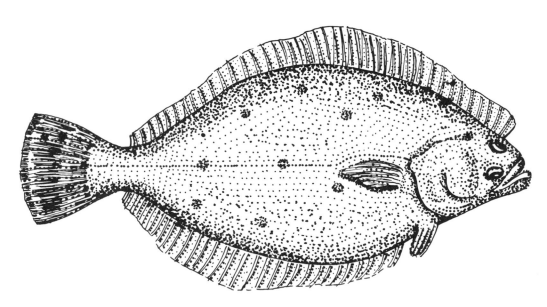

Winter flounder, flatfish with small mouths. COURTESY OF THE RHODE ISLAND DEPARTMENT OF ENVIRONMENTAL MANAGEMENT.

by their small mouth and teeth and the gill slit that extends from the right side to the center of the fish.

Season: Can be caught most of the year; however, the best catches are in the cooler months since winter flounder avoid water temperatures above 59°F.

Size: Most commonly 12 to 15 inches in length and 1½ to two pounds and at times reaching 18 inches and four pounds.

Edibility: One of the best.

Fishing methods: Minimum legal size was 11 inches in 1989. Flounder feed on an incoming tide. Bottom fish with light tackle—eight-pound test line and #10 long shank hooks to suit the flounder's small mouth. Bait your hooks with sandworms, blood worms, clams, or cut bait.

Filleting

1) Lay the fish on a cutting board. With a *sharp* knife, make an incision through the skin from the top of the head arcing down behind the gill and pectoral fin then continuing to just behind the pelvic fin.

2) At the top of the head, slice through the skin and into the flesh along the backbone all the way to the tail. Repeat this incision several times, slicing deeper into the flesh as you shave the knife blade just over the ribs.

3) Carefully free the fillet, leaving the rib bones attached to the backbone. If done properly, all entrails will be left intact in the fish. You now have a fillet free of most, if not all, bones, but with skin still attached. Flip the fish over and repeat the procedure.

4) Lay the fillets skin side down on the board. Hold the blade of the knife flat and start a cut between the skin and flesh at the tail. Grip the skin and slice with the blade of the knife still held flat against the skin. The fillet will peel away from the skin. Finger the fillet for any tiny bones that may need to be removed.

BAY
FISH
AND
HOW
TO
CATCH
THEM

167

Shellfish of the Bay

Quahog. This hardshell clam, pronounced "KO-hog," is the state shell of Rhode Island. Indians made their purple wampum from the edge of this shell. Quahogs are the most plentiful bivalve in Narragansett Bay, supporting a large commercial industry. Quahogs live in mud and sand at all depths of Narragansett Bay by filter-feeding on plankton from the water. At two years old they reach legal size of one-inch hinge width. These small, tender quahogs are called "littlenecks." Medium-size quahogs are known as cherrystones. The oldest quahogs, which can live up to 25 years and grow to five to six inches, are called chowder clams. Quahogs can be dug using special deepwater rakes, but the best way for recreational fishermen to catch them is to don a mask and snorkel and unearth them from the bay bottom. They usually lie exposed or just beneath the surface of the sand or mud, and lightly fanning the area with your hands will reveal them.

The quahog, the state shell of Rhode Island. COURTESY OF THE RHODE ISLAND DEPARTMENT OF ENVIRONMENTAL MANAGEMENT.

Soft-Shell Clam. These clams, also called "steamers," live buried in sand and mud in the intertidal zone, where they are exposed to air twice a day. At low tide, walking over a soft-shell's territory causes the frightened clam to withdraw its siphon creating a minigeyser of water to spew into the air, revealing its position. When you see a geyser, turn up the sand in the area with a shovel or pitchfork and then dig around the resulting hole with a smaller trowel to unearth the steamer clams. At one year steamers attain the legal size of 1½ inches across their longest axis. These clams are as delicious as smaller quahogs; however, the cleaner the shore and surrounding water, the better the flavor will be.

The oyster, once the basis of a huge bay industry. COURTESY OF THE RHODE ISLAND DEPARTMENT OF ENVIRONMENTAL MANAGEMENT.

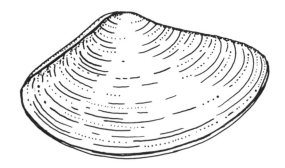

The soft-shell clam, delicious as "steamers." COURTESY OF THE RHODE ISLAND DEPARTMENT OF ENVIRONMENTAL MANAGEMENT.

Surf Clam. Surf clams live buried in sand where there is heavy breaking surf. These clams can grow to seven inches and are the largest bivalve on the north Atlantic Coast. The minimum size for the taking of surf clams is 5½ inches across the longest axis. The flavor is as good as the quahog.

Blue Mussel. In America, mussels are an underutilized food source. Mussels live attached to rocks and pilings in intertidal zones where clean tidal flows exist, and can be easily handpicked at low tide. Blue mussels grow to three inches and may be harvested if they are at least 1½ inches long. When steamed, the blue mussel has an excellent flavor, enjoyed by those who prefer a fuller, less delicate flavor than the quahog.

Ribbed Mussel. This mussel lives in muddy flats, brackish, and often times polluted water. Because of its less clean environment, the flavor is inferior to the blue mussel. Ribbed mussels grow to two to four inches across. Legal size for harvesting is 1½ inches.

Oyster. Before the turn of the century, oysters supported a huge commercial industry on Narragansett Bay. Today, harvest season is from September 15 to May 15. Oysters grow to eight inches in length in intertidal zones. For harvesting, oysters must be at least three inches long, and they can be handpicked—if you can find them!

Bay Scallop. Unlike other shellfish, scallops can swim through the water and over the bay floor. By snapping their shells together, they produce a jet of water that propels them in a jerky motion in the direction of the shell's hinge. At one time, Greenwich Bay supported the largest East Coast scallop fishery. Scallops live in eelgrass beds three to five feet deep and grow to four inches in diameter. As the eelgrass disappeared, so did the scallops. Today, there is a short harvest season beginning in October.

Baby scallops, jet-propelled swimmers with a short harvest season. COURTESY OF THE RHODE ISLAND DEPARTMENT OF ENVIRONMENTAL MANAGEMENT.

Polluted Shellfish Areas, May 1988

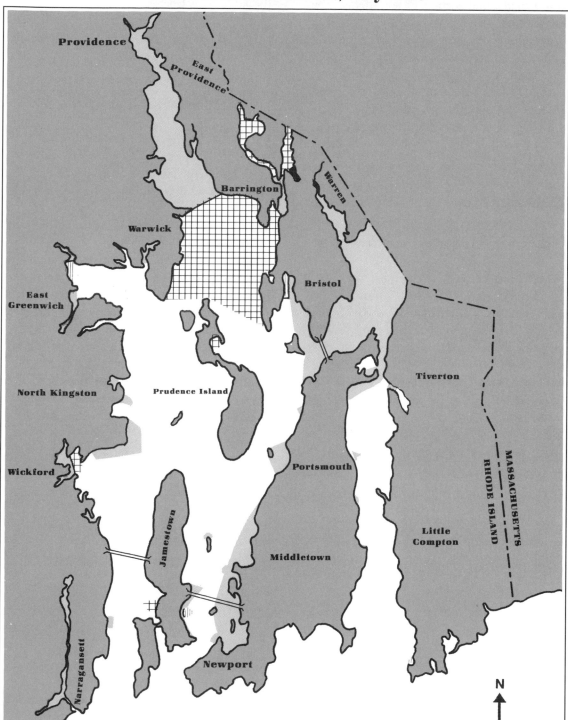

SCALE: 1″=3.6 MILES **Polluted Area** **Conditional Area**

Seasonal Closures (May 28 to September 30) **Approved Shellfishing Area**

BAY

FISH

AND

HOW

TO

CATCH

THEM

169

Whelk. Known locally as conch, this is the largest snail found north of Cape Hatteras, growing to nine inches. Whelk travel the bottom throughout Narragansett Bay, feeding on other shellfish, and are easily picked from the bottom where they rest. The meat is marinated and appears on seafood restaurant menus as "snail salad," although not everyone considers the whelk palatable. In no way does the flavor of the whelk compare to the Queen Conch found in Florida and Bahamian waters.

Opening a Bivalve

To open a bivalve such as a clam or mussel, which will be eaten raw, the shellfish must be thoroughly chilled in a refrigerator or iced for half an hour. The cold numbs the incisor muscle which holds the shells together. Hold the shell in the palm of one hand. With the other hand, force a dull bladed knife between the shells at the large, more rounded, end of the shell. Use the forefinger of the hand holding the shell to help pull the blade of the knife all the way to the hinge. As the knife moves between the shells, the incisor muscle will be severed. When the knife blade reaches the hinge, give the knife a twist to force the shells away from each other.

A Word About "Red Tide"

In other parts of New England, shellfish beds are periodically closed each summer season due to a proliferation or "bloom" of tiny organisms called dinoflagellates that stain the sea a nasty red color and taint shellfish in surrounding waters. This so-called red tide can poison humans who ingest infected shellfish.

While red tides occur frequently in Connecticut, Massachusetts and Maine, the phenomenon fortunately is not a problem in the waters of Narragansett Bay. Though state biologists are hard-pressed to explain why, there has never been an outbreak of red tide in the confines of the bay. Although the organisms that cause the tide have been seen in bay water, concentrations have never reached levels acute enough to cause closure of shellfishing areas or threaten anyone's health.

Beachcombing

Around

the

Bay

On the Narragansett Bay shoreline, there is a tremendous amount of marine life, vegetation, and bird and animal life to be discovered at the water's edge. The following guide will help you identify marine life, intertidal grasses and interesting treasures at the shore.

Crushing and grinding their way to the sea, glaciers deposited the first sugary sands along the shores of Narragansett Bay. The whiteness of our beaches comes mainly from crushed white quartz interspersed with particles of clam and snail shells as well as minerals, rocks, and gems of various colors. More sand is added and erosion continues with the influence of tides and currents carrying sand from the continental shelf to our shores, and with the help of rainfall and rivers carrying eroded material from inland. Wave and wind action deposits the finer grains of sand high on shore, leaving larger grains and rocks to be buffeted and scoured in the eternal motion of the surf. Prime examples of the process in action are rocks called "cabochons," which have become rounded from rolling to and fro in the surf. Often, pinkish cabochons are all that remains of a red clay brick; cabochons formed from coal and glass bottles make colorful collectibles and are fun to find while combing through the sand.

Farther up on the beach, strong onshore winds pile up sand to form sand dunes, where sand-binding plants stabilize the shifting grains. There are times when man helps nature by installing sand fences or burying discarded Christmas trees to help secure sand dunes till plants can take root.

Beach grass along the shore of Greene Island in the Upper Bay. LYNDA CHILDRESS PHOTO.

Shore grasses and plants grow where conditions are favorable for individual plants. Tolerance to sea salt is particularly important.

Shore Grasses and Seaweeds

Tall salt marsh cordgrass is generally the first line of vegetation found on shore, as it can tolerate exposure to tidal flooding. Once rooted, underground stems spread out quickly to help stabilize the shore.

Salt meadow cordgrass is a shorter variety of cordgrass found where sea water floods for a shorter period of time.

Eelgrass is a thin, long vascular plant that grows in great beds in shallow water. As depth increases and light penetration decreases, the beds of eelgrass become less extensive. Eelgrass beds are a hatchery and nursery for all forms of marine life as well as a permanent home for crabs, shrimp, shellfish, and other inhabitants.

Seaweed washed ashore is generally representative of what is living immediately offshore. Here are a few seaweeds that are commonly seen during a walk along the shore:

Rockweeds are some of the most common types of seaweeds sighted along the shoreline. These vary from weeds that have bladders filled with air that can be popped with the fingers to shiny brown weed with a spiraling, ribbony appearance. This seaweed was used by the Indians in shoreside clambakes and still is used to surround shellfish in clambakes today.

Although it is a fast growing, tough seaweed, *kelp* is actually a brown algae. Kelp does not grow in sufficient quantity along the Rhode Island coast to warrant harvesting as is done in California, but is a prevalent sight while beachcombing nonetheless.

Found in shallow water, the green, broad-leafed *sea lettuce* is actually an algae. It, too, is a frequent sight while strolling the shores of Narragansett Bay.

Marine Life

In the intertidal zone (the beach area between high and low tide) an abundance of marine life lies buried in the sand or can be found nestled among the clam, oyster and scallop shells on the beach.

The *razor clam* gets its name from its resemblance to the handle of an old fashioned straight razor. The shell is four to 10 inches long and conceals a powerful digging foot which can expand to half the length of the shell. When the razor clam senses threatening vibrations from the feet of beachcombers or their shovels, it can dig its way to safety almost as fast as the approaching shovel. If you are able to out-dig the razor clam, its meat can be cooked and eaten the same way as the soft-shelled clam. The flavor of the razor clam is said to be superior to all other clams.

Slipper shells are often found living stacked on top of one another and are one of the most common shells found along shore. They are also called "boat shells," because an individual shell can be floated on calm water. The large gastropod on the bottom of the pile is always a female; lone shells are always female, and they attract males, which stack up on top of the female. When one of the females dies, the next male in line will conveniently change gender, turning into a female to keep the situation balanced. All of these gastropods begin life as males and convert to female as necessary.

The *skate* has a shape similar to that of a stingray, and is closely related. A skate has a cartilaginous skeleton, but does not have the stingray's barb at the base of its tail. Skates live on the bay floor, feeding on fish, crabs, and lobsters.

When mythical mermaids were believed to inhabit the world's oceans, it was supposed that this black leathery case was a *"mermaid's purse."* Actually, it is the egg case of a skate that broke free of its attachment on the bay bottom before the skate hatched.

The *whelk egg case* is a string of pouches that

once was attached to the bay bottom by the whelk. Before the young shellfish hatched, the string was dislodged and washed ashore to dry in the sun. You can shake this parchment-like string and hear the rattle of the small whelks inside.

The *horseshoe crab* is not a crab at all. It is a living fossil that has not evolved in 200 million years, and its contemporary relatives are spiders and scorpions. Contrary to popular belief, the horseshoe crab is completely harmless and live horseshoe crabs should be protected by the beachcomber. Horseshoe crabs feed on young clams and sea worms on the bottom of the bay. When the crabs molt their shells, the discarded armor is often found intact, washed up on shore, and often is mistaken for a dead horseshoe crab. The blood of the horseshoe crab is extremely valuable; it is being used in medical experiments to detect harmful bacteria in the blood of humans.

Periwinkles live on boulders, pilings and rocks in the intertidal zone, feeding on algae. The tiny shellfish were carried to New England from Nova Scotia as passengers on the hulls of sailing ships.

Although most periwinkles found in Narragansett Bay are small, they are eaten by some and are said to have a pleasing flavor. After collecting a bucket of periwinkles, some folks steam or boil them and dip them in garlic butter. Periwinkles should not be eaten raw and should be cooked soon after collecting. The shellfish can grow as large as an inch across and can be any shade of green, brown or yellow.

Chitons are the most primitive mollusk in Narragansett Bay. They are found in shaded crevices and on the underside of smooth rocks. Smooth surfaces aid their great suction ability, making them nearly impossible to pry loose. At night, or on very cloudy days, chitons come out of hiding to feed on algae. They can be loosened from their rock with a sharp sideways blow or pried loose with a knife. Chitons can be prepared as food in the same way as periwinkles.

Commonly—and erroneously—called "starfish," *sea stars* live at all depths of Narragansett Bay and can be found in shaded areas of tide pools. They travel across the bottom on hundreds of tube feet and can hover just above the bay bottom allowing currents to carry them to new feeding grounds. Sea stars are destructive to commercial shellfish beds, since their strong arms and suction feet can pull open even the strongest quahog. The sea star's stomach envelops the soft flesh of its prey and quickly digests it. At one time, sea stars were deliberately harvested from the bay to help save the shellfish beds. They were disposed of ashore or ground into fertilizer or poultry feed.

Sea urchins live in all oceans of the world. These relatives of the sea star can be found in shaded areas of tide pools. They feed on seaweeds, shellfish, and other sea urchins. Sea urchins are not poisonous; however, some species of urchins have brittle, sharp spines that will break off easily in human skin if stepped on or handled. In Japan, raw sea urchins are a delicacy.

Sand dollars are related to sea stars and sea urchins. The thin, white, three-inch circular chips found along the shore are the skeletons of the sand dollar. Sand dollars live just buried in sand in all depths of water and feed on small worms and other organisms. A rattling noise is heard when the bleached out skeleton of the sand dollar is shaken. The noise is caused by five loosened teeth, called "Aristotle's lanterns," because the teeth resemble old Greek oil lamps used when Aristotle first studied the creature. The teeth are also called "doves of peace" by beachcombers, who liken them to tiny white birds.

Jellyfish are the most primitive form of multicelled animals. Although they can swim, their movements are more influenced by tides and currents. Stinging cells are located on the tentacles of all jellyfish although not all jellyfish have stingers capable of penetrating the skin of humans.

Although they are transparent and look something like a small jellyfish, the *sea walnut* and *sea gooseberry* are not related to the jellyfish. They have tentacles, but they do not have stinging cells. Biologically, they are more advanced than the jellyfish. At night, when bay water is disturbed by an outboard engine or the splashing of an oar, much of the bioluminescence you see is created by the sea walnut and gooseberry.

Narragansett Bay Birdlife and Wildlife

During a cruise on Narragansett Bay you will encounter a diversity of bird life, sea life and, during hikes ashore, large and small wildlife. Because Narragansett Bay is an estuary, it has a large population of shore birds, some of which are rarely seen elsewhere in New England.

On shoreside hikes through wildlife refuges near the water, you're likely to see a variety of small mammals including cottontail rabbits, red foxes, chipmunks, and gray squirrels. On Prudence Island, which harbors one of New England's densest populations of white-tailed deer, sighting one of these timid creatures with unusually long and doglike white tails is practically guaranteed.

We carry aboard a library of nature guides to help us identify and enjoy the birds, animals and fish we see while cruising the bay. We include here descriptions of some of the most common birds and animals you're likely to encounter during a cruise on Narragansett Bay.

Shore Birds

Gulls are long-winged, square-tailed swimming birds with slightly hooked beaks for catching prey. They survive by eating plant and marine animal life and by relentless scavenging. They don't dive for their seafood as do terns and pelicans. *Herring*

Herring gulls are plentiful around the bay. LYNDA CHILDRESS PHOTO.

gulls are abundant in and around Narragansett Bay. The herring gull eats mollusks after carrying them aloft and then dropping them to crack open the shells. Flocks of these raucous creatures are apt to materialize begging for handouts the minute they spy a cockpit gathering. This is the most common seagull, and has a gray back, white head and tail feathers, dark wing tips and a yellow beak with a red spot. Slightly larger than herring gulls, *black-backed gulls* have an unmistakable black back, and are seen in increasing numbers in and around Narragansett Bay. This gull's wing beats are slow and its cry is lower-pitched and more even than that of the herring gull. Once a rare sight around the bay, the pixieish *laughing gull* is now a common sight here in summer months. The laughing gull has a black-capped head, reddish beak, dark gray back and solid, dark wing tips. The gull gets its name from its distinctive voice, a chuckling "ha-ha-ha-ha" sound.

The *American oystercatcher* is an exotic-looking bird and a rare but thrilling sight on Narragansett Bay. In the Upper Bay, we were lucky enough to sight a pair of these unusual birds on tiny Spar Island in Mount Hope Bay. Oystercatchers are shy birds and prefer unpopulated mudflats and sandy beaches, where they feed on shellfish by breaking them open with their long, orange beaks—hence their name. Oystercatchers are loners and flocks are usually small and segregated from other shore birds. Oystercatchers have black heads, grayish backs and wingspans with a distinctive white V when in flight. If you hear this bird's call you'll take notice—its voice is a shrill "eeep eeep eeep" that stands apart from the calls of other shore birds.

Plovers are small shore birds that can be seen scurrying about near the shoreline, often taking small, rapid steps and then stopping before repeating the process. They feed on insects and small marine animals along the shore and have shorter bills than similar looking sandpipers.

The less common *piping plover* recently caused a flap on Narragansett Bay with the closure of one of the south coast's more popular beaches to protect its nests. The small birds have pale backs, dark neck bands, and yellow legs and feet.

Bodies are rather plump. Piping plovers can be seen on dry sandy beaches and its musical, two-noted call is distinctive.

Also seen along the shore, *sandpipers* have longer beaks and longer legs than plovers. Plumage is more mottled. Along Narragansett Bay shores, the spotted sandpiper is the most commonly seen. Like the plover, the sandpiper feeds on shore insects, mollusks, and worms. Spotted sandpipers bob their tails almost non-stop while foraging along the shore; their call is shrill and multi-noted.

Terns are small, slight birds with forked tails, long wings with a distinctive crook, and pointed bills. They fly low over the water searching for small fish and insects, and dive for their prey from the air.

Friendly little *common terns* are a familiar sight on a summer bay cruise, especially in the Upper Bay. The small gray and white birds have bright reddish orange bills and black wing tips, with a partial black cap on the head. Their call, a high-pitched chirr, usually precedes them. *Least terns* are less frequently seen than common terns, but are sometimes sighted along sandy beaches. The least tern's bill is yellow, and the tail is not forked, which distinguishes it from the common tern. This tern is smaller than other terns, and is also called a *little tern*.

Double-crested cormorants are very commonly seen in large flocks around the bay perched on rocks, pilings or isolated docks, these 27-inch-tall, black-brown birds with orange bills eat fish. Cormorants swim partially submerged with necks tilted upward, periscope-like. They have webbed feet and dive and swim under water in search of prey. These long-necked birds often dry their wings by spreading them out to either side like a cape as they sit sunning on rocks or docks. On Narragansett Bay, cormorants are almost as plentiful as seagulls, and are present in just about any anchorage.

NARRAGANSETT
BAY
BIRDLIFE
AND
WILDLIFE

175

Herons and Egrets

Herons and egrets are large, wading birds with long legs, necks and bills that stalk the shallows of coastal shallows searching for fish, mice, insects, and other aquatic life. The birds are seen with their long necks either extended or curled down on their shoulders in an "s" shape.

Near the bay's many marshy areas, and on rivers and streams that feed the bay, *great egrets* can sometimes be glimpsed stalking the shallows. Look for these majestic birds in Prudence Island's Coggeshall Cove. Plumage is white, legs are black, and bill is yellow. This is the largest egret, and looks almost prehistoric with its large body and long neck. Mature birds stand almost three feet tall.

Smaller than the great egret, the *snowy egret* is a frequent sight near the shores of the bay, especially in or near marshy areas. Its name undoubtedly has much to do with its snow white feathers. This bird has a black bill and black legs, but its feet are startlingly yellow. Often, snowy egrets can be seen perched on docks or pilings alongside seagulls and cormorants.

Until recently, *cattle egrets* were rare on Narragansett Bay. While less frequently seen than snowy egrets, chances are good you'll encounter one of these birds while exploring the marshy areas of the bay. The cattle egret is distinguished from others by its shorter neck and more hunched posture. Legs are shorter as well, and are yellowish in color. The bird gets its name because it is fond of feeding on insects in coastal pastureland as well as marshes, and sometimes is seen perched on cows' backs.

The spectacular *great blue heron* never fails to impress, no matter how many times you see one. Great blues favor marshes, swamps, shores, and tidal flats around Narragansett Bay, and if you look carefully in these areas, chances are you'll spot one. The great blue is the largest North American heron, standing more than three feet tall. The head is whitish, with a dark crop of

A snowy egret in flight. STEVEN KROUS PHOTO.

NARRAGANSETT
BAY
BIRDLIFE
AND
WILDLIFE

177

A great blue heron looks almost prehistoric perching in a small tree. STEVEN KROUS PHOTO.

trailing feathers, and it has a light-colored bib of spiky feathers and large, yellow-orange beak. From a distance, the body feathers of the great blue appear blue, hence the name. These birds are often seen standing stock-still or stalking the shallows with head hunched forward searching for fish.

Darker and smaller than the great blue, the *little blue heron* is less frequently seen. It has dark gray coloration with a brownish head and neck. The bill has a distinctive black tip and legs are blueish green. Like the great blue, this heron favors marshy areas near the shore. Its height is just under two feet.

Abundant but not often seen, the *green heron* is sometimes glimpsed when it is immature, during which time it has a brown, mottled appearance. Mature birds have blueish-gray plumage with a brownish neck, a dark cap of stringy head feathers and orange legs. Its call is sharp. The bird stands just over a foot tall.

The exotic-looking *black crowned night heron* is always a treat to see in tidal marshy areas and along the shore, sometimes roosting in nearby trees. It is often seen hunting in the shallows at night or early in the morning. This heron stands 20 inches high, has a white breast and gray and black back, and a black crown with a flowing trail of light-colored feathers down its back. We sighted one of these birds on Hope Island very early one morning, perched on a rock in the warm sun searching surrounding waters for fish.

Similar to the black crowned heron in appearance, the *yellow-crowned night heron* is less frequently seen in Narragansett Bay. To distinguish it, look for a speckled back, grayer breast feathers, a distinctive white patch under the eye and a larger black crown accented by a tuft of trailing yellow feathers on the very top of its head. This bird also has longer legs than the black crowned night heron.

Waterfowl

Waterfowl, or various types of ducks, geese, and swans, are characterized by short legs, webbed feet, long necks and narrow, pointed wings. Their bills are flat, and are equipped to strain what the bird eats.

Large flocks of *Canada geese* are common on Narragansett Bay, and you will often hear their honking as they pass overhead before you are aware they are approaching. These geese are fond of open fields and pastureland near the coast, but can often be seen enjoying the water in quiet coves and harbor corners as well. The geese are large, standing up to 25 inches high, and are quite plump. Long, black necks are marked by a distinctive white chin strap on the throat, and body feathers are shades of brown merging to whitish at the breast and black-tipped at the tail. The Sakonnet River was named "place of the black goose" by the Indians for these prevalent fowl.

There is no more regal sight than the large,

A mute swan: always picture-perfect posture. STEVEN KROUS PHOTO.

white, orange-billed *mute swan* especially common in the waters of the Middle and Upper Bay. This swan looks as if it is permanently posing, and holds its neck in a graceful curve while paddling quietly about. This swan emits a low grunt, and hisses when provoked. Flocks of these birds often will paddle by to beg for food, and some can be quite aggressive once fed, craning their long necks into the cockpit and nipping at unwary fingers. They can deliver a nasty bite, so be careful if you feed them. In flight, the swans' wings create a low reverberating hum that is unmistakable when they pass overhead.

Ducks, like swans, are a common sight while cruising the waters of the Middle and Upper Bay. Colorful *mallard* males have a green head, white neck and reddish orange breast with a classic yellow bill. The female is spotted brown. Mallards are often seen in flocks with other types of ducks. When they fly, both male and female have a blue strip at the base of each wing. These ducks eat vegetation, but sometimes consume mollusks, fish and insects.

The modest-looking *American black duck* is found in shallow coastal waters and is actually brown, not black, except for its white wing patches, visible in flight. The head is paler than the body and like the mallard, its call is a loud quack. The black duck is the most common Atlantic Coast duck.

Hawks and
Birds of Prey

Osprey, large, regal birds, also called "fish hawks," once were so common on the waters of Narragansett Bay they were considered a nuisance. Decimated in later years by increasing use of the pesticide DDT, their population in Rhode Island dropped to a low of seven birds in 1974. Today, thanks to the ban on DDT, they are back in the bay and their numbers are increasing steadily, with 31 known nests counted in 1988. The soaring fish hawks are especially common along the Sakonnet River, where they are often seen hunting high in the sky. Ospreys flying overhead are distinguishable from seagulls by their wing beat, which is a dogged, slow and consistent flapping, only occasionally pausing to glide. Wings are long with ragged feathers on the tips, and have conspicuous crooks marked by black spots. Coloration is dark on the back, white on the breast with stripes of white and dark feathers on the underside of wings and tail in flight. When perching, it stands about two feet tall. The head of the osprey is similar to that of the bald eagle, but with a black band on the cheek. The bird's beak is hooked downward, and it catches prey by diving for it feet first. The osprey's call is a loud and clear whistle.

The venerable *red-tailed hawk* can be seen perched in tall trees near Narragansett Bay anchorages, particularly in early morning, or soaring above pastureland and marshes near the water. Red-tailed hawks prey on rabbits and small rodents, and are distinguished by their size—18 inches tall—and reddish colored tail. In flight, they are distinguished from the osprey by their soaring, as well as a less pronounced crook in the wing.

The *American kestrel*, a small falcon, can be seen near open country along the shores of the bay and along the banks of its many marshy rivers and ponds. Just 8½ inches tall, the kestrel often hovers waiting for prey to appear, with fast, hummingbird-like wing beats. The male is colorful with a black, white, and reddish head and back, and blueish wing feathers. The breast is white with dark spots, and the face is black and white.

The *marsh hawk* (or *Northern harrier*) is common in marshes, as its name suggests. In flight, it has a whitish underbelly; feathers on its back and wing tops are brownish in females, gray in males, but both have a white spot just above the tail. Males are more gray than females.

NARRAGANSETT
BAY
BIRDLIFE
AND
WILDLIFE

179

Dangerous Sea Life

Fortunately, there is little in the way of threatening sea life to encounter while cruising Narragansett Bay. Several types of non-stinging jellyfish are present as the water warms up in mid to late summer. You may notice blooms of *"sea walnuts"* or comb jellies when you dive in for a swim. Small, about the size and shape of a walnut, these are often felt rather than seen, and are completely harmless. In large numbers, they may keep the squeamish from diving overboard, but they certainly are no threat. *Moon jellyfish* may also be sighted, and these, while they may look more threatening, are not harmful to humans either. Moon jellies are larger, up to almost a foot across, with small tentacles. They propel themselves upward and downward through with water by flapping slowly. The only jellyfish to be concerned about in these waters are *Portuguese man-of-war*, which infrequently ride the Gulf Stream north from the tropical waters that are their normal habitat. The Portuguese man-of-war looks like a purplish floating bleach bottle and has an unmistakable ridge or "sail" that rides just above the water's surface. These jellyfish have very long, poisonous tentacles that can extend to a surprising 165 feet from their bodies. Their sting is toxic, painful, and can cause serious symptoms that can include shock and interference with heart and lung function. While there have been no recorded fatalities resulting from a Portuguese man-of-war sting, it should certainly be avoided at all costs. If these jellyfish are spotted in the area, avoid swimming; and avoid touching any found on shore. If you are seriously stung, seek medical attention immediately.

Unlike in many areas, *sharks* are not a worry on Narragansett Bay. Harmless nurse sharks sometimes meander into the bay from the waters of Rhode Island Sound, and larger sharks have been caught off Block Island, but in the bay there has never been a recorded shark attack.

Wildlife around the Bay

Although there is other wildlife present in the state, these are the animals you are most likely to encounter on a visit to the bay by water:

Once almost extinct in much of New England, the *white-tailed deer* is now more abundant than ever. Prudence Island is home to one of the most dense herds of white-tails in New England, and chances are you'll be lucky enough to catch a glimpse of one or more of these shy animals while hiking ashore on the island. White-tails are reddish brown with white on the belly, nose, neck, eyes, and inside their ears. Their long, doglike tails are white on the underside, and stand straight up when the deer is alarmed. Signs of deer as you walk ashore include paths through grassy areas, depressions in underbrush where deer have bedded down, scars or oblong sections of trees where bark has been rubbed off, and tracks and droppings. Deer tracks are abundant on Prudence. Look for depressions in the mud shaped like split hearts with a deeper imprint made by the front of the foot. Droppings are dark, oblong pellets. Most likely sighting times are late afternoon or early evening when deer emerge from the thickets to feed on woody vegetation and green plants. The white-tail is mainly nocturnal, and goes to sleep around dawn, sleeping most of the day. The deer are fast runners and excellent swimmers, which explains how they reached the islands of Narragansett Bay from the dense woodlands of the mainland years ago.

You may not catch a glimpse of the shy *red fox* during a cruise on the bay, but you may notice signs of it during hikes ashore. The red fox is small and doglike in appearance, with reddish brown fur and a large, bushy tail. The animals

A white-tailed deer is startled by a photographer on Prudence Island.

COURTESY OF THE RHODE ISLAND DEPARTMENT OF ENVIRONMENTAL MANAGEMENT, DIVISION OF FISH AND WILDLIFE.

are skittish, and primarily hunt at night, though you may glimpse one near dawn or dusk if you're lucky. Red foxes were brought to the area from England as hunting objects; released foxes interbred with native strains and the population spread. Foxes favor wooded areas and areas of low, dense brush. Tracks are doglike, with four toes in front of a pad, and are about two inches long.

The fairly large, tawny *eastern cottontail rab-*bit is a common sight when strolling near underbrush or fields on the shores of Narragansett Bay. Feet are white, and ears long. Cottontails emerge from the brush to feed in late afternoon, and often you will surprise them feeding on grass in open areas. These rabbits usually take short hops, but are capable of leaping up to 15 feet. Tracks are in clusters of four, with round forefoot prints and oblong hind prints.

NARRAGANSETT
BAY
BIRDLIFE
AND
WILDLIFE

181

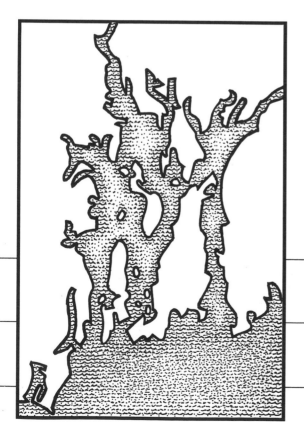

Appendices

Further Reading About Narragansett Bay

There are volumes written about the bay's history, and most are available at libraries or bookstores in the area. Try browsing the local history stacks during rainy days on your cruise. Here are some of our favorite volumes.

From the Library

Bacon, Edgar Mayhew. *Narragansett Bay, Its Historic and Romantic Associations and Picturesque Setting.* New York: G.P. Putnam's Sons, 1904.
> Out of print, but available at libraries and, if you're lucky, at area used-book stores. One of the most delightful treatments of Narragansett Bay we've ever read, this tome provides an excellent and witty glimpse of the bay and its people as they were almost 100 years ago. It is also full of history, folklore, and legends about the bay.

Livermore, S.T. *History of Block Island.* Hartford: Case, Lockwood & Brainard Co., 1877.
> A solid history of the island with an enlightening perspective.

Longfellow, Henry Wadsworth. "The Skeleton in Armor."
> This poem can be found in anthologies and separately bound editions at libraries and bookshops around the bay.

Maytum, Charles. *Paragraphs on Early Prudence Island.* Self published.
> Everything you ever wanted to know about the island, from history to local lore, written by an islander. Well worth browsing through, this book is out of print but can be found in some libraries and historical societies.

Oppel, Frank, ed. *Tales of New England Past.* Secaucus, N.J.: Castle, Division of Book Sales, Inc.
> Only one section focuses on Aquidneck Island, but this digest of magazine articles from the turn of the century is worth a read.

Rhode Island Department of Public Schools. *Handbook of Historical Sites in Rhode Island.* Providence: 1936.

Out of print but still available at some libraries. If you can get your hands on a copy, this is a highly informative guide to interesting sites around the state.

Ritchie, Ethel Colt. *Block Island Lore and Legends*. Block Island: F. Norman Associates, 1955.

If you can find a copy, it's fun to have aboard during a visit to Block Island. A wonderful book full of information for fans of Block Island.

From the Bookstore

In addition to history books, more than a few works of fiction or fun have been set in Narragansett Bay. Here are a few fiction titles and other entertaining suggestions you might enjoy reading during your cruise of the bay.

Bousquet, Don. *The Best of the Quahog Trilogy*. Westerly: Narragansett Graphics, 1987.

Bousquet is Rhode Island's own cartoonist, whose brilliance has the biting edge of "The Far Side"'s Gary Larson. His collections of locally aimed wit are hilarious; he has written several volumes and his work appears frequently in newspapers and other publications. This book is his best anthology, perfect for a taste of Narragansett Bay humor and a good sampler for a bay cruise.

Conley, Patrick T. *An Album of Rhode Island History, 1636–1986*. Norfolk: The Donning Company, 1986.

This glossy coffee-table book is not only attractive, it is jam-packed with photos, drawings, and tidbits of information about the bay, as well as solid and well written history.

Providence Journal Bulletin. *Rhode Island Almanac*.

A Rhode Island reference book compiled and published by the Providence newspaper. It's full of fun facts and figures about the state and the bay for the trivia fan.

Stockenberg, Antoinette. *The Challenge and the Glory*. New York: Bantam Books, Inc., 1987.

This enjoyable historical romance–suspense is set in Newport and revolves around the America's Cup. A page-turner, this well-written paperback is perfect summer reading.

Updike, John. *The Witches of Eastwick*. New York: Fawcett, 1987.

A strange, funny, and twisted tale about life in a small Rhode Island town based on a fictionalized version of the town of Wickford.

Vanderbilt, Gloria. *Once Upon A Time*. New York: Fawcett Gold Medal, 1985.

The true story of the emotional upbringing of a poor little rich girl, set in such glamorous locales as Newport and Monte Carlo, is fascinating and sad.

Welch, Wally. The Lighthouses of Rhode Island. Apopka, Florida.: Lighthouse Publications, 1987.

This is a full-color book with photographs and historical information about lighthouses around the bay. The book contains a wealth of interesting facts about the structures you pass on a cruise of Narragansett Bay, and is worth carrying aboard as a reference.

Wilder, Thornton. *Theophilus North*. New York: Carroll & Graff Publishers, Inc., 1987.

Set in Newport in the Roaring Twenties, this charming story is told through the eyes of an ambitious young man on the fringe of the glitz and glamour of this exclusive resort. John Huston turned this novel into the movie "Mr. North," and filmed it on location in Newport in 1987.

Wright, Marion I., and Sullivan, Robert J. *The Rhode Island Atlas*. Providence: Rhode Island Publications Society, 1962.

A compendium of useful and interesting information ranging from history to area weather patterns.

From the University
of Rhode Island

The University of Rhode Island (URI) publishes a series of excellent pamphlets, booklets and books about Narragansett Bay that often aren't available in bookstores and are not generally known. These

FURTHER
READING
ABOUT
NARRAGANSETT
BAY

185

are *excellent* references for anyone cruising the bay, visitors or natives. A free catalog is available that lists the entire collection. To obtain a copy write to Publications Office, Rhode Island Sea Grant, URI Bay Campus, Narragansett, RI 02882. Phone (401) 792-6800. Publications can be ordered through the same address and phone number. Below is a selection of our favorites.

Ely, Eleanor. *An Overview of Narragansett Bay.* Rhode Island Sea Grant, June 1988.

> This small pamphlet is full of facts about the bay and is well worth having aboard.

Hale, Stuart O. *Narragansett Bay: A Friend's Perspective.* University of Rhode Island Marine Bulletin 42; Marine Advisory Service, NOAA Sea Grant.

> A pleasant and informative overview of the bay; available from the University of Rhode Island for $15; also available at libraries.

Keiffer, Elisabeth. *Weather Information for Boaters, Cape Cod to Watch Hill.* NOAA Sea Grant, URI Marine Bulletin 47.

> A highly informative booklet about area weather patterns and how they affect boaters.

Olsen, Stephen, Robadue Jr., Donald D., and Lee, Virginia. *An Interpretive Atlas of Narragansett Bay.* Coastal Resources Center, URI Marine Bulletin 40.

> A chance to delve deeper into the natural and geologic history of the bay.

Spaulding, Malcolm and Swanson, Craig. *Tides and Tidal Currents of Narragansett Bay.* URI Sea Grant.

> A series of charts for recreational boaters showing tidal current and their values for 600 locations in Narragansett Bay. Calculated with the aid of a computer.

Further Study. Rhode Islanders can learn more about the bay by taking advantage of informal classes focused on all aspects of Narragansett Bay. The University of Rhode Island offers many courses each spring and fall on topics ranging from sharks and seafood to boating, birding, diving, beach walking, clambaking, and more. The courses are non-credit and available at minimal cost. For further information, contact the Narragansett Bay Classroom, Marine Resources Building, URI Narragansett Bay Campus, Narragansett, RI 02882.

Narragansett Bay Marina Listings

LOWER BAY

NEWPORT

MARINA	SERVICES
Christie's Restaurant and Marina 351 Thames Street Newport, RI 02840 847-5400	40 transient slips. No guest moorings. Ice, garbage, phone, showers, electricity. Reservations suggested. 10–20 ft. at dock MLW. Max. LOA 240 ft. Sail & power.
Goat Island Marina Goat Island Newport, RI 02840 849-5655	VHF Channel 16. Transient slips. No guest moorings. Gas, diesel, ice, garbage, phone, showers, electricity, ship's store, laundry. Reservations suggested if over 100 feet. 18 ft. at dock MLW. Max. LOA 250 feet. Sail & power.
Navy Marina Navy Base Newport, RI 02840 841-2311	Active duty or retired personnel only. No facilities for transient civilians.
New York Yacht Club Harbor Court Newport, RI 02840 846-1000	No transient slips. 9 guest moorings. Gas, phone, showers. Reservations suggested. 12 ft. at dock MLW. Sail & power.
Newport Marina Lee's Wharf Newport, RI 02840 849-2293	VHF Channel 16. 35 transient slips. Ice, phone, showers, laundry, electricity, pool. Reservations preferred. Max. LOA 80 ft. Sail & power.

MARINA	SERVICES
Newport Offshore Boatyard 1 Washington Street Newport, RI 02840 846-6000	VHF Channel 16. 4 transient slips, subject to change. No guest moorings. Ice, garbage, phone, showers, electricity, ship's store. Full-service marina. 70-ton travel lift. Reservations suggested. 10 ft. at dock MLW. Max. LOA 50 ft. Sail & power.
Newport Yacht Club Long Wharf Newport, RI 02840 846-9410	VHF Channel 9. Transient slips, number varies. No guest moorings. Ice, garbage, phone, showers, electricity. Reservations suggested. 9–10 ft. at dock MLW. Max. LOA 40–65 ft. Sail & power.
Newport Yachting Center 4 Commercial Wharf Newport, RI 02840 846-1600	VHF Channel 16, 9. 100 permanent transient slips. No guest moorings. Gas, diesel, ice, garbage, phone, showers, electricity. 40-ton travel lift. Reservations suggested. 10–15 ft. at dock MLW. Max. LOA 170 ft. Sail & power.
Oldport Marine Services Sayer's Wharf Newport, RI 02840 847-9109	VHF Channel 68. No transient slips. 25–30 guest moorings. Ice, garbage, phone, launch. No reservations. Max. LOA 60 ft.
Treadway Resort and Marina 49 America's Cup Avenue Newport, RI 02840 847-9000	VHF Channel 16. Transient slips, number varies. Guest moorings. Ice, garbage, phone, showers, electricity. Reservations suggested. 15 ft. at dock MLW. Max. LOA 100 ft. Sail & power.

JAMESTOWN OR CONANICUT ISLAND

MARINA	SERVICES
Dutch Harbor Shipyard 252 Narragansett Avenue Jamestown, RI 423-0630	No transient slips. 5–10 guest moorings. Gas, diesel, ice, garbage, showers. 10-ton crane. Reservations suggested. 9 ft. at dock MLW. Max. LOA 50 ft.
Clark Boat Yard 110 Racquet Road Jamestown, RI 423-1545	No transient slips. 4 guest moorings. Garbage disposal. Max. LOA 65 ft. Sail & power.

MARINA	SERVICES
Conanicut Marina 1 Ferry Wharf Jamestown, RI 423-1556	VHF Channel 71. 15 permanent transient slips. Cost $1.50/foot/night. 20 guest moorings. Gas, diesel, ice, garbage, phone, showers, electricity, launch, ship's store. 12-ton travel lift. Full service marina. Reservations suggested. 9 ft. at dock MLW. Max. LOA 90ft.
Jamestown Boat Yard Racquet Road Jamestown, RI 423-0600	VHF Channels 16 and 72. 3 work slips. 3–5 guest moorings. Garbage, phone. 50-ton travel lift. Reservations suggested. 10–30 ft. at dock MLW. Max. LOA 75 ft. Sail & power.

POINT JUDITH

MARINA	SERVICES
Billington Cove Marina 557 Pond Street Wakefield, RI 783-1266	VHF Channel 6. 5–10 transient slips, number varies. No guest moorings. Gas, ice, garbage, showers, ship's store. Full service marina. Reservations suggested. 2.5 ft. at dock MLW. Max. LOA 26 ft. Power.
Pt. Judith Marina 360 Goosebury Road South Kingstown, RI 789-7189	VHF Channels 16, 68, 74. 2 transient slips. No guest moorings. Gas, diesel, ice, garbage, phone, showers, electricity, ship's store. 30-ton travel lift. Full service marina. 10 ft. at dock MLW. Max. LOA 60 ft. Sail & power.
Ram Point Marina William Schmid Drive Wakefield, RI 783-4535	VHF Channels 9, 16. Transient slips, number varies. 3 Guest moorings. Gas, diesel, ice, garbage, phone, showers, electricity, ship's store, laundry. Full service marina. Reservations suggested. 6 ft. at dock MLW. Max. LOA 50 ft.
Snug Harbor Marina 510 Gooseberry Road Wakefield, RI 783-7766	VHF Channel 9. 2 transient slips. No guest moorings. Gas, diesel, ice, garbage, phone, electricity, ship's store. No reservations. 3 ft. at dock MLW. Max. LOA 42 ft. Power.

BLOCK ISLAND

MARINA	SERVICES
Block Island Boat Basin New Harbor Block Island, RI 02807 466-2631	VHF Channel 16. 90 transient slips. Gas, diesel; LPG, CNG, groceries, ice, showers, restaurant, electricity, gift shop, moped, bike and auto rentals, ship's store. 10 ft. at dock MLW. Max. LOA 110 ft. Sail & power.
Champlin's Marina New Harbor Block Island, RI 02807 466-2641	VHF Channel 68. 100 transient slips. Gas, groceries, ice, showers, laundromat, pump-out station, restaurant, pool, cocktail bar, gift shop, launch service, ship's store. 20 ft. at dock MLW. Max. LOA 150 ft. Sail & power.
Payne's Dock New Harbor Block Island, RI 02807 466-5572	VHF Channel 68. 50 transient slips. Gas, diesel, groceries, ice, showers, cocktail bar, gift shop, restaurant. 20 ft. at dock MLW. Max. LOA 100 ft. Sail & power.
Smuggler's Cove Ocean Avenue New Harbor Block Island, RI 02807 466-2828	VHF Channel 68. 16 transient slips. Groceries, ice, restaurant. 10 ft. at dock, approach 6 ft. MLW. Max. LOA 64 ft. Sail & power.
Old Harbor Dock Old Harbor Block Island, RI 02871 466-2526	VHF Channel 16. 30 transient slips. Gas, diesel, LPG, groceries, ice, shower, laundromat, restaurant. 15 ft. at dock MLW. Max. LOA 80 ft.

MIDDLE BAY

WICKFORD

MARINA	SERVICES
Johnson's Boat Yard 3 Esmond Avenue Wickford, RI 294-3700	Transient slips, number varies. No guest moorings. Gas, diesel, garbage disposal, electricity, ship's store. Full service marina. Reservations suggested. 6 ft. at dock MLW. Sail & power.

MARINA	SERVICES
Pleasant Street Wharf 160 Pleasant Street North Kingstown, RI 02852 294-2791	Transient slips, number varies. Guest moorings vary. Gas and diesel. Ice, garbage disposal, phone, showers, electricity, small ship's store. 25-ton travel lift. Reservations suggested. 12 ft. at dock MLW. Max. LOA 35 ft. Sail & power.
Wickford Cove Marina P.O. Box 436 Wickford, RI 884-7014	Transient slips, number varies. Guest moorings, number varies. Gas, diesel, ice, garbage disposal, phone, showers, electricity, ship's store. Full service marina. 70-ton travel lift. No reservations. 9 ft. at dock MLW. Max. LOA 70 ft. Sail & power.
Wickford Shipyard 125 Steamboat Avenue Wickford, RI 294-3361	Transient slips, number varies. No guest moorings. Gas, diesel, ice, garbage disposal, phone, showers, laundry, ship's store, electricity. Full service marina. Reservations suggested. 7 ft. at dock MLW. Max. LOA 60 ft. Sail & power.
Wickford Yacht Club 165 Pleasant Street Wickford, RI 294-9010	No transient slips. 4 guest moorings. Showers. 10 ft. at dock MLW. Max. LOA 40 ft. Sail & power.

GREENWICH COVE

MARINA	SERVICES
East Greenwich Marina 28 Water Street East Greenwich, RI 885-2911	Transient slips, number varies. No guest moorings. Ice, garbage disposal, phone, electricity. Reservations suggested. 5 ft. at dock MLW. Max. LOA 60 ft. Sail & power.
East Greenwich Yacht Club Water Street East Greenwich, RI 02818 884-7700	VHF Channel 9. Transient slips and moorings, number varies. Gas, diesel, ice, garbage, phone, showers, electricity, launch. 10 ft. at dock MLW. Max. LOA 100 ft. Sail & power.
Harborside Lobstermania Water Street East Greenwich, RI 884-6363	20 transient slips, for dinner only. Phone. 8 ft. at dock MLW. Max. LOA 50 ft.

MARINA	SERVICES
Norton's Shipyard and Marina P.O. Box 106 East Greenwich, RI 02818 884-8828	VHF Channel 16. 15 transient slips, numbers vary. Guest moorings vary. Gas, diesel, ice, garbage disposal, phone, showers, electricity, launch, ship's store. Full service marina. 35-ton travel lift. Reservations suggested. 8 to 15 ft. at dock MLW. Max. LOA 300 ft. Sail & power.

GREENWICH BAY

MARINA	SERVICES
Apponaug Harbor Marina 17 Arnold's Neck Drive Warwick, RI 739-5005	Transient slips occasionally available. Garbage disposal, phone, showers, electricity, ship's store. Full service marina. Reservations suggested. 5 ft. at dock MLW. Sail & power.
Brewers Yacht Yard 100 Folly Landing Warwick, RI 884-0544	Transient slips, number varies. No guest moorings. Diesel, ice, garbage disposal, phone, showers, ship's store, electricity. Full service marina. 35-ton travel lift. Reservations suggested. 6 ft. at dock MLW. Max. LOA 60 ft. Sail & power.
C-Lark Marina 252 Second Point Road Warwick, RI 739-3871	Transient slips, number varies. No guest moorings. Gas, diesel, ice, garbage disposal, phone, showers, electricity ($5), ship's store, restaurant. Full service marina. 25-ton travel lift. Reservations suggested. 6 ft. at dock MLW. Max. LOA 45 ft. Sail & power.
Carlson's Marina 125 Wharf Road Warwick, RI 738-4278	VHF Channel 16. Transient slips, number varies. No guest moorings. Ice, garbage disposal, phone, showers, electricity, ship's store. Full service marina. 25-ton travel lift. Reservations suggested. 6 ft. at dock MLW. Max. LOA 41 ft. Sail & power.
Frank Pettis Boat Yard 1 Baylawn Avenue Warwick, RI 467-8982	VHF Channel 65. Transient slips occasionally available. No guest moorings. Garbage disposal, phone, electricity. Full service marina. 10-ton travel lift. Reservations suggested. 2–3 ft. at dock MLW. Max. LOA 40 ft. Sail & power.

MARINA	SERVICES
Harbor Light Marina 200 Gray Street Warwick, RI 737-6353	VHF Channel 16. Transient slips, number varies. No guest moorings. Garbage disposal, phone, showers, electricity. Full service marina. 60-ton travel lift. Reservations suggested. 9 ft. at dock MLW. Max. LOA 52 ft. Sail & power.
Masthead Marina 1 Masthead Drive Warwick, RI 884-1810	VHF Channels 16, 68. 10 transient slips, number varies. No guest moorings. Ice, garbage disposal, phone, showers, ship's store, electricity. Full service marina. 35-ton travel lift. Reservations suggested. 8 ft. at dock MLW. Max. LOA 60 ft. Sail & power.

PORTSMOUTH (EAST PASSAGE) MARINAS

MARINA	SERVICES
East Passage Yachting Center 1 Lagoon Road Portsmouth, RI 02871 683-4000	VHF Channels 16, 74. 40 transient slips. No guest moorings. Gas, diesel, ice, garbage disposal, phone, showers, electricity, ship's store. 165-ton travel lift. Full service marina. Reservations suggested. 7–15 ft. at dock MLW. Sail & power.
Little Harbor Marine 1 Little Harbor Landing Portsmouth, RI 02871 683-5700	VHF Channels 16, 9. 50 permanent transient slips. No guest moorings. Diesel, ice, garbage disposal, phone, showers, electricity, ship's store. 160-ton travel lift. Full service marina. 15 ft. at dock MLW. Max. LOA 130 ft. Reservations suggested. Sail & power.

UPPER BAY

BARRINGTON

MARINA	SERVICES
Barrington Yacht Club Barton Avenue Barrington, RI 02806 245-1181	VHF Channel 68. No transient slips, number varies. 2 guest moorings. Diesel, gas, ice, garbage disposal, phone, showers, electricity, launch. Reservations suggested. 7 ft. at dock MLW. Max. LOA 40 ft. Sail & power.

MARINA	SERVICES
Cove Haven Marina 101 Narragansett Avenue Barrington, RI 02806 245-5090	VHF Channel 9. Transient slips, number varies. No guest moorings. Gas, ice, garbage disposal, phone, electricity. Ship's store. 150-ton travel lift. Full service marina. Reservations suggested. 12 ft. at dock MLW. Max. LOA 65 ft.
Stanley's Boat Yard 17 Barton Avenue Barrington, RI 02806 245-5090	Transient slips. No moorings. Gas available. No diesel. Ice, garbage, phone, electricity. 35-ton travel lift. Ship's store. Full-service marina. Reservations suggested. 5 ft. at docks MLW. Max. LOA 25 ft. Sail & power.

CRANSTON

MARINA	SERVICES
Edgewood Yacht Club Shaw Avenue Cranston, RI 02910 941-9810	VHF Channel 16. Transient slips; number varies. Ice, garbage disposal, phone, showers, electricity, launch. Reservations suggested. 5–7 ft. at docks MLW. Maximum LOA 50 ft. Sail & power.
Pawtuxet Cove Marina 75 Rear Fort Avenue Cranston, RI 02910 467-4519	4 transient slips. No guest moorings. Diesel, ice, garbage disposal, phone, showers, electricity. Reservations suggested. 4 ft. at dock MLW. Max. LOA 50 ft. Power only.
Rhode Island Yacht Club 1 Ocean Avenue Cranston, RI 02910 941-0220	Transient slips. Ice, garbage, phone, showers, electricity. 5 ft. at docks MLW. Max. LOA 80 ft. Sail & power.

FALL RIVER

MARINA	SERVICES
Borden Light Marina 251 Bank Street Fall River, MA (508) 678-7547	30 transient slips. No guest moorings. Gas, diesel, ice, garbage disposal, phone, showers, electricity, ship's store. Reservations suggested. 8–27 ft. at dock MLW. Max. LOA 90 ft. Sail & power.

PROVIDENCE

MARINA	SERVICES
Old Harbor Marina 525 South Water Street Providence, RI 02903 751-SLIP	6 transient slips. No guest moorings. Gas, diesel, ice, garbage disposal, phone, showers, laundry, electricity. Reservations suggested. 11 ft. at dock MLW. Max. LOA 75 ft. Power only.
Oyster House Marina 28 Water Street East Providence, RI 434-0400	3 transient slips for restaurant. No guest moorings. Garbage disposal, phone, electricity. Reservations suggested. 6–20 feet at dock MLW. Max. LOA 40 ft. Sail & power.

SAKONNET RIVER

LITTLE COMPTON

MARINA	SERVICES
Sakonnet Point Marina Bluff Head Avenue Little Compton, RI 635-4753	3 transient slips. No guest moorings. Gas, diesel, ice, garbage disposal, phone, showers, electricity. Reservations suggested. 7 ft. at dock MLW. Max. LOA 45 ft. Sail & power.

PORTSMOUTH

MARINA	SERVICES
Brewer's Sakonnet Marina Narragansett Boulevard Portsmouth, RI 02871 683-3551	Transient slips, number varies. No guest moorings. Gas, diesel, ice, garbage disposal, phone, showers, electricity. 35-ton travel lift. Ship's store. Full service marina. Reservations suggested. 8–10 ft. at dock MLW. Max. LOA 60 ft. Sail & power.
Pirate's Cove Marina Point Road Portsmouth, RI 02871 683-3030	VHF Channel 16. 50 permanent transient slips, number varies. Guest moorings. Gas, diesel, ice, garbage disposal, phone, showers, electricity. Ship's store. 45-ton lift. Full service marina. Reservations suggested. 9 ft. at dock MLW. Max. LOA 60 ft. Sail & power.

MARINA	SERVICES
Stonebridge Marina 17 Point Road Portsmouth, RI 02871 683-1011	1 transient slip. No guest moorings. Ice, garbage disposal, phone, electricity. Reservations suggested. 9 ft. at dock MLW. Max. LOA 40 ft. Sail & power.

TIVERTON

MARINA	SERVICES
Standish Boat Yard Main Road Tiverton, RI 02878 624-4075	2 to 3 transient slips, number varies. 6 Guest moorings. Gas, diesel, ice, garbage disposal, phone, electricity. Ship's store. 12½-ton travel lift. Full service marina. 12 ft. at dock MLW. Max. LOA 50 ft. Sail & power.

Some

Cruise

Suggestions

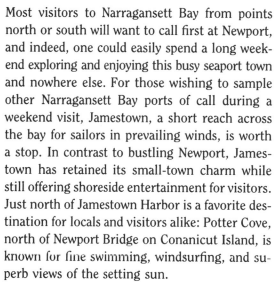

A Long Weekend on

the Bay . . .

Most visitors to Narragansett Bay from points north or south will want to call first at Newport, and indeed, one could easily spend a long weekend exploring and enjoying this busy seaport town and nowhere else. For those wishing to sample other Narragansett Bay ports of call during a weekend visit, Jamestown, a short reach across the bay for sailors in prevailing winds, is worth a stop. In contrast to bustling Newport, Jamestown has retained its small-town charm while still offering shoreside entertainment for visitors. Just north of Jamestown Harbor is a favorite destination for locals and visitors alike: Potter Cove, north of Newport Bridge on Conanicut Island, is known for fine swimming, windsurfing, and superb views of the setting sun.

Should you want a longer sail, try heading up the bay to yet another Potter Cove, on Prudence Island, perhaps with a stop at the south end of the island for lunch, a swim and a hike. A word of warning, however: Get north to Prudence well before evening or you may have to drop the hook in the anchorage outside the cove due to crowded conditions. If the tide allows, you will also want to allow time to forage for steamer clams to have as an appetizer (or in a shore dinner, as a meal in itself).

If you've got a day to visit, weigh anchor and head the short distance east to the bight at Hog Island for lunch, a swim, and a walk along the shell strewn beach before heading to Bristol for the night. Plan to have a meal ashore in one of Bristol's excellent shoreside eateries, and save time the next morning for a walking tour of the historic and picturesque town. Sailors should allow a few hours for the beat back down the bay on their way home; the wind typically won't fill in until around noon, anyway, so the time spent ashore in the morning will be well spent. Note that when sailing south toward the mouth of the bay in prevailing southwesterlies, the best course is to stay west of Dyer Island to avoid being temporarily becalmed in its lee on the east side.

The Week-Long Cruise . . .

Visiting yachts spending a week cruising Narragansett Bay will have ample time to explore some of its less frequented ports of call. Newport or Jamestown are logical first stops for boats arriving from Rhode Island Sound, but after you've had your fill of the more popular cruising stops, you may wish to head to calmer regions for a few days' R&R.

Weigh anchor from Newport or drop your mooring at Jamestown and head for Dutch Island, leaving early enough in the morning to allow time for a stop at Mackerel Cove on Conanicut Island for lunch. Mackerel is a perfect lunch stop, with a fine swimming beach and pleasant scenery, but is too rolly for an overnight anchorage. After lunch and a swim, weigh anchor once again and head south and west around Beavertail Light, then north for Dutch Island, a downwind sail in the prevailing winds. In predictable southwesterlies it is safe to anchor on the northeast end of Dutch, but if a wind shift to the north or east is forecast, a better option is to pick up a guest mooring in Dutch Harbor, not far away. Allow plenty of time the next day for exploring the natural and historic wonders of deserted Dutch Island, perhaps planning a long hike and picnic lunch ashore before departing.

From Dutch, head north under the Jamestown Bridge (watch for obstacles caused by construction of a new span) to the village port of Wickford. You may wish to pick up a mooring in the outer cove and spend the rest of the day exploring tiny Cornelius Island, or taking a walk through one of Rhode Island's most picture-perfect colonial towns. When you've had your fill of browsing the village's quaint antique book and gift shops, head back to the boat for sundowners and dinner aboard.

After breakfast in the morning, set sail for Prudence Island's Potter Cove, a prime midweek destination. Head east between the north tip of Conanicut Island and the south tip of Prudence before turning northward, perhaps stopping at the park at South Prudence for lunch, swimming and excellent hiking during the hottest part of the day. South Prudence is the best place on the island for cruising folks to spot white-tailed deer, and if you venture ashore chances are you'll catch a glimpse of one of these timid creatures. South Prudence is a bit exposed for overnight stays, so head north to Potter Cove on the island's opposite end to spend the night. Potter is such a pleasant place during the week you may want to allot two days to spend here, since you are likely to have it mostly to yourselves Monday through Thursday before the weekend crowds hit. There are plenty of hiking trails nearby, a good swimming beach and excellent shellfishing to be had, so you won't have trouble filling your hours here.

From Prudence, visitors with only a week to spend exploring the bay have two choices for the last two days of a cruise: Either head west to East Greenwich or east to Bristol. East Greenwich offers a nice combination of swimming and hiking at Goddard Park and Beach and a series of shoreside restaurants and facilities, while Bristol offers some of the bay's more interesting history as well as shady, tree-lined streets and impressive architecture that is quintessentially New England. Bristol also offers a variety of excellent restaurants and other shoreside activities both day and night. Either of these interesting ports of call will provide a pleasant finale to a week-long bay cruise for visitors who have arrived from the south. Those exploring the bay from points north in Massachusetts or Rhode Island might simply reverse the order of the stops above and end the cruise with a stop at Newport or Jamestown before heading north toward home.

. . . Or Longer

Those with more than a week to spend may wish to sample some of the generally more urban delights of Upper Bay ports of call and will certainly not want to miss the delightful Sakonnet River. At the outset, you can follow the same itinerary as the week-long cruise, but instead of choosing between East Greenwich or Bristol, visit both, first heading west to East Greenwich from Potter Cove on Prudence Island. From East Greenwich, those with more time might enjoy spending a day at Rocky Point Park, particularly if children are aboard, and those cruising under power might wish to continue northward after a day at the park to dock overnight at Providence Harbor, partaking of the fine dining and nightlife within walking distance of the marina. Cruisers on a tighter schedule would be better advised to head directly from East Greenwich to Bristol, sailing around the north tip of Prudence and south-southeast around the tip of Popasquash Neck toward Bristol. To break up the sail, you might try a stop at Hog Island for a swim and some shell collecting before heading into Bristol Harbor.

After enjoying historic Bristol, head out of the harbor and turn north under the Mount Hope Bridge, enjoying a day sail or motor cruise around the scenic bay, perhaps making a bird-watching stop at tiny Spar Island before threading your way through the narrow entrance of the wide Kickamuit River for the night. There are no restaurants or facilities here, so plan a stern rail barbecue for dinner and then enjoy your night under the stars. The lovely Kickamuit offers excellent swimming, shellfishing, and fine conditions for boardsailing as well as abundant wildlife and plenty of opportunity for exploration down various creeks and crannies by dinghy, so plan to spend at least a day there. Just a short sail or motor from the river mouth is Fall River, a good choice for your next overnight if you're in the

mood for a change of pace. The museums near the harbor, the Battleship *Massachusetts* and the submarine *Lionfish* are all worth a visit, and provide endless amusement for adults and kids alike. A spacious park and boardwalk allow ample room to stretch your legs or picnic in pleasant surroundings ashore.

From Fall River, visitors will most likely wish to head south toward the blue Sakonnet, making Fogland Harbor a next port of call. Here, you'll find a white sand beach on one side of the small peninsula and excellent shellfishing on the other; the site is also popular with scuba divers. There are no facilities here, either, so if you're low on fuel or groceries, stop for fuel and supplies at Tiverton or Portsmouth in Pirate's Cove first.

Farther south on the Sakonnet are two harbors that offer excellent jumping off points for boats heading toward Buzzards Bay, Rhode Island Sound or Long Island Sound. Third Beach Cove, on the west side of the river, has one of the area's best swimming beaches, and is also a prime spot for windsurfing, hiking and beachcombing. On the opposite shore, Sakonnet Harbor offers less room for transients, but provides a healthy dose of downeast charm and one of the best views of the open Atlantic to be had anywhere from the shore south of the harbor and breakwater. This quiet harbor is especially popular as an overnight for boats heading toward Cuttyhunk Island and points east; boats bound for Block Island and points west may wish to opt for Third Beach Cove.

It would be easy to spend an entire summer exploring Narragansett Bay's many anchorages. But for the visitor with limited time, these ports of call will be well worth a stop . . . and remember, there will always be new anchorages to explore on your next visit.

Tidal

Current

Charts

for

Narragansett

Bay

The following tidal current charts for the bay are taken from a 1936 Coast and Geodetic Survey publication. No more-recent measurements exist, but these charts adequately serve the needs of small boat owners.

Mean current velocities are shown to the nearest tenth of a knot, and the arrows indicate direction of flow. The observations used in preparing the charts were taken within 14 feet of the water surface under normal weather conditions. Strong winds or freshets may modify considerably the velocities and directions shown.

The velocities shown on the charts represent the current for a mean range of tide (3.4 to 3.6 feet) at Newport. For a different mean tidal range, proceed as follows: Obtain from the tide tables the predicted heights of high and low waters at Newport for the date in question. Subtract the mean of the two low-water heights from the mean of the two high-water heights. This difference gives the mean range of tide for the day. With this range enter the following table and find the corresponding correction factor. Multiply any charted velocity by this factor to obtain the velocity for the day in question.

Factors for Correcting Velocities

When range of tide for day at Newport is	Multiply velocity on chart by - factor
1.6–1.9 feet	0.5
2.0–2.2 feet	0.6
2.3–2.6 feet	0.7
2.7–2.9 feet	0.8
3.0–3.3 feet	0.9
3.4–3.6 feet	1.0
3.7–4.0 feet	1.1
4.1–4.3 feet	1.2
4.4–4.7 feet	1.3
4.8–5.0 feet	1.4
5.1–5.4 feet	1.5
5.5–5.7 feet	1.6
5.8–6.1 feet	1.7
6.2–6.4 feet	1.8
6.5–6.8 feet	1.9

Four of the 13 charts now published by the National Ocean survey are reproduced here. The complete series is available in a 9-inch by 14-inch booklet from authorized NOAA chart agents.

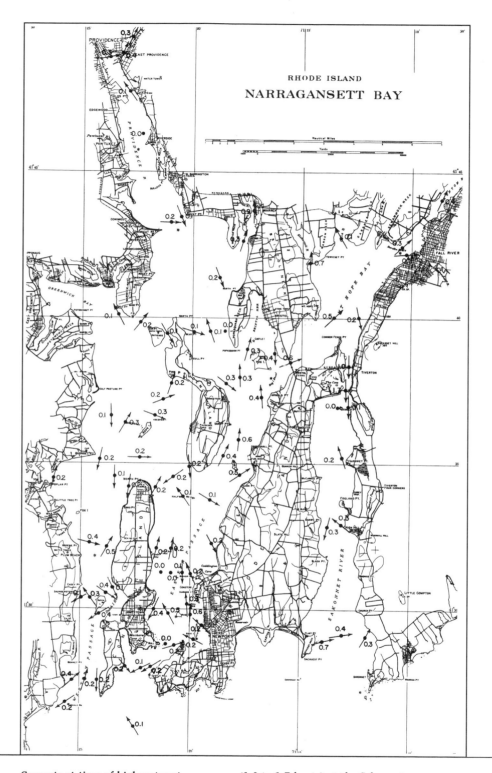

RHODE ISLAND
NARRAGANSETT BAY

Currents at time of high water at Newport. Although current velocities are mostly small and directions variable, there is a strong ebb (1.0 to 1.7 knots) at the Sakonnet River bridges at Tiverton. The ebb velocity there peaks at 2.4 to 2.6 knots one hour after high water.

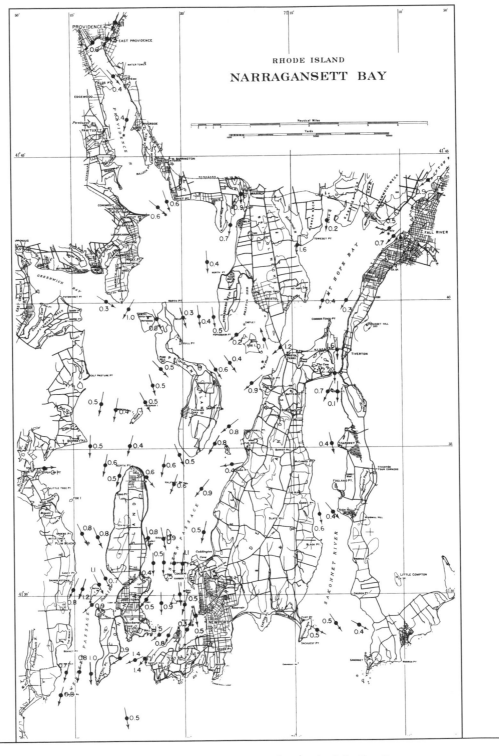

Currents three hours after high water at Newport. Ebb velocities in the mouth of the bay peak at this hour, then begin to decrease within the next hour in the mouth of the East Passage, and within the next two hours in the mouth of the West Passage.

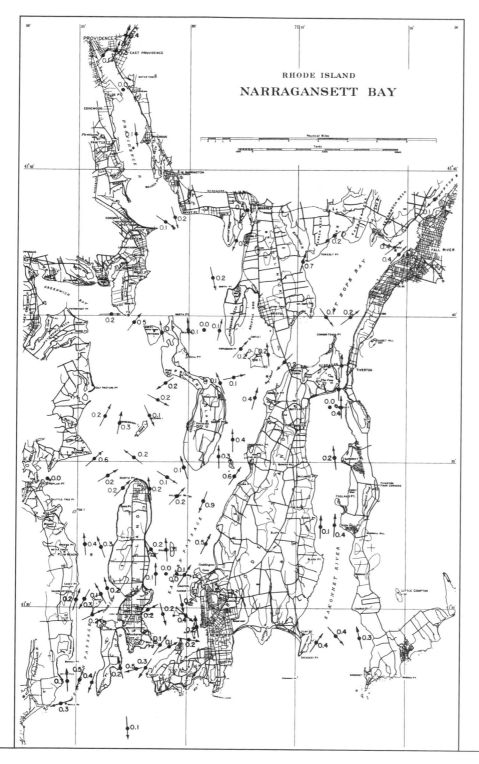

RHODE ISLAND

NARRAGANSETT BAY

Currents six hours after high
water at Newport. Velocities are low
and directions variable near the
time of the low-water stand.

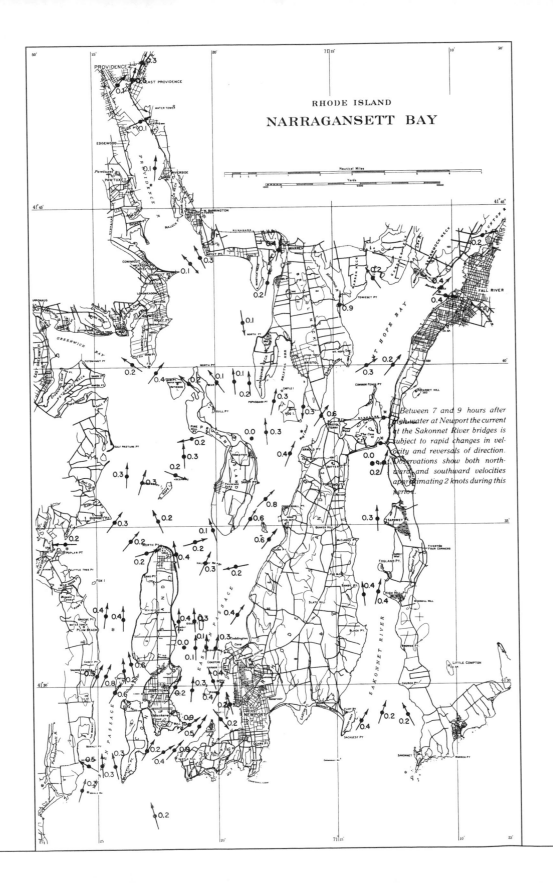

RHODE ISLAND
NARRAGANSETT BAY

Between 7 and 9 hours after high water at Newport the current at the Sakonnet River bridges is subject to rapid changes in velocity and reversals of direction. Observations show both northward and southward velocities approximating 2 knots during this period.

Currents nine hours after high water at Newport. The flood current just off The Neck in the East Passage remains at 0.9 to 1.0 knots between hours eight and ten after high water. Flood velocity never exceeds 0.6 knot in the mouth of the West Passage, but reaches 1.1 knots in the constriction between Dutch Island and Saunderstown in hours 10 through 11, and 0.9 knot off Greene Point in hour 11. Between seven and nine hours after high water at Newport, the current at the Sakonnet River bridges is subject to rapid changes in velocity and reversals of direction. Observations show both northward and southward velocities approximating 2 knots during this period, with northward velocities of up to 2.3 knots in hours 10 and 11. By hour 12 the velocity there is southward again.

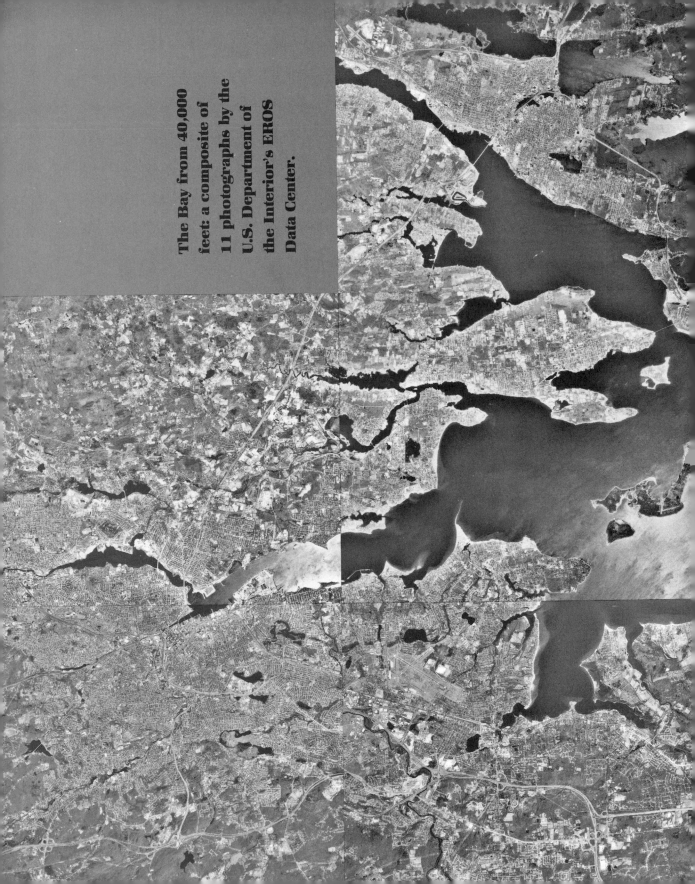

The Bay from 40,000 feet: a composite of 11 photographs by the U.S. Department of the Interior's EROS Data Center.

Index